Constituent Power

Constituent Power

Law, Popular Rule and Politics

Edited by Matilda Arvidsson,
Leila Brännström and
Panu Minkkinen

EDINBURGH
University Press

Edinburgh University Press is one of the leading university presses in the UK. We publish academic books and journals in our selected subject areas across the humanities and social sciences, combining cutting-edge scholarship with high editorial and production values to produce academic works of lasting importance. For more information visit our website: edinburghuniversitypress.com

Edinburgh University Press Ltd
The Tun – Holyrood Road
12 (2f) Jackson's Entry
Edinburgh EH8 8PJ

First published in hardback by Edinburgh University Press 2020

Typeset in 11/13 Adobe Garamond Pro by
IDSUK (DataConnection) Ltd, and
printed and bound by CPI Group (UK) Ltd,
Croydon, CR0 4YY

A CIP record for this book is available from the British Library

ISBN 978 1 4744 5497 1 (hardback)
ISBN 978 1 4744 5498 8 (paperback)
ISBN 978 1 4744 5499 5 (webready PDF)
ISBN 978 1 4744 5500 8 (epub)

This collection has been generously supported by the Kone Foundation, a charitable trust registered in Finland (No. 0213537-1).

Contents

Part 3 Democracy and Populism

Editors' Introduction

Matilda Arvidsson, Leila Brännström and
Panu Minkkinen

The notion 'constituent power' is an answer to the question about the origins of the constitution and the legal order. Within democratic-constitutional thought, it expresses the conviction that power is ultimately vested in an entity known as 'the people' which is the fundamental source of all political authority. Accordingly, a constitution is deemed legitimate only if 'the people' has both created it and continues to endorse it.

As a concept, constituent power emerged during the Enlightenment period as an articulation of the revolutionary right of a political community to alter or to replace its form of government.[1] Emmanuel Sieyès, the classic theorist of constituent power, emphasised the sovereignty of the people, or in his words 'the nation', in the traditional sense of being unlimited. Constituent power is consequently superior to the constitution and any constituted powers and may subvert or alter them at any time. In Sieyès's well-known words:

> Tyranny needs no more than a single moment of success to bind a people, through devotion to a constitution, to forms which make it impossible for them to express their will freely and, as a result, to break the chains of despo-tism. Every nation on earth has to be taken as if it is like an isolated individual outside all social ties or, as it is said, in a state of nature. The exercise of their will is free and independent of all civil forms. Since they exist only in the natural order, their will needs only to have the *natural* character of a will to produce all its effects. However a nation may will, it is enough for it to will. Every form is good, and its will is always the supreme law.[2]

---

[1] For a historical overview, see e.g. Andrew Arato, *The Adventures of the Constituent Power. Beyond Revolutions?* (Cambridge: Cambridge University Press, 2017). For a more subversive take, see e.g. Antonio Negri, *Insurgencies. Constituent Power and the Modern State*, trans. Maurizia Boscagli (Minneapolis, MN: University of Minnesota Press, 1999).

[2] Emmanuel-Joseph Sieyès, 'What is the Third Estate?' [1798], in Emmanuel-Joseph Sieyès, *Political Writings. Including the Debate between Sieyès and Tom Paine in 1791*, trans. Michael Sonenscher (Indiana, IN: Hackett Publishing, 2003), pp. 92–162, at pp. 137–138 (Sieyès's emphasis).

The idea originally put forward by Sieyès that constituent power would some-how survive its constituted institutions – 'above' them, 'within' them, 'beside' them[3] – perhaps in the form of a 'dormant' superior extra-constitutional pop-ular sovereign, is not merely a historical curiosity. It is more or less explicitly present in, for example, Carl Schmitt's notion of 'constitution-making power'[4] that, in turn, has inspired many more contemporary elaborations on democ-racy and politics.[5] Such a radical idea of constituent power is not only trou-bling for those with a liberal and result-oriented take on constitutionalism.[6] Hannah Arendt feared the unsettling proclivity of the notion and made her point by scrutinising the instability that popular sovereignty imposed on the French Revolution.[7] Similarly, Claude Lefort stressed the totalitarian dangers attached to the figure of a unitary people, of a 'People-as-One' (*peuple-un*), that will always have to be embodied by someone or some group, and he illustrated his worries with the examples of, *inter alia*, the French revolution, the Soviet Union, and neoliberal capitalism.[8]

The promise of popular sovereignty – that of a rule 'of the people, by the people, for the people' – is, however, not easy to let go of, bound up as it is with creative, egalitarian and participatory impulses that are proper to democracy itself. While a liberal constitutional lawyer like Ernst-Wolfgang Böckenförde is willing to endorse some kind of unitary notion of the people[9], the radical political theorist Antonio Negri gladly embraces the instability that the concept introduces.[10] However, most contemporary

---

[3] See Mikael Spång, *Constituent Power and Constitutional Order. Above, Within and Beside the Constitution* (Basingstoke: Palgrave Macmillan, 2014).

[4] See Carl Schmitt, *Constitutional Theory*, trans. Jeffrey Seitzer (Durham, NC: Duke University Press, 2008), pp. 125–135.

[5] See e.g. Matilda Arvidsson, Leila Brännström and Panu Minkkinen (eds), *The Contemporary Relevance of Carl Schmitt. Law, Politics, Theology* (Abingdon: Routledge, 2016).

[6] David Dyzenhaus would be a clear-cut contemporary example of such a constitutionalist position. See e.g. David Dyzenhaus, 'The Politics of the Question of Constituent Power', in Martin Loughlin and Neil Walker (eds), *The Paradox of Constitutionalism. Constituent Power and Constitutional Form* (Oxford: Oxford University Press, 2007), pp. 129–146; and David Dyzenhaus, 'Constitutionalism in an Old Key: Legality and Constituent Power', *Global Constitutionalism* 1:2 (2012), pp. 229–260.

[7] See e.g. Hannah Arendt, *On Revolution* (London: Faber and Faber, 1963), pp. 141–165.

[8] See e.g. Claude Lefort, 'The Image of the Body and Totalitarianism', in Claude Lefort, *The Political Forms of Modern Society. Bureaucracy, Democracy, Totalitarianism*, trans. Alan Sheridan et al. (Cambridge: Polity, 1986), pp. 292–306.

[9] E.g. Ernst-Wolfgang Böckenförde, 'The Constituent Power of the People: A Liminal Con-cept of Constitutional Law', in Ernst-Wolfgang Böckenförde, *Constitutional and Political Theory. Selected Writings*, eds. Mirjam Künkler and Tine Stein (Oxford: Oxford University Press, 2017), pp. 169–185.

[10] E.g. Michael Hardt and Antonio Negri, *Multitude. War and Democracy in the Age of Empire* (London et al: Penguin Books, 2006).

proponents of the constituent power of the people would prefer to renegotiate and re-articulate the people's oneness and its sovereign rule. Andrew Arato, for example, wishes to differentiate between constitutions that are imposed on a people and constitutions that can, in a meaningful sense, be considered as the product of a people's self-government. In order to achieve this, he has developed a notion of constituent power that survives under its constituted framework, but only as a 'post sovereign, pluralistic, always limited power whose authority is due to both its legitimacy and, even during legal breaks, its legality'.[11] Hans Lindahl, on the other hand, defines the work of constituent power as 'normative innovation and rupture . . . [that] proceeds from a radical outside no political community succeeds in domesticating', and continues to argue that the collective identity of the people must be understood reflexively.[12] And finally, Martin Loughlin, stressing the need for the people in its non-instituted manifestation to irritate instituted power, argues that constituent power 'exists only when [a] multitude can project itself not just as the expression of the many (a majority) but – in some senses at least – of the all (unity)'.[13]

The aim of this collection is not to revisit the debates on constituent power at a general or historical level. Rather, we wish to ask the central questions about the place and composition of the people in liberal democracies anew, in light of what the current political situation may suggest. Over the last few years, right-wing forces claiming to speak for the people against liberal elites, thematically often focusing on immigration, minorities and/or feminism, have either surged to power or gained considerable ground in almost all European states, as well as in the United States, Brazil and a number of other liberal democracies around the globe. There is widespread uncertainty as to how to characterise and name this ascending family of parties and politicians, suggestions range from 'fascism' and 'new authoritarianism' to 'illiberal democracy' and 'enraged majority rule'. But most scholars and pundits refer to the phenomenon as 'right-wing populism'. The increasing concern about

[11] Andrew Arato, *Post Sovereign Constitution Making. Learning and Legitimacy* (Oxford: Oxford University Press, 2016), p. 10.

[12] Hans Lindahl, 'Constituent Power and Reflexive Identity: Towards an Ontology of Collective Selfhood', in Loughlin and Walker, *The Paradox of Constitutionalism: Constituent Power and Constitutional Form* (Oxford: OUP 2007), pp. 22–24.

[13] Martin Loughlin, 'The Concept of Constituent Power', *European Journal of Political Theory* 13:2 (2013), pp. 218–237, at p. 232. For further elaborations along these lines, see e.g. Andreas Kalyvas, 'Popular Sovereignty, Democracy, and the Constituent Power', *Constellations* 12:2 (2005), pp. 223–244; Joel I. Colón-Ríos, *Weak Constitutionalism. Democratic Legitimacy and the Question of Constituent Power* (Abingdon: Routledge, 2012); and Dieter Grimm, *Sovereignty. The Origin and Future of a Political Concept*, trans. Belinda Cooper (New York, NY: Columbia University Press, 2015).

the current political trajectory is reflected in the trending numbers of related academic engagements. According to the British Library catalogue, the number of books published this millennium with words related to 'populism' in the title had been around ten to fifteen titles a year up until 2015, with a sudden increase to 35 in 2016, and a record high of 65 in 2018. The dramatic increase, of course, marks Donald Trump's rise to power as the President of the United States, which gave a recognisable face to developments that had gradually been taking place.

Populism, whatever else one could say about it, is a politics that claims to make good on the founding ideal of democracy, that is, to let the people rule. And so populism is intimately associated with the idea of constituent power and popular rule. It should, therefore, not come as a surprise that assessments of populism often mirror those made of constituent power.

For some like Jan-Werner Müller, German-born political scientist at Princeton, populism is unequivocally a threat to democracy. He argues that populism lacks any potential to function as a useful corrective for a democracy that has somehow become too 'elite-driven'. Populism is, Müller concludes, always an exclusionary and anti-pluralist form of identity politics.[14] A similar argument is reduplicated in more or less elegant forms in much of the literature on populism, and it reflects the reservations that many constitutionalist scholars have about 'radical democratic' interpretations of constituent power, as well.

The Belgian-born political theorist Chantal Mouffe has a more positive view. Perhaps inspired by some Latin American experiences, Mouffe claims that populism is not primarily substance, but strategy. And as strategy, it can serve potentially progressive aims, as well. Right-wing populism claims to support popular rule, but its definition of 'the people' is factually a narrow ethnoracial entity that excludes categories of individuals that are seen as a threat to its identity or prosperity. Mouffe's left populism, by contrast, would attempt to broaden and deepen democratic rule by including groups that are not adequately represented in the politics of neoliberal societies. The strategic aim of left populism is to align the possibly conflicting demands of multiple social groups – workers, immigrant communities, the middle class, the LGBT community, and so on – into a collective will that will be able to function as the foundation of a 'people' confronting the oligarchy as its common adversary.[15] This reflects well positions that even other post-Marxist 'radical democrats' developed in relation to constituent power and popular rule.[16]

---

[14] Jan-Werner Müller, *What is Populism?* (Philadelphia, PA: University of Pennsylvania Press, 2016).

[15] Chantal Mouffe, *For a Left Populism* (London: Verso, 2018).

[16] See e.g. Adrian Little and Moya Lloyd (eds) The Politics of Radical Democracy (Edinburgh: Edinburgh University Press, 2009).

Finally, Mexican political theorist Benjamin Arditi has noted populism's familial relation to democracy by describing it as the 'internal periphery' of democratic politics. Populism, he suggests, is a 'spectral' companion that haunts the workings of a healthy democracy in three different forms. First, it can appear as a mode of representation. Populist representation is less about the positions a politician takes, and more about trusting a charismatic individual and favouring what he or she symbolises. Populist representation is also about creating a sense of identification, connection and closeness, often staged and media-communicated. Think of, for example, the televised rallies in which President Trump addresses his 'base'. Arditi suggests that populism as a mode of representation has gone mainstream and has become commonplace in media-enhanced democracies as recent elections in Austria bear witness. Second, populism can arrive as a mode of political participation in which 'improper' subjects not only depart from conventional political etiquette but also challenge the credentials of formal democracy. By mobilising improper subjects, populism can claim to expand the scope of citizen involvement in public affairs which mainstream opponents will have problems in criticising. Populist mobilisations may, however, not be easily distinguishable from the desire for mob rule. Think of, once again, the reported hostility and aggression of the fired-up audience at Trump's rallies. In this second mode, the populist spectre, Arditi notes, causes tangible discomfort for mainstream politics. Third, populism also materialises as the ominous shadow of democracy and its potential destroyer. In this mode, populists fully embrace and act out the fantasy about the social body as a unitary one by dispelling pluralism and toleration, using state resources as patrimony for the in-group, by dismissing accountability as an issue, and by engaging in authoritarian behaviour and rule by decree. President Trump's frequent threats of executive orders that are meant to circumvent the will of a democratically elected legislature is an instance of populism's third guise as the 'underside of democracy'.[17]

Some might question whether the term 'populism' best describes the current political situation. Be that as it may, the widespread and somewhat muddled use of the word is to us a symptom of the heightened tensions between constituent power and constituted politics that are typical of our times. In this light, the collection at hand examines the troubled relationships between the people and constitutions, law, human rights and democracy. While we make no claims about our ability to find cures for social ills, we have put the emphasis on the ability of multidisciplinary scholarship to understand and explain the complicated issues slightly better than before. The following chapters will accordingly approach the topic from without the liberal

---

[17] Benjamin Arditi, *Politics on the Edges of Liberalism. Difference, Populism, Revolution, Agitation* (Edinburgh: Edinburgh University Press, 2007).

framework that usually informs this type of research. The contributions engage with classic works on constituent power, such as Carl Schmitt's, Hannah Arendt's and Claude Lefort's, but also with more contemporary thinkers such as Jacques Rancière, Judith Butler and Alain Badiou.

In a lead essay that follows this introduction. Benjamin Arditi highlights and analyses two ways in which 'the etiquette of public discourse' has changed in today's liberal democracies. On the one hand, confirmation bias has become a respectable mode of political reasoning (i.e. privileging belief over evidence), and on the other, shamelessness has become normalised (i.e. the willingness to accept behaviour that used to be unthinkable). These shifts in public discourse foster what Arditi labels 'an exclusionary *demos* of *ressentiment*', immune to embarrassment.

The main bulk of the book is organised around three interrelated themes.

As the rubric 'The Ambiguities of Constituent Power' indicates, the elusive notion of constituent power is at the centre of the first part of the book. Unlike constituted power, which is represented in the established political and legal institutions as defined by a constitution, constituent power is thought to be the 'raw' and formative power of popular sovereignty in a democracy 'of the people, by the people, for the people'. Constituent power is the constitution's source of legitimacy and, at the same time, not easy to pin down because the people does not appear as a single subject. The individual chapters of this first thematic subdivision investigate who and what might play the part of constituent power in contemporary liberal democracies. The chapters focus on topical issues such as the 'activist' role of the judiciary in democracies (Minkkinen), the compatibility of strongly entrenched constitutional provisions with popular sovereignty (Vinx), and the 'world-stabilising' capacity of constitutions (Zakin).

The second part of the book, 'Popular Identity and its Others', discusses the boundaries that establish the identity of 'the people', as well as the practices that destabilise and renegotiate these boundaries. The relationship between 'the people' and notions such as race, ethnic group and nation is at the very centre of discussion. The chapters of this section investigate the ethnoracial construction of 'the people' as a constitutional subject in the contemporary Western and Northern Europe (Brännström), the paradoxical relationship between constituent power and democratic representation (Lukkari), how the coming together of 'the people' may be mediated by culture and neoliberal rationality (Turpeinen), and whether, and under what conditions, human rights can be seen as constitutive of 'the people' rather than as a medium restraining its will (Gill-Pedro).

The focus of the third part of the book, 'Populism and Democracy', is populist politics and the impact of such politics on democratic life and practices. The individual chapters address the reasons why the current political crisis cannot be reduced to merely a conflict between technocracy and populism as forms of rule, but that it may also involve a theologically framed 'katechontic' democracy intended to hold back the advent of the Antichrist (Falk), the ways in which the musings of contemporary political theorists like Jacques Rancière and Alain Badiou about popular sovereignty draw on the tradition of political philosophy (Hirvonen – Lindroos-Hovinheimo), the extent to what, and the possible senses in which, the current political trajectory is, in fact, related to what has historically been labelled 'populism' (Vergara), and how Carl Schmitt's ideas concerning the protective, concrete and physical borders of communities involving curious entanglements between law, customs and sacred rituals remain relevant even today (Wittrock).

This book has come about as part of the work of a collaborative network. The individual chapters have been chosen and developed from a range of presentations given originally at a workshop organised by the network in Helsinki in June 2017 entitled 'The People: Democracy, Populism, and the Constituent Popular Sovereign', with keynotes by philosopher and Nietzsche-scholar Christa Davis Acampora[18], political theorist and feminist theoretician Bonnie Honig[19], and legal philosopher Hans Lindahl[20]. During the course of the workshop, all keynote speakers gave invaluable feedback to the paper presenters. The editors wish to thank the keynote speakers for their support and their inspiration.

[18] See e.g. Christa Davis Acampora, *Contesting Nietzsche* (Chicago, IL: University of Chicago Press, 2013).
[19] See e.g. Bonnie Honig, *Public Things. Democracy in Disrepair* (New York, NY: Fordham University Press, 2017).
[20] See e.g. Hans Lindahl, *Authority and the Globalisation of Inclusion and Exclusion* (Cambridge: Cambridge University Press, 2018).

Politics, Shamelessness and the People of *Ressentiment*

Benjamin Arditi

> Everyone is entitled to his own opinion, but not his own facts.
>
> *Daniel Patrick Moynihan, former US Senator*

> Honestly, people are definitely dumber. They just keep passing stuff around. Nobody fact-checks anything anymore—I mean, that's how Trump got elected. He just said whatever he wanted, and people believed everything, and when the things he said turned out not to be true, people didn't care because they'd already accepted it. It's real scary. I've never seen anything like it.
>
> *Paul Horner, professional fake-news writer*

The quote from Moynihan is an indirect vindication of decency in public life. It tells us that politicians in liberal democracies shouldn't go around lying, cheating, or smearing their adversaries with baseless charges, and ought to feel ashamed if they did. More sceptical observers would take this in stride, for embarrassment is contingent on being caught. The liberal concern with good political table manners might sound even less credible when you factor in pork-barrel politics and deceit, familiar staples of congressional and governmental activity, or when you ask yourself what kind of facts gave support to the long cohabitation of the liberal state with slavery and the genocide of the indigenous people. Decency is also questionable when considered in conjunction with capitalism, the economic leg of liberal states. For every success story of rags to riches, there are countless more about the chronic collateral damages of the market. This is because inequality is not an accident. Those with wealth, privilege and connections play with loaded dice and, in the absence of rules imposed and enforced by governments, markets will fall short of a level playing field. Advocates of deregulation simply ignore this, putting their trust in an invisible hand whose proof of existence, like that of the Holy Ghost, requires a leap of faith, not evidence.

If self-interest, political opportunism, demagogy and inequality make a mockery of Moynihan's quote, why should anyone be moved by it? Because stating that there ought to be some kind of line between evidence and belief doesn't mean that the line is uncontroversial, or that it won't be crossed. The line expresses a normative preference, the 'as if' of a moral claim, not the actual behaviour of people.

The quote from the late Paul Horner paints a very different image of public life. His assessment of the present is brutal. It dispenses with the pretence that politicians seek the moral high ground, or that people really mind that they don't. Donald Trump 'just said whatever he wanted', and people didn't care if what he said wasn't true because 'they'd already accepted it'.[1] Horner knew a thing or two about this; he was a hoax artist who made a living from posting plausible or outright deceitful stories. He called them fake news before Trump popularised this expression, and presented them as if they were bona fide news. Trump's supporters were the least likely to verify what they shared. Says Horner: 'His followers don't fact-check anything—they'll post everything, believe anything. His campaign manager [at the time, Corey Lewandowsky, B.A.] posted my story about a protester getting paid $3,500 as fact. Like, I made that up. I posted a fake ad on Craigslist'.[2]

We can't explain away Horner's talk of dumbness as a matter of ignorance. It's good to verify information before accepting it, but equating dumbness with ignorance alone would be too easy, and wrong. The worldly and cultivated elites often don't bother to fact check either. We also need to factor in the confusion caused by the incessant bombardment of information from conspiracy sites and false account profiles in social media platforms. They mislead people by concocting conversations, retweets, followers, and likes and dislikes, to shore up or attack a policy proposal or candidates. Most of us find it difficult to distinguish between endogenous and targeted opinion making.

So, what do we make of the claim that people are dumber? Horner complains that our fact-checking standards are lax. Isn't this a way of saying that something is blowing the fuse of acceptable public discourse? Let me give an example. Toni Holt Kramer was the public face of The Trumpettes, a group of women that supported Trump during his 2016 campaign. All were rich, most of them were white. When asked about Hillary Clinton's tax reform proposal, Holt said confidently: 'I think Hillary's tax plan will defeat the country'. The

---

[1] Quoted in Caitlin Dewey, 'Facebook fake-news writer: "I think Donald Trump is in the White House because of me"', *The Washington Post*, November 17, 2016. Available at https://www.washingtonpost.com/news/the-intersect/wp/2016/11/17/facebook-fake-news-writer-i-think-donald-trump-is-in-the-white-house-because-of-me/ (accessed October 2018).

[2] Quoted in Dewey, 'Facebook fake-news writer'.

interviewer then asked: 'What do you know about Hillary's tax plan?'. Her response: 'I know nothing about her tax plan'.[3] Holt was obviously unaware of her performative contradiction. Maybe it was plain stupidity or an exercise in political bad faith that backfired on her. What is noteworthy is that she was unembarrassed, didn't expect to face the consequences for what she said, and considered her feelings for and against candidates to be a source of discursive legitimacy on par with evidence. She pushed the bounds of what we thought counted as valid public discourse.

The outrageousness of Holt and others, not to mention their impunity, corrodes the political table manners of liberal democracies. These polities were supposed to be better than autocracies, populist regimes, or illiberal democracies. My explanation for what is going on is that confirmation bias and shamelessness are freeing many from the burden of embarrassment, and that this is creating a mode of public reason that distrusts evidence and gives an aura of respectability to a conspiratorial fringe. Shamelessness is also fostering an exclusionary *demos* of *ressentiment*. I don't mean a *demos* in Jacques Rancière's sense of the word. Politics for him is always about emancipation; it sets up an apparatus of dissensus aimed to redress a wronging of equality.[4] *Ressentiment* is different. It is a negative emotion close to pettiness that feeds a *demos* that is resistant to embarrassment. This *demos* harnesses the power of *ressentiment* to mount a politics of redemption that is more exclusionary than inclusive.

In what follows, I will look at confirmation bias and shamelessness to discuss changes in the etiquette of public discourse. I will then examine the *demos* of *ressentiment* using the Guaraní language to distinguish two forms of the pronoun we, *oré* and *ñandé*, to distinguish the exclusionary and inclusive we of redemption and emancipation, correspondingly.

Confirmation Bias

Descartes might have got it wrong epistemologically – there is no absolute certainty – but he wasn't off the mark in an existential register: the promise of certainty helps to counterbalance the anxiety of having to make sense of the world in the wake of the death of God. Certainty is often sought precisely because there is no ultimate ground for truth, justice, etc. We might prefer to appeal to solidarity and the desire for a better world, but xenophobia, racism,

---

[3] 'Embed with Desi – Meet the Trumpettes', *The Daily Show with Trevor Noah*, November 2, 2016. Available at http://www.cc.com/video-clips/chosjm/the-daily-show-with-trevor-noah-embed-with-desi---meet-the-trumpettes (accessed June 2019).

[4] Jacques Rancière, *Disagreement: Politics and Philosophy,* trans. Julie Rose (Minnesota: The University of Minnesota Press, 1998).

or something just as bad can also be sources of certainty. The opinions and beliefs characteristic of confirmation bias are mundane equivalents of Cartesian certainty: they help us navigate through a chaotic and ever-changing world without feeling so lost.

Joel Mathis describes confirmation bias as the predisposition 'to uncritically accept stories that line up with preexisting beliefs'.[5] We take for granted whatever confirms what we already believe. Any number of us will retweet negative stories about people we dislike simply because they coincide with what we already thought about them. It's like gossiping. One can shrug it off in private conversations, but not on platforms like Facebook or Twitter, which blur the distinction between public and private. Confirmation bias becomes even more of a problem when those involved are show hosts, politicians, CEOs, columnists, public intellectuals, academics, social media influencers, financial advisers, and the rest of the global chattering classes. I am not talking about old-fashioned demagogy, of saying whatever it takes to please an audience in exchange for applause or votes. There is something of this, but confirmation bias is transversal to many styles of politics, both on the left and right. Its normalisation, that is, the mainstreaming of this bias in public discourse, helps to explain Horner's claim that people pass things around without bothering to check if they are true.

Daniel Kahneman maps confirmation bias at a cognitive level. He distinguishes two systems of thought. One is system 1, that functions as a rapid response mechanism to process information, the other System 2, a more reflective way of dealing with information. It only kicks in later, if ever. System 1 is a mode of reasoning based on beliefs and intuitions. Unlike the slower and more logical System 2, it is immediate and 'does not keep track of alternatives that it rejects, or even of the fact that there were alternatives. Conscious doubt is not in the repertoire of System 1'.[6] System 1 is our cognitive automatic pilot, or, as Kahneman calls it, a machine for jumping to conclusions. We would like to think that economic and political reasoning put System 1 on the sideline, but Kahneman sees both systems as part of who we are, not ideal types to designate different kinds of people, some intuitive and others logical. There are those who buy stocks on a hunch that their price will go up, or because they heard an expert praise them in a morning talk show, ignoring available market research about the company's financial

---

[5] Quoted in John Blake, 'How an internet mob falsely painted a Chipotle employee as racist', CNN, May 27, 2019. Available at https://edition.cnn.com/2019/05/25/us/false-racism-internet-mob-chipotle-video/index.html (accessed May 2019).

[6] Daniel Kahneman, *Thinking, Fast and Slow* (New York: Farrar, Strauss and Giroux, 2011), p. 80.

performance. Health officials can make decisions about birth control funding based on what they feel is right, without considering its impact on teenage pregnancies. Both are examples of System 1 driving decisions among people we would have expected to operate primarily through System 2.

Marshall McLuhan's line, 'I wouldn't have seen it if I hadn't believed it', is shorthand for the confirmation bias lodged in System 1: we tend to see what we already believe. System 1 has always been our cognitive first responder; it might be on its way to becoming the preferred frame of reference to filter and assess information, making logic and verification the exception. Confirmation bias, or System 1, is a rebellion against the spirit of the Enlightenment; it operates through beliefs that are resistant to the test of evidence. A critical assessment of the present can't ignore this.

The Politics of Shamelessness

The second change in public discourse falls outside the opposition between jumping to conclusions and a reflexive mode of reasoning. People like Moynihan were capable of experiencing embarrassment because their conduct had at least a veneer of honour. In the scenario Horner describes, people take confirmation bias as a virtue and are far more willing to ditch embarrassment by embracing shamelessness.

Ruth Wodak speaks of shamelessness and post-shame to signal the mainstreaming of terms previously associated with fringe groups. She says: 'the boundaries of what can be said have significantly shifted; this has led to a *normalization* of right-wing extremist, formerly taboo contents and terminology . . . Many existing conventions (concerning politeness, conversation maxims, conventional norms and rules governing discussions, negotiations, conflict management and so forth) are increasingly being jettisoned in political debates . . . Apologies no longer seem necessary, insults are left standing'.[7] Her example to illustrate these changes is the Austrian People's Party (ÖVP). Within the party, says Wodak, 'rational discussion is mostly substituted by symbolic politics, impoliteness, eristic argumentation or denial . . . scientific empirical evidence is frequently neglected or ridiculed. It seems as if the ÖVP . . . has either ignored or quietly accepted the kind of non-democratic ideologues they have aligned themselves with, thus normalising the previously unsayable and unacceptable'.[8] I take this last phrase, 'normalising the previously unsayable and unacceptable', to be the decisive aspect of post-shame politics. It

---

[7] Ruth Wodak, '"The Boundaries of What Can Be Said Have Shifted": An Expert Interview with Ruth Wodak (questions posed by Andreas Schulz)', *Discourse & Society* 31:2 (2020), pp. 235–244, at pp. 238–239.

[8] Ruth Wodak, 'Entering the "Post-Shame Era": The Rise of Illiberal Democracy, Populism and Neo-Authoritarianism in Europe', *Global Discourse* 9:1 (2019), pp. 195–213, at p. 207.

involves ignoring or having a cavalier attitude towards moral and ethical considerations when stating something as true or making decisions that will affect people's lives. Shamelessness turns that attitude into something acceptable.

Wodak is right in stating that shamelessness changes the terms of political discussion. It supplements confirmation bias but differs from it because it doesn't rest on belief. It is also different from political realism, which takes as its rule that in the affairs of a state, principles will always give way to interests: in shameless behaviour, there is often no discernible interest of a state, a political party or an organisation. It can be about something banal or corrupt. It is also different from lying. Former US President Richard Nixon lied and trampled with electoral etiquette during the Watergate scandal. His actions fell short of basic standards of public morality. He resigned to avoid the embarrassment of impeachment by Congress. Trump has taken lying to such a disturbing level that it ceases to be an issue. By this I mean that Nixon was immoral, but Trump is amoral about the truth, and about the boundaries between his personal business and political interests on the one hand, and, on the other, between those interests and the public good. His sycophantic appointees and party supporters justify his outrageous claims because they act shamelessly to stay in the game.

To reiterate their difference, in confirmation bias, belief suspends critique, whereas shamelessness entails a willingness to accept behaviour that used to be unthinkable, and to exchange dignity for power, glory, money, jobs, etc. In its most extreme form, distinctions between right and wrong don't really enter into the equation because neither the value of what is right nor the guilt of doing the wrong thing are strong enough to function as deterrents. Shamelessness is a form of amorality whose object is irrelevant. The most absurd claims can become valid points of debate. President Jair Bolsonaro of Brazil said that Amazonian wildfires in 2019 were caused by NGOs assisted by actor Leonardo di Caprio to discredit his government, not because he encouraged landowners to burn the forest to clear land.[9] The Hungarian Civic Alliance party (Fidesz) of prime minister Viktor Orbán passed a law to punish the Central European University (and force its de facto emigration to Vienna), founded by financier and philanthropist George Soros, as part of Orbán's feud with Soros for funding organisations helping refugees.[10] Fox

---

[9] Leah Asmelash, 'Leonardo DiCaprio responds after Brazil's President blames actor for Amazon forest fires', CNN, December 1, 2019. Available at https://edition.cnn.com/2019/11/30/world/leonardo-dicaprio-bolsonaro-amazon-fires-trnd/index.html (accessed December 2019).

[10] Cas Mudde, *The Far Right Today* (Cambridge: Polity, 2019), p. 128; Susan Adams, 'Why Hungary Forced George Soros-Backed Central European University to Leave the Country', *Forbes*, December 4, 2018. Available at https://www.forbes.com/sites/susanadams/2018/12/04/why-hungary-forced-george-soros-backed-central-european-university-to-leave-the-country/#5ce05b9e533e (accessed October 2019).

News blurs the line between information and entertainment, often through narratives provided by right-wing, white supremacist and conspiracy-theory sources unconcerned about veracity. This is the new normal in many polities.

Others have picked up on Wodak's notion of shamelessness and see it as a result of the highly focused and persistent messages of politicians, particularly around migration. 'A process of normalization', say two policy researchers, 'is taking place among these actors. They do not like the shift, and many feel a sense of personal moral outrage at the crossing of the normative boundaries, but they accept the change in political rhetoric as something that they cannot influence directly'.[11] They cite from private conversations about illiberal practices with policy actors. One told them: 'Be realistic, see what we can get through the Council [of Europe] when the Orbáns and Salvinis say what many others are thinking.'[12] The acceptance of something you can't influence sounds good, almost like a declaration of political realism among policy actors, but it is really nothing more than an alibi for not speaking up to the Orbáns and Salvinis, whether for fear of losing their jobs, looking bad, fear of reprisals, or other reasons. It helps to understand how people's inaction contributed to the success of radical right-wing parties in pushing the unthinkable into the political mainstream, especially exclusionary policies towards immigrants and all kinds of minorities, not complying with European Union rules, as well as questioning pluralism and the objectivity of the critical media. The capitulation of the Republican Party to Trump for the sake of power is another example: it puts their morally abject behaviour on display.

Mudde reinforces this argument. He says that the populist radical right has managed to set the political agenda in many European countries, moving *all* of the mainstream parties, even those on the left, 'significantly to the right in terms of their discourse on corruption, crime, European integration, and immigration, but made mainly cosmetic policy changes.'[13] He adds that this changed after the so-called refugee crisis and jihadist attacks that 'quickly closed the gap between discourse and policy.'[14] The media played a role by interviewing far right politicians for their spectacle value and readership, but by doing so, it gave them and their ideas an air of respectability.[15] The 'respectable' media had a role in 'normalizing populist radical right and

---

[11] Heather Grabbe and Andreas Aktoudianakis, 'Response to Ruth Wodak's Paper', *Global Discourse* 9:1 (2019), pp. 215–219, at p. 215.

[12] Grabbe and Aktoudianakis, 'Response to Ruth Wodak's Paper', p. 216.

[13] Mudde, *The Far Right Today*, pp. 121–122.

[14] Mudde, *The Far Right Today*, p. 122.

[15] Mudde, *The Far Right Today*, p. 109.

Islamophobic politicians by employing them as columnists and occasional op-ed writers', to the extent that the *Wall Street Journal* endorsed Bolsonaro in the Brazilian elections of 2018.[16] Mudde's reasoning coincides with Wodak's in relation to the normalisation of the radical right in public discourse, which, by moving into the mainstream, redefines the very meaning of that mainstream. The success of the nativist Brexit advocates is a reminder of this.

We shake our heads in disbelief, but we are growing accustomed to the normalisation of speech and behaviour that we once considered outrageous. How far can one push the limits of acceptability? It is difficult to tell, but shamelessness, even in its less strident forms, already has an impact on our lives and institutions. The will of the people has become less relevant in the US political process due to careful gerrymandering and laws that disenfranchise felons. Both are generally targeted to minorities to limit their electoral voice. And while Trump's tirades might seem bizarre, he is reshaping the US judiciary by filling vacancies in the Supreme Court and appointing new judges. 'With the help of Senate Republicans, Donald Trump spent the first three years of his presidency remaking the federal judiciary in his own image. The president has appointed 133 district court judges, 50 appeals court judges, and two Supreme Court justices—meaning about one-fifth of the nation's federal trial judges, and one-fourth of its federal appellate judges, are Trump appointees'.[17] Most of them were hand-picked for their conservative views on issues like abortion, immigration, mandatory health coverage, or law enforcement.

The novelty of Wodak's post-shame politics lies in the normalisation or mainstreaming of previously unacceptable behaviour. This is true, but maybe voters always cared more about their representatives delivering the goods or wanted politicians to embrace emotionally charged issues that mattered to them, be it immigration, race, jobs, or the dominance of their preferred religion. Hitler emerged from a rarefied liberal democratic regime. Germans voted for an openly racist bully that promised them great things. They didn't really seem to mind, or didn't mind enough, that greatness happened at the expense of the humiliation of Jews, stripping them of citizenship, taking away their property, and eventually murdering them as part of a carefully planned genocidal policy. Neither did they seem to care that this was also happening to other undesirables, like communists, social democrats, union activists and eventually all kinds of dissenting voices. Even Carl Schmitt, one of the

[16] Mudde, *The Far Right Today*, p. 109.

[17] Marc Joseph Stern, 'What Happened When Trump Reshaped a Powerful Court', *Slate*, December 26, 2019. Available at https://slate.com/news-and-politics/2019/12/fifth-circuit-trump-judges-devastating.html (accessed December 2019).

most brilliant legal and political thinkers of the Weimar Republic, supported the purge of his Jewish colleagues from universities and the burning of their books out of shameless opportunism.

Those who think that this is not an appropriate example because Germany in the 1930s was an outlier should think twice. What happened there was not circumscribed to a bad apple. All polities experience bursts of shamelessness. Sometimes they last longer. One can't forget the liberal state's cohabitation with slavery. This punches a hole in the gentrified view of liberalism as the epitome of tolerance and due process. And during the Cold War, the House Un-American Committee embarked in an anti-communist witch hunt led by Senator Joseph McCarthy and seconded by Roy Cohn, an unscrupulous young lawyer who later mentored Trump. McCarthy and Cohn destroyed reputations and careers by attacking perceived adversaries without much regard for evidence. Anti-communist hysteria offered them cover. McCarthyism normalised shamelessness in the US in the name of national security, even if this meant compromising due process and the presumption of innocence.

Add to this the red lines crossed every day in plain view: racial profiling; the separation of children from their asylum-seeking parents; President Trump's claim that there are very fine people among neo-Nazi white supremacists; calling the mainstream media fake news; mocking a handicapped reporter in an electoral rally; or redefining waterboarding as a legitimate form of interrogation. As Wodak says, 'The state itself, the entire political system, is challenged, like in reality TV: shamelessness, humiliation of other participants, defamation, lies and ad hominem attacks dominate.'[18]

One can see that liberal democracies have no immunitarian privilege shielding them from the challenge Wodak describes. This doesn't mean that one has to endorse Giorgio Agamben's claim that the state of exception and bare life of concentration camps have become the analogical model for electoral democracies.[19] We just have to accept that liberal democracies might be preferable to other types of regimes, but that their polished political table manners are more of a comforting bedside story than an actuality. Even more when looking at things from the vantage point of the poor, women, gays, blacks, youth, or immigrants. Their everyday experience is full of tales of discrimination. This is why calling Trump, Bolsonaro, or Brexit's Nigel Farage political outliers is a misnomer. They are vehicles that supercharged the worst of what was already there, in the backrooms of institutions and among common citizens.

---

[18] Wodak, 'Entering the "Post-Shame Era"', p. 197.
[19] Giorgio Agamben, *State of Exception*, trans. Kevin Attell (Chicago: University of Chicago Press, 2005).

'What was already there' is not a psychological or essentialist argument about dormant qualities stored in our subconscious and then triggered by the right message or political climate. The already there are sedimented beliefs, meanings and practices. Those who had grudgingly curtailed their xenophobia and sexism in public now feel empowered. Bolsonaro told a member of congress that she was too ugly to deserve being raped by him.[20] Trump said that a US-born judge, the son of Mexican parents and bearing a Latino name, should have recused himself from presiding over a fraud lawsuit against his Trump University because 'he's a Mexican'.[21] Both became presidents despite making statements that normalise stereotypes and emboldened people to express their prejudice openly. Districts that voted heavily for Trump in 2016 have the highest reported hate crimes: perpetrators saw his victory as a validation of his incendiary campaign rhetoric, and hate crimes increased 226 per cent in counties where he held campaign rallies.[22] Post-shame is a sign of the times.

The People of *Ressentiment* and Redemption vs. Emancipation

Two corollaries follow from this discussion. One is that privileging belief over evidence leads to a demise of textbook expectations about what counts as sound public reasoning. Confirmation bias and shamelessness nourish this demise, making a travesty of the idea of the public use of reason. If it is not brazen lying, the new normal cuts argumentative corners by jumping to conclusions without paying much attention to evidence, refutation, or alternatives. Shamelessness corrodes the liberal ethos. It does so by letting go of embarrassment, and by granting mainstream respectability to those who

---

[20] Zing Tsjeng, 'Brazil's New President Once Told a Politician She Was Too Ugly to Rape', *Vice*, October 29, 2018. Available at https://www.vice.com/en_us/article/j53wx8/jair-bolsonaro-elected-president-brazil (accessed November 2019). As president, in his weekly broadcast in Facebook, he declared: 'Indians are undoubtedly changing . . . They are increasingly becoming human beings just like us'. Quoted in Tom Phillips, 'Jair Bolsonaro's racist comment sparks outrage from indigenous groups', *The Guardian*, 24 January 2020. Available at https://www.theguardian.com/world/2020/jan/24/jair-bolsonaro-racist-comment-sparks-outrage-indigenous-groups (accessed January 2020).

[21] Griffin Sims Edwards and Stephen Rushin, 'The Effect of President Trump's Election on Hate Crimes' (14 January 2018). Available at https://ssrn.com/abstract=3102652 or http://dx.doi.org/10.2139/ssrn.3102652 (accessed November 2019).

[22] Edwards and Rushin, 'The Effect of President Trump's Election on Hate Crimes', and Ayal Feinberg, Regina Branton and Valerie Martinez-Ebers, 'Counties that hosted a 2016 Trump rally saw a 226 per cent increase in hate crimes', *The Washington Post*, March 22, 2019. Available at https://www.washingtonpost.com/politics/2019/03/22/trumps-rhetoric-does-inspire-more-hate-crimes/ (accessed June 2019).

promote conspiratorial views of out-groups because of how they look, dress, or pray. This enhances an exclusionary pattern in the polity. The problem is not that the practice of liberal democracies doesn't match the high moral standards they claim to embody. That would be a banal truism, for no political praxis lives up to its well-polished discourse. Checks and balances, due process, and the accountability of public servants are only normative goals, like Moynihan's primacy of facts over opinions. But one cannot downplay outrageous practices as occasional misfires or as something that happens to others. Shamelessness and confirmation bias are the petri dish for a *demos* of *ressentiment*.

A second corollary refers to this *demos* and shows the prolific nature of the people. There is a *demos* that resists injustice and mounts a critique of inequality, and another one structured around the thinly virtuous citizenry Moynihan had in mind. These are the people as event and as re-presentation, correspondingly. But there is also a third, less virtuous one. I referred to the people in Nazi Germany as an example. Anti-Communism during McCarthyism was another. A third one, under the military regimes in Argentina and Chile, is about people who were shameless enough to justify the torture, disappearances and exile of fellow citizens in the name of patriotism. These three modes of being of the people are a reminder that any 'we' is always fissured, like political systems, which have parties, or parts, except in the oxymoronic expression of 'one party system'. While all these parts/parties strive to command the will of the state, the third variety of the *demos* poses the question of fissures that make some parts more insidious than others.

One example of a heterogeneous 'we' is the preamble to the US Constitution. The capitalised 'we' in 'We, the People', can, and does, mean all of us, but it also can, and does, mean a more exclusionary 'we' that is less than all. Slaves didn't count in that founding 'We' of 1787 – they were someone's property, not deliberating agents – and neither did native Americans, who were considered savages, or women, at least not with their own voices and rights of citizenship. The language of the Tupí Guaraní people of Paraguay and its surrounding countries uses two pronouns to describe this fissured we. One is *oré*, the exclusionary us/we, as in Borussia Dortmund fans or members of the Communist Party. They exclude other political parties and football teams without necessarily ceasing to engage with them. The other is *ñandé*, the inclusive we, as in Mexicans, democrats and, ultimately, humans. If we leave aside the all-inclusive humans (which can also be contentious), the contours of *oré* and *ñandé* oscillate and there is no fixed criterion to determine which is less inclusive and which more: hamburger lovers and vegans are *oré*, despite the difference in magnitude of their respective populations. *Oré* is simply the tribal form of the 'we'. The reach of the ecumenical we of *ñandé* is also contextual. Finally, the distinction between the exclusionary and inclusive 'we' does not necessarily presuppose an a priori moral hierarchy between *oré* and *ñandé*.

The exclusionary *oré* is a good thing when accompanied by toleration. It has often worked well when it refers to something like political parties that stick to democratic rules of engagement. But it signals trouble when the exclusionary identity of the *oré* turns the difference of out-groups into negativity, making the in-group feel threatened by a real or imaginary danger posed by others. The Nazis dissolved the distinction between *oré* and *ñandé* by trying to make Germany the home of a sanitised Aryan *oré-as-ñandé*. The Jewish *oré* didn't fit into this picture, yet it was one of its conditions of possibility. Migrants from so-called shithole countries are present-day Jews, although things are not nearly as dire as they were in Nazi concentration camps. I already made clear my reservations about Agamben's use of the state of exception as the truth of liberal democracies. There is nonetheless a *demos* that feeds off the less virtuous variants of the exclusionary *oré*. It is the *demos* of *ressentiment*, which has a complex, ambiguous, and at times hostile relation with the inclusive *ñandé*.

What is this *ressentiment*? The literature uses the French word rather than resentment to indicate something in excess of its linguistic definition. Resentment is a weakness of character that leads to expressions of hostility toward the object of one's frustration. It's like harbouring anger towards immigrants because a non-native colleague got the promotion that you thought you deserved. It is a negative emotion, close to pettiness. Politically, however, *ressentiment* is an emotion that can turn frustration into a productive force. Sometimes it is for the greater good. At other times, like in the case of the fear of strangers, or the demonisation of Jews under Nazism, it is not.

Ressentiment was an object of thought for Nietzsche and Kierkegaard, and taken up by existential philosophers later. Nietzsche was critical of *ressentiment* because it 'promises blessedness, advantage, privilege to the most insignificant and humble; it fills poor little foolish heads with an insane conceit, as if *they* were the meaning and the salt of the earth—'.[23] *Ressentiment* gives hope to the undeserving weak, something 'one cannot sufficiently despise'.[24] Gilles Deleuze says that for Nietzsche, *ressentiment* upturns a natural hierarchy where stronger spirits should dominate over weaker ones. It 'gives revenge a means: a means of reversing the normal relation of active and reactive forces. This is why

---

[23] Friedrich Nietzsche, *The Will to Power*, ed. Walter Kaufman, trans. Walter Kaufman and Stuart Hollingdale (New York: Random House, 1967), p. 104.

[24] Nietzsche, *The Will to Power*, p. 104.

ressentiment itself is always a revolt and always the triumph of this revolt. *Ressentiment* is the triumph of the weak as weak, the revolt of the slaves and their victory as slaves'.[25] It is a story about a reversal of the normal state of things: *ressentiment* is the victory of the weak that remain weak even in victory.

I find it difficult to go along with this quasi-aristocratic understanding of the normal state of affairs. One could dismiss comments about 'the foolish little heads' of the meaningless, insignificant and humble folks if they came from someone less prestigious, but the proper name 'Nietzsche' is awe-inspiring and many embrace them because they are his. It's fine to criticise the pettiness of the weak and their revenge when victorious, but why not acknowledge the generative force of *ressentiment*?

A line from Lewis Carroll's *Through the Looking Glass* helps to introduce what I mean by this: '"The question is," said Humpty Dumpty, "which is to be master – that's all"'. The intent of the open-ended 'which is to be master' is quite clear: to undermine the naturalness of mastery and the fixity of the positions of those who are dominant and subordinate. Once the dice of the Nietzschean wars of interpretation begin to roll, nothing guarantees which narrative will win. You might root for a Nelson Mandela but get stuck with Nigel Farage. Nietzsche was more interested in validating the role of the warrior caste, exemplary individuals that are precursors of the overman, and lost track of the consequences of his own claims about the primacy of becoming and the contingency of all being. Or rather, he realised that the weak could win, but found this revolting. And their winning matters. People whose *ressentiment* fills their 'poor little foolish heads with an insane conceit' may be unworthy, but their victory means that the vital, superior, midnight men and women that Nietzsche celebrates as worthy of dominion have been defeated by their inferiors. Looking down at the winners is no consolation. Trump won, the Democratic National Committee conspired so Bernie Sanders wouldn't be nominated in 2016, Orbán was re-elected multiple times, the British voted for Brexit, and Bolsonaro became president of Brazil. Nietzsche's aristocratic dismissal of unworthy victors is simply not political. It resembles the voyeurism of the chattering classes, who resort to irony to tell themselves that their superiority persists even in defeat. A more plebeian variant of this consolation shares memes to sublimate powerlessness. The noble folks can be political in defeat if their irony is accompanied by a willingness to fight back.

The most unpalatable traits of today's people of *ressentiment* include a nativist distrust of immigrants; a perception of non-Christians as dangerous; a fear that non-binary sexuality and female empowerment threatens masculinity; and a view of the traditional family that is out of step with

---

[25] Gilles Deleuze, *Nietzsche and Philosophy*, trans. Hugh Tomlinson (London: Continuum, 2002), p. 117.

the reality of older grooms and brides, the delay in parenthood among women, young people staying with their parents until an older age, stay at home dads, and a long etcetera. Most of these were present in the now-defunct Tea Party in the US, a collection of predominantly Christian, flag-waving, mostly non-college educated and at times racist white people (many of whom demonised Barack Obama, the first black US president) that challenged the political establishment with an aggressive agenda to reduce public spending and make us suspicious of the very idea of government.[26] As they believed in the sovereignty of the market, they considered healthcare as something to be dealt with by individuals, not government programmes, or, in their jargon, not through handouts. Their representatives cut taxes on the wealthy, questioned environmental policies on the grounds that climate change was unproven, and generally made shamelessness a virtue. We live in the aftermath of that victory, that is also Trump's. The Tea Party assembled a *demos* of *ressentiment* that challenged the status quo in an exclusionary manner.

The *ressentiment* of the Tea Party, but mainly Trump voters, was also an expression of frustration for the anxieties of a less secure, less white, less Christian, and more unstable world in matters of jobs, relationships or gender. *Ressentiment* functioned as an affirmative force for this coalition. Trump nurtured its *ressentiment* and offered himself as its vehicle. Many of his supporters were casualties of rentier capitalism stuck in a mystifying denial of the harm that market forces and policies (like lowering the tax rate for the wealthy) were doing to them. They looked elsewhere for explanations about the loss of jobs from global trade, industrial relocation, technological innovation, or the obsolescence of some occupations and industries. Their weakness in victory was to confuse the poison for the remedy. They wanted salvation, no matter how it would be achieved, or who could be affected, even if salvation through the market was a mirage. That's why a *demos* of *ressentiment* can champion the causes of class, occupational, ethnic, or religious *oré*, but is less concerned about the fate of the *ñandé* than with making a given *oré* better off. Members of Trump's coalition, for example, put the reduction of poverty and the improvement of racial equality at the bottom of their priorities, just slightly above combatting climate change, and restricting immigration as their main concern.[27] They sought relief through redemption, not necessarily emancipation.

[26] Joseph Lowndes, 'Populism and Race in the United States from George Wallace to Donald Trump', in Carlos de la Torre (ed.), *Routledge Handbook of Global Populism* (London: Routledge, 2018), pp. 190–200, at pp. 196–197.

[27] Emily Ekins, 'The Five Types of Trump Voters. Who They Are and What They Believe', *The Voter Study Group*, June 2017, https://www.voterstudygroup.org/publication/the-five-types-trump-voters (accessed November 2017).

A politics of emancipation shares the concern for secular relief found in narratives of redemption, but it involves other things too. One is inclusiveness: emancipation is rooted in the modern quest for universality. Another is the relation to the impossible, understood as something that might seem unfeasible in the present field of experience yet nonetheless moves people to act as if it might happen. For example, demanding democracy under authoritarianism, gender equality in patriarchal settings, and so on. Emancipation also involves a polemic about whether existing social relations enable or hamper greater freedom, equality, or solidarity and whether a better world is possible. Those who say that the status quo is good don't pose the question of emancipation. Others, who think that society is not great, but believe that the odds of changing things are slim, have a decent normative position (more equality is good), not a political one. Emancipation combines the critique of existing social relations with acting to change them. Those who do so may fail, but there will have been emancipatory politics even in failure.

Emancipation takes 'We, the People', in the strong sense of the ecumenical *ñandé* championed by the French Revolution. This 'we' is transversal to class, gender and race. One of its iconic representations is 'The People United Will Never be Defeated', a song associated with Salvador Allende's socialist government in Chile and used as an anthem during the resistance to Pinochet's dictatorship. Today it energises protests against injustice and for equality in many parts of the world. Emancipation is nonetheless compatible with the *oré* when it is not encased in a tribal demand. Drawing from Rancière, there is a politics of emancipation among immigrants, women and other *oré* when they claim that their equality has been wronged by discrimination, and mount a dispute to verify the universality of that equality.

Redemption is slightly different. Michael Oakeshott speaks of the politics of faith, a human effort to achieve salvation without the intervention of divine providence, and normally disregarding scruples.[28] Jacobins are an archetypical example. Canovan rebrands faith as redemption, 'the promise of a better world through action by the sovereign people'.[29] This is a good start for understanding redemption. Some adjustments can develop it further. One is that while salvation is an opening to the promise of a better world, 'better' might not include all the people, or even most of them. The lack of scruples makes redemption something more selfish than emancipation because sometimes our redemption doesn't contemplate theirs. There's

---

[28] Michael Oakeshott, *The Politics of Faith and the Politics of Scepticism*, ed. Timothy Fuller (New Haven and London: Yale University Press, 1992), p. 22–23.

[29] Margaret Canovan, 'Trust the People! Populism and the Two Faces of Democracy', *Political Studies* 47:1 (1999), pp. 2–16, at p. 12.

also the question of whether the disregard for scruples is an inescapable feature of redemption. One could simply say that it is part of its structure of possibilities. This still places the lack of scruples within the semantic field of redemption, but without the weight of necessity: there *can* be a politics of redemption that is not unscrupulous. Finally, while it is true that redemption involves a secular notion of salvation, why must we exclude religion by default? The oxymoronic combination of secular and religious markers works as long as we understand redemption as worldly relief, not as salvation in the eschatological sense of the intervention of divine providence.

A politics of redemption pursues mundane relief from perceived or imaginary burdens of one's existence. It can draw from a religious imaginary or not, it can be scrupulous or unscrupulous, and its invocation of the sovereign people might embrace inclusiveness or advocate the exclusion of some. A people of *ressentiment* emerges whenever there is a politics of redemption that is primarily (although perhaps not only) exclusionary. The Tea Party's advocacy of small government and lower taxes in the US was done at the expense of the chronic collateral damages of the market – the old, the sick and the vulnerable. Fidesz sees secular salvation as something pertaining to ethnic Hungarians, not immigrants, and is as unscrupulous as the Khmer Rouge was in Cambodia, where salvation was possible only among the zealots of revolutionary truth. The Gilets Jaunes in France illustrate a politics of redemption that at times can be violent yet scrupulous, and also emancipatory through the universal claim to equality. The theology of liberation and its preferential option for the poor in Latin America too: it addresses the wronging of the equality of the dispossessed as a matter of worldly relief, not divine salvation. As a general rule, redemption is more *oré* than *ñandé* when it downplays claims to the universality of equality.

Shamelessness, confirmation bias and the *demos* of *ressentiment* show that Horner's reference to people being dumber can't be reduced to ignorance. Instead of dismissing the generative force of *ressentiment*, and of the *demos* it produces, one should look for new weapons to resist its excesses and invite them to break away from redemption to embark in a politics of emancipation.

Part 1

The Ambiguities of Constituent Power

1

'Enemies of the People'? The Judiciary and Claude Lefort's 'Savage Democracy'

Panu Minkkinen

Democratic 'Enemies'?

Thomas Stockmann, the protagonist of Henrik Ibsen's play *An Enemy of the People* (1882), is an educated and civilised physician who is, among other things, responsible for monitoring the health standards at the baths of his home town on the Norwegian coast. Stockmann suspects that the thermal waters are contaminated. When tests verify his suspicions, he announces his intention to disclose the facts to the public. He is subsequently confronted by his brother Peter, the Mayor, who insists that revealing the poor quality of the waters would do no good and would, in fact, be detrimental to the livelihood of the town. As an inflexible man of principle, Stockmann is, however, adamant that the truth must prevail at all costs.

A town meeting is called together. As he realises that the publication of his results are being managed and manipulated by the local press, by his brother the Mayor, as well as by other municipal authorities, Stockmann becomes ever more agitated about the narrow-mindedness of not only those who are trying to prevent him from disclosing the facts, but also of the general public that does not seem to share his own appetite for the truth. The public, so it seems to Stockmann, will settle for what is convenient, for 'majority truths' that are 'like last year's cured meat—like rancid, tainted ham; and they are the origin of the moral scurvy that is rampant in our communities'.[1] And the general public's right to take lies for the truth is supported by a 'doctrine':

> that the public, the crowd, the masses, are the essential part of the population—that they constitute the People—that the common folk, the ignorant and incomplete element in the community, have the same right to pronounce judgment and to approve, to direct and to govern, as the isolated, intellectually superior personalities in it.[2]

---

[1] Henrik Ibsen, *An Enemy of the People*, trans. R. Farquharson Sharp (Mineola, NY: Dover Publications, 1999), p. 60.

[2] Ibsen, *An Enemy of the People*, p. 60.

The confrontation with the town earns Stockmann his epithet as an 'enemy of the people'.

This narrative has a more contemporary parallel, as well.

On 3 November 2016, the High Court of Justice of England and Wales ruled in *R (Miller) v Secretary of State for Exiting the European Union*[3] that the notification to initiate the formal two-year process for the UK's withdrawal from the European Union, as prescribed in Article 50 of the Treaty on European Union (TEU), must be triggered by an act of Parliament, and not by the Prime Minister under the Crown's prerogative. The ruling, upheld by the Supreme Court the following year, was widely considered a victory for parliamentary sovereignty over cabinet executive powers.[4]

On the day after the High Court ruling, the *Daily Mail* published a full-page cover with facial portraits of each of the three justices involved in the case in court dress and wigs, and the words 'Enemies of the People' were printed as the main heading below the portraits.[5] The images and the heading suggested that these unelected judges represented a small privileged minority, and that their ruling undermined the democratic will that had been expressed by 'the People' in the Brexit referendum. The power of a social elite, described further down as 'out of touch', one judge identified as founding member of 'a club of lawyers and academics aiming to "improve" EU law', another as 'openly gay' and a former Olympic fencer, is set against majority rule by 'the People'.

The juxtaposition is the same in both instances, even if the narrative perspectives are diametrically opposite. The implied author of Ibsen's play, that is, the 'playwright', celebrates the 'aristocratic heroism' of the defiant middle-class individual with 'truth' on his side,[6] whereas the 'journalist' ridiculing the High Court justices demands deference in the face of democratic majority rule by 'the People'.

Indeed, the democratic accountability of the judiciary to the elected branches representing 'the People' is usually portrayed through the restraint that the word 'deference' as a metaphor implies.[7] In liberal democracies, the

---

3   R (Miller) v Secretary of State for Exiting the European Union [2016] EWHC 2768 (Admin).

4   E.g. Damian Chalmers, 'Gina Miller and the last Gasp of Parliamentary Sovereignty?', *Maastricht Journal of European and Comparative Law* 24:1 (2017), pp. 3–5.

5   'Enemies of the people: Fury over "out of touch" judges who have "declared war on democracy" by defying 17.4m Brexit voters and who could trigger constitutional crisis.' *Daily Mail*, 4 November 2016. Available at https://www.dailymail.co.uk/news/article-3903436/Enemies-people-Fury-touch-judges-defied-17–4m-Brexit-voters-trigger-constitutional-crisis.html (accessed 8 June 2020).

6   On Ibsen's Nietzschean affiliations, see Ralph Leck, 'Enemy of the People: Simmel, Ibsen, and the Civic Legacy of Nietzschean Sociology', *The European Legacy* 10:3 (2005), pp. 133–47.

7   On deference broadly, see e.g. Matthew Lewans, *Administrative Law and Judicial Deference* (Oxford: Hart Publishing, 2016).

role of unelected justices is often limited to the application of – at most the interpretation of – laws that have been passed by a democratically elected legislator representing 'the People'. The aim of this chapter is to question the democratic plausibility of this admittedly simplified claim. In many European jurisdictions, domestic courts have, for instance, taken it upon themselves to actively monitor the ways in which state parties comply with their positive obligations in 'securing Convention rights' as per Article 1 of the European Convention on Human Rights (ECHR), a task that cannot, at least not without some reservation, be subsumed under the rubrics of mere 'application' and 'interpretation'.[8] In this sense, the judiciary takes on 'activist' democratic functions that can be said to go beyond the traditional 'deference' paradigm.[9]

But in discussing these democratic functions, this chapter will not adopt the usual focus that views the judiciary as an institution or social agent with, perhaps, a particular political agenda.[10] Instead, it will discuss the nature of the rights that the courts must adjudicate on, and how the adjudication of actionable rights by necessity positions the judiciary into a democratic landscape that goes beyond traditional accounts of 'deference' and disinterested application. This applies particularly to the basic and human rights that, over the last half-century or so, have saturated practically all areas of judicial decision-making, especially in transnational contexts.[11] To make my argument, I will first clarify the position of human rights in Claude Lefort's unique blend of phenomenologically and psychoanalytically inspired political theory. Human rights are in Lefort's account an integral element of a 'savage democracy' that he envisions as the only plausible political challenge to the totalitarian tendencies of neoliberalism. If my analogy is plausible, this will apply by extension to all actionable rights. In dealing with actionable rights, the judiciary, so I suggest, takes on democratic functions that are not compatible with the much narrower notion of adjudication that the 'deference' paradigm implies.

From this starting point, I will then continue to discuss in more detail the position of the judiciary in contemporary democracies and with special

[8] See e.g. Helen Keller and Alec Stone Sweet (eds.), *A Europe of Rights. The Impact of the ECHR on National Legal Systems* (Oxford: Oxford University Press, 2008).

[9] E.g. Graham Gee, Robert Hazell, Kate Malleson, and Patrick O'Brien, *The Politics of Judicial Independence in the UK's Changing Constitution* (Cambridge: Cambridge University Press, 2015). For a critical view of judicial empowerment, see Ran Hirschl, *Towards Juristocracy. The Origins and Consequences of the New Constitutionalism* (Cambridge, MA: Harvard University Press, 2004).

[10] E.g. Kate Malleson, *The New Judiciary. The Effects of Expansion and Activism* (Aldershot: Dartmouth, 1999).

[11] E.g. Nico Krisch, *Beyond Constitutionalism. The Pluralist Structure of Postnational Law* (Oxford: Oxford University Press, 2010).

reference to its role in a separation of powers doctrine. Standard accounts of the doctrine reduce the judicial powers of unelected courts to the application and interpretation of laws passed by an elected legislator representing 'the People' as the subject of a constituent power. But as the relationship between the legislature and the executive branch has factually changed in contemporary democracies, so too has the *relative position* of the judiciary. A strong executive as the engine of legislative initiatives, supported by the weak parliamentary scrutiny of a 'rubber-stamp' legislature, has highlighted the need for a more active judiciary, a more democratically self-reflexive 'People's' judiciary, that reaches beyond the 'deferential' role that standard accounts offer.

Lefort and the Body Politic

The main reason why Claude Lefort's name comes up so often in discussions about politics, ranging from Ernesto Laclau and Chantal Mouffe's critical theory of the hegemony of radical democracy,[12] to the post-Heideggerian analyses of Philippe Lacoue-Labarthe and Jean-Luc Nancy,[13] is the distinction that he popularised between *le politique* as a form of political regime, usually translated into English as 'the political', and *la politique* or social agency conflict-ridden by opposing and often irreconcilable interests, usually translated simply as 'politics'.[14] Many seem to think that the distinction was specifically introduced by Lefort, but its origins in French political theory can be traced to Julien Freund and Régis Debray[15] through an emphatically philosophical reception of Max Weber.[16]

   While 'politics' in the second, apparently more conventional, sense can be understood as the antagonist competition for power in all of its

---

[12] Ernesto Laclau and Chantal Mouffe, *Hegemony and Socialist Strategy. Towards a Radical Democratic Politics*, 2nd edn. (London: Verso, 2001).

[13] Philippe Lacoue-Labarthe and Jean-Luc Nancy, *Retreating the Political*, trans. Simon Sparks (London: Routledge, 1997).

[14] See also Martin Plot (ed), *Claude Lefort: Thinker of the Political* (Basingstoke: Palgrave Macmillan, 2013), Oliver Marchart, *Post-Foundational Political Thought. Political Difference in Nancy, Lefort, Badiou and Laclau* (Edinburgh: Edinburgh University Press, 2007), Martin Breaugh, Christopher Holman, Rachel Magnusson, Paul Mazzocchi, and Devin Penner (eds.), *Thinking Radical Democracy. The Return to Politics in Post-War France* (Toronto: University of Toronto Press, 2015), and Gill-Pedro's chapter in this volume.

[15] See Julien Freund, *L'Essence du politique* (Paris: Dalloz, 2003), and Régis Debray, *Critique of Political Reason*, trans. David Macey (London: Verso, 1983).

[16] In particular Raymond Aron, *Main Currents in Sociological Thought. Volume 2: Durkheim, Pareto, Weber*, trans. Richard Howard and Helen Weaver (New Brunswick, NJ: Transaction Publishers, 1999), pp. 219–346, and Julien Freund, *The Sociology of Max Weber*, trans. Mary Ilford (London: Routledge, 1998).

usual guises, Lefort's use of the term 'the political', in turn, refers to how a society represents its unity to itself as a collectivity. It could, then, be understood as a form of collective identity, a representation of the body politic through which society identifies itself, claiming to be, for example, a 'liberal democracy'. Commenting on Raymond Aron, who is a major source of inspiration here,[17] Lefort notes how the term 'the political' is used in at least two ways:

> In a first meaning, this term designates a particular domain of the social ensemble; it delimits the source of authority, the conditions and means of its exercise, and the range of its competences. In a second meaning, the *political* refers to the social ensemble itself, for the entire collectivity is affected by conceptions of the nature of power and the mode of the exercise of government. . . . decisions made at the top have repercussions in all domains of social life but also . . . the representation of authority in the particular sector of politics circulates in some manner throughout the social ensemble. It is in this second sense that it becomes relevant to affirm a 'primacy of the political,' no matter the society under consideration.[18]

So in the first meaning, 'the political' refers to the institutional framework of a polity that we may call, for instance, 'liberal democracy'. This framework includes constitutional 'branches' and state authorities, their legally defined competences, the regulations covering political participation, as well as the 'softly normative' expectations that the regularities of political conventions create. But in the second, more important meaning, 'the political' also includes the ways in which social actors, be they institutional or individual, self-reflexively act in relation to each other as constituent elements of a particular polity. An institutional 'liberal democratic' actor like the judiciary will, then, understand its relationship with other institutions and individuals through a certain rationale that usually aims at maintaining its relative position in the overall framework.

Lefort's complex notion of the body politic is not easily accessible as he draws inspiration from both the phenomenology of his mentor

---

[17] Especially Raymond Aron, *Democracy and Totalitarianism*, trans. Valence Ionescu (London: Weidenfeld and Nicolson, 1968).

[18] Claude Lefort, 'The Political and the Social', in Claude Lefort, *Complications. Communism and the Dilemmas of Democracy*, trans. Julian Bourg (New York, NY: Columbia University Press, 2007), pp. 113–23, at pp. 113–14. There is an echo here of the way in which Carl Schmitt makes a distinction between the constitution in its relative and absolute senses. See Carl Schmitt, *Constitutional Theory*, trans. Jeffrey Seitzer (Durham, NC: Duke University Press, 2008), pp. 59–74.

Maurice Merleau-Ponty[19] and the psychoanalytic theory of Piera Aulagnier.[20] Lefort suggests that as a representation, 'the political' not only shapes (*mise-en-forme*) collective life into more or less permanent social relations, but that it also stages (*mise-en-scène*) individual interpretations of those relations as politics. Only these relations and the ways in which they are interpreted as politics can together provide form and meaning in society (*mise-en-sens*).[21] In this sense, the dimensions of 'the political' and 'politics' are interwoven into one another. The antagonistic or conflictual element of political action, of 'politics', is always reflected in a given society's representation of itself, in 'the political', and vice versa. Neither dimension can exist independently of the other.

The two modern ideal-typical regimes of 'the political' that Lefort has looked at in more detail, namely totalitarianism and democracy, share a common source. But they operate in diametrically opposite ways. In both, 'the political' functions as a symbolic constitution in so far as it locates society's unity at a particular point of power. As regimes, both totalitarianism and democracy are responses to the same question in so far as they attempt to come to terms with the empty space that has been left behind after the monarchy, with its claim to the transcendental nature of the monarch's divine power, has lost its capacity to represent the corporeal unity of the body politic. Following the symbolic decapitation of the monarch and the consequent dissolution of the kingdom that she represented, power appears as an empty space. Democracy, Lefort emphasises, leaves that space empty. In the absence of monarchs, those who exercise power can henceforth only be mortals who occupy positions of power temporarily or who can invest themselves in it only by force or cunning. Such a fragile unity is unable to erase the underlying social divisions. For Lefort, these divisions represent

---

[19] Especially the posthumous Maurice Merleau-Ponty, *The Visible and the Invisible. Followed by Working Notes*, trans. Alphonso Lingis (Evanston, IL: Northwestern University Press, 1968). See also Bernard Flynn, *The Philosophy of Claude Lefort. Interpreting the Political* (Evanston, IL: Northwestern University Press, 2005).

[20] See Piera Aulagnier, *The Violence of Interpretation. From Pictogram to Statement*, trans. Alan Sheridan (Hove: Brunner-Routledge, 2001). Aulagnier was originally trained by Jacques Lacan, but later co-founded the so-called 'Fourth Group' that split away from Lacan's EFP in 1969 over disagreements concerning training protocols. See e.g. Cornelius Castoriadis, 'Epilegomena to a Theory of the Soul Which Has Been Presented as Science', in Cornelius Castoriadis, *Crossroads in the Labyrinth*, trans. Kate Soper and Martin H. Ryle (Cambridge, MA: MIT Press, 1984), pp. 3–45. Aulagnier was at one point married to Castoriadis, Lefort's collaborator from the *Socialisme ou Barbarie* period, 1947–1958. See Cornelius Castoriadis et al, *Socialisme ou barbarie. Anthologie* (La Bussière: Acratie, 2007).

[21] Claude Lefort, 'The Permanence of the Theologico-Political?', in Claude Lefort, *Democracy and Political Theory*, trans. David Macey (Cambridge: Polity, 1988), pp. 213–55, at pp. 217–21.

the true nature of democracy as a political regime: 'Democracy inaugurates the experience of an ungraspable, uncontrollable society in which the people will be said to be sovereign, of course, but whose identity will constantly be open to question, whose identity will remain latent.'[22]

In other words, the antagonistic and conflictual nature of 'politics' that keeps the symbolic space of power empty is what characterises 'the political' of the democratic regime. In democracy, 'politics' prevents 'the People' from becoming a fixed sovereign in the monarch's stead.

Totalitarianism, on the other hand, is an attempt to fill that space, to unify society by placing society itself into the emptiness left behind after the regicide and the consequent dissolution of the body politic. With violence and repression totalitarianism attempts to 'weld power and society back together again, to efface all signs of social division, to banish the indetermination that haunts the democratic experience',[23] or, in other words, to suppress the 'politics' that would maintain the emptiness of that space and prevent 'the People' from coagulating into a fixed sovereign.

Lefort's notion of democracy also has a legal dimension. For democracy:

> goes beyond the limits traditionally assigned to the *état de droit*. It tests out rights which have not yet been incorporated in it, it is the theatre of a contestation, whose object cannot be reduced to the preservation of a tacitly established pact but which takes form in centres that power cannot entirely master.[24]

Political Rights Beyond the Rule of Law

In other words, Lefort's interpretation allows us to see how the judiciary operates on a stage on which contradictory and often irreconcilable interests are played out as actionable rights. So the claim does not follow the usual line of argument that begins with a politicised 'counter-majoritarian' judiciary that then goes on to adjudicate on rights in a political way,[25] but

---

[22] Claude Lefort, 'The Image of the Body and Totalitarianism', in Claude Lefort, *The Political Forms of Modern Society. Bureaucracy, Democracy, Totalitarianism*, trans. Alan Sheridan et al. (Cambridge: Polity, 1986), pp. 292–306, at pp. 303–04.

[23] Lefort, 'The Image of the Body and Totalitarianism', p. 305.

[24] Claude Lefort, 'Politics and Human Rights', in Claude Lefort, *The Political Forms of Modern Society. Bureaucracy, Democracy, Totalitarianisn*, trans. Alan Sheridan et al. (Cambridge: Polity, 1986), pp. 239–72, at p. 258.

[25] See e.g. Scott E. Lemieux and David J. Watkins, *Judicial Review and Contemporary Democratic Theory. Power, Domination, and the Courts* (New York, NY: Routledge, 2018), and Luís Roberto Barroso, 'Reason Without Vote: The Representative and Majoritarian Function of Constitutional Courts', in Thomas Bustamante and Bernardo Gonçalves Fernandes (eds.), *Democratizing Constitutional Law. Perspectives on Legal Theory and the Legitimacy of Constitutionalism* (New York, NY: Springer, 2016), pp. 71–90.

that rights themselves are by their very nature political, and that adjudicating on them necessarily positions the adjudicator – the judiciary – in a 'democratic' way.

Lefort's rather optimistic take on the democratic potential of rights may seem curious bearing in mind that his background is in critical political theory. This view has a very particular history. French representatives of the so-called 'post-Marxist' or 'radical democratic' movement would entertain a somewhat more positive view on the revolutionary potential of human rights than their Anglophone and German counterparts.[26] After decades of Marxist human rights critique, the discussion in France took this decisive turn in 1980, specifically with Lefort's seminal article 'Politics and Human Rights'.[27] For Lefort, human rights – and, as I wish to suggest here, rights more generally – are a *politics* of rights equivalent to democratic politics. Lefort rejects the critique of the early Marx who famously declared that human rights 'are nothing but the rights of the *member of civil society*, that is, of egoistic man, of the man who is separated from other men and from the community'.[28] So Marx sees rights merely as a consequence of the decomposition of society into isolated monadic individuals. But for Lefort, even social separation is a modality of man's relation to others.

Views in this debate were far from uniform. A fitting counterpoint for Lefort would be his former student Marcel Gauchet who is, perhaps, better known for his historical analyses of democracy or the relationship between

---

[26] Generally, see Justine Lacroix, 'A Democracy Without a People? The "Rights of Man" in French Contemporary Political Thought', *Political Studies* 61:3 (2013), pp. 676–90, Stephen W. Sawyer and Iain Stewart (eds.), *In Search of the Liberal Moment. Democracy, Anti-Totalitarianism, and Intellectual Politics in France since 1950* (Basingstoke: Palgrave Macmillan, 2016), and Natalie Doyle, 'Democracy as Socio-Cultural Project of Individual and Collective Sovereignty: Claude Lefort, Marcel Gauchet and the French Debate on Modern Autonomy', *Thesis Eleven* 75:1 (2003), pp. 69–95. In addition to Lefort, Marcel Gauchet and Miguel Abensour discussed below, a fourth protagonist in this French debate would be Pierre Rosanvallon. See Pierre Rosanvallon, *Democracy Past and Future*, trans. Samuel Moyn (New York, NY: Columbia University Press, 2006), Pierre Rosanvallon, *Counter-Democracy. Politics in an Age of Distrust*, trans. Arthur Goldhammer (Cambridge: Cambridge University Press, 2008), and Pierre Rosanvallon, 'The Test of the Political: A Conversation with Claude Lefort', *Constellations* 19:1 (2012), pp. 4–15. See also Wim Weymans, 'Freedom through Political Representation: Lefort, Gauchet and Rosanvallon on the Relationship between State and Society', *European Journal of Political Theory* 4:3 (2005), pp. 263–82, and James R. Martin, 'Pierre Rosanvallon's *Democratic Legitimacy* and the Legacy of Antitotalitarianism in Recent French Thought', *Thesis Eleven* 114:1 (2013), pp. 120–33.

[27] Lefort, 'Politics and Human Rights'.

[28] Karl Marx, 'On the Jewish Question', in Karl Marx, *Marx. Early Political Writings*, trans. Joseph O'Malley and Richard A. Davis (Cambridge: Cambridge University Press, 1994), pp. 28–56, at p. 44.

religion and politics.[29] Following the publication of Lefort's article, Gauchet published his own intervention with the provocative title 'Human rights are not a politics'.[30] Gauchet opens his essay with an almost scornful stab at the renewed interest in human rights in France, a stab that is clearly aimed at, among others, his former teacher and friend:

> and so the old becomes new, what was once the very definition of something suspect resurfaces as something beyond all suspicion, and so our antiquated, waffly and hypocritical human rights regain grace, innocence and a sulphurous audacity in the eyes of the most subtle and exigent members of the avant-garde.[31]

This stab reflects the rift that developed between political theorists like Lefort who, despite being 'post-Marxist' in the aftermath of the hugely divisive '*choc Soljénitsyne*',[32] still relied on Marx in his attempts at creating a social theory, and Gauchet who quickly became one of the key figures of the liberal left. As Samuel Moyn convincingly illustrates, Gauchet's disagreement is not so much about human rights per se, but about the notion of individualisation.[33] Apart from that, Gauchet, the historian, has no explicit 'theory of rights' on the basis of which he could disagree with Lefort. He seems far more concerned – and quite rightly so – about the factual ability of human rights to promote social justice and about the willingness of the courts to participate in this political work.

For Lefort, the situation is, however, quite different. He seems to be less interested in whether rights can successfully deliver on what they promise. His focus is more on the *potential* of an 'agonistic' understanding of rights and what that would imply for democracy as an ideal-typical regime. The 'state of right', an *état de droit*, as Lefort understands it, introduces a

---

[29] Marcel Gauchet, *The Disenchantment of the World. A Political History of Religion*, trans. Oscar Burge (Princeton, NJ: Princeton University Press, 1997).

[30] Marcel Gauchet, 'Les droits de l'homme ne sont pas une politique', *Le Débat* 3 (1980), pp. 3–21. To my knowledge, the article has not been translated into English. Twenty years later Gauchet wrote a reassessment of the debate, but still just as critical of any positive or emancipatory potential of human rights. See Marcel Gauchet, 'Quand les droits de l'homme deviennent une politique', *Le Débat* 110 (2000), pp. 258–88, and Marcel Gauchet, *La Révolution des droits de l'homme* (Paris: Gallimard, 1989). See also Geneviève Souillac, *Human Rights in Crisis. The Sacred and the Secular in Contemporary French Thought* (Lanham, MD: Lexington Books, 2005), pp. 1–50.

[31] Gauchet, 'Les droits de l'homme ne sont pas une politique', p. 3 (my translation).

[32] See e.g. Michael Scott Christofferson, *French Intellectuals Against the Left. The Antitotalitarian Moment of the 1970's* (New York, NY: Berghahn Books, 2004), pp. 89–112.

[33] Samuel Moyn, 'The Politics of Individual Rights: Marcel Gauchet and Claude Lefort', in Raf Geenens and Helena Rosenblatt (eds.), *French Liberalism from Montesquieu to the Present Day* (Cambridge: Cambridge University Press, 2012), pp. 291–310.

'disincorporation' of both power and right rather than their complete separation from each other. And so the 'state of right' will always include within itself an 'opposition in terms of right':

> The rights of man reduce right to a basis which, despite its name, is without shape, is given as interior to itself and, for this reason, eludes all power which would claim to take hold of it whether religious or mythical, monarchical or popular. Consequently, these rights go beyond any particular formulation which has been given of them; and this means that their formulation contains the demand for their reformulation, or that acquired rights are not necessarily called upon to support new rights.[34]

Democracy is, then, a regime in which rights are always external in relation to power. In Lefort's 'savage democracy', the law as the institution of right is, as Miguel Abensour, another former student and colleague, explains, no longer thought of as an instrument of social conservation, but as a potentially revolutionary source of authority for a society that constitutes itself as the indeterminate entity it is and will always be. In this sense, a right is always in excess of what it may have established. And once constituted into institutional forms, a constituent force will always re-emerge in order to either reaffirm existing rights or to create new ones:

> A political stage opens according to which there is a struggle between the domestication of rights and its permanent destabilization-recreation via the integration of new rights, new demands that are henceforth considered as legitimate. According to Lefort, it is the existence of this incessantly reborn protest, this whirlwind of rights, that brings democracy beyond the traditional limits of the 'State of right' [*État de droit, Rechtsstaat*].[35]

The term 'savage democracy' that Abensour accredits to Lefort is apparently a direct reference although the English editions available of Lefort's

---

[34] Lefort, 'The Image of the Body and Totalitarianism', p. 258. See also Claude Lefort, 'Human Rights and the Welfare State', in Claude Lefort, *Democracy and Political Theory*, trans. David Macey (Cambridge: Polity Press, 1988), pp. 21–44, Claude Lefort, 'International Law, Human Rights, and Politics', *Qui Parle* 22:1 (2013), pp. 117–37, and Raf Geenens, 'Democracy, Human Rights and History: Reading Lefort', *European Journal of Political Theory* 7:3 (2008), pp. 269–86.

[35] Miguel Abensour, '"Savage Democracy" and the "Principle of Anarchy"', in Miguel Abensour, *Democracy Against the State. Marx and the Machiavellian Moment*, trans. Max Blechman and Martin Breaugh (Cambridge: Polity, 2011), pp. 102–24, at p. 108 (translation modified). These French and German expressions are not entirely compatible with what we mean by the 'rule of law' in English. See e.g. Martin Loughlin, *Foundations of Public Law* (Oxford: Oxford University Press, 2010), pp. 312–41 and The Principle of the Rule of Law. Resolution of the Parliamentary Assembly of the Council of Europe No. 1594 (2007).

work seem to bear little or no evidence of it.[36] Abensour, however, emphasises that the 'savagery' implied in the term is neither a reference to Hobbes nor to the political anthropologist Pierre Clastres whose seminal work on the political structures of so-called primitive societies was a major influence for the young Lefort.[37] Instead, Abensour claims that Lefort's democracy is 'the form of society that, through the play of division, leaves the field open for the question the social asks of itself ceaselessly, a question in perpetual want of resolution but that is here recognised as interminable'.[38] In this interminable quest for answers, rights play a dual role both as the question being asked and as something that enables the asking.

Although Abensour here seemingly professes allegiance to his old teacher and colleague, James Ingram cautions that especially two features in Abensour's reading of Lefort cannot be easily reconciled with Lefort himself.[39] First, Abensour defines democracy through a notion of popular rule that Lefort would find difficult to accept. For Lefort, 'the People' cannot act as a unified collective subject in the way in which Abensour would have to assume because no society is able to master its own development in a way that would suggest such a notion of 'the People'. Indeed, it would go against the gist of Lefort's agonistic premises. This also applies to Abensour's interpretation of how rights function in democracy and would undermine the 'revolutionary instrumentalism' that Abensour assigns to them.

Second, for Abensour, the state and its institutions are always a totalitarian threat to democracy. Lefort, on the other hand, seems to suggest that the state can, in fact, advance democratic interests, as well. Hence his positive outlook *vis-à-vis* human rights. And so if the democratic actors of rights in Abensour's scheme can only be representatives of 'the People' set against a necessarily totalitarian state, Lefort would be more interested in how these rights-related

---

[36] Justine Lacroix traces this expression to an article from 1979. See Justine Lacroix, 'The "Right to Have Rights" in French Political Philosophy: Conceptualising a Cosmopolitan Citizenship with Arendt', *Constellations* 22:1 (2015), pp. 79–90, at p. 89, fn. 47. Most commentators only refer to Abensour.

[37] See Pierre Clastres, *Society Against the State. Essays in Political Anthropology*, trans. Robert Hurley (New York, NY: Zone Books, 1989), and Pierre Clastres, *Archeology of Violence*, trans. Jeanine Herman (Los Angeles, CA: Semiotext(e), 2010). See also Samuel Moyn, 'Of Savagery and Civil Society: Pierre Clastres and the Transformation of French Political Thought', *Modern Intellectual History* 1:1 (2004), pp. 55–80, and Samuel Moyn, 'Savage and Modern Liberty: Marcel Gauchet and the Origins of New French Thought', *European Journal of Political Theory* 4:2 (2005), pp. 164–87.

[38] Abensour, '"Savage Democracy" and the "Principle of Anarchy"', p. 105.

[39] James D. Ingram, 'The Politics of Claude Lefort's Political: Between Liberalism and Radical Democracy', *Thesis Eleven* 87:1 (2006), pp. 33–50, at p. 44.

struggles are staged in, for example, state-run courtrooms where the identity of the democratic actors is more fluid.

An Agonistic Separation

So in Lefort's overall view, democracy is not merely the *absence* of an external authority once God has been pronounced dead. A mere absence would simply be a repetition of the post-theological vacuum from which both political regimes, both totalitarianism and democracy, follow as archetypal variations of modernity. If totalitarianism is the frenzied attempt to fill that empty space with unifying structures that would abolish all social divisions of politics, then democracy, by contrast, is measured by the ability of politics – as, for example, actionable rights – to keep that space empty. Democracy is, in other words, marked by the *resistance to* or *opposition against* the totalitarian tendencies of modern capitalism. One name for that resistance is 'right'.

What would the implications of Lefort's notion of rights be for the decision-makers that are tasked to put them into effect, that is, for the judiciary? What are the democratic characteristics of a judiciary of 'the People'?

The standard account of the position of the judiciary in a democratic environment is, as has been indicated earlier, usually framed through the notion of 'deference'. Although this is a mere approximation of the more complex issue at hand, the task of unelected courts is to *apply* laws that have been passed by a democratically elected legislator to individual cases. Unelected courts do not have a mandate to legislate on behalf of 'the People.'[40] In principle, the independent discretion of the courts is said to be limited to situations where discretionary powers have either explicitly been delegated by the legislature, or where interpretation is needed to resolve cases in which the law remains ambiguous. Other than that, the courts are expected to defer any decisions that may seem 'political' to the elected branches. This standard account of a 'passive' or 'deferential' judiciary – as opposed to an 'activist' one – is dependent on a very specific understanding of rights as a question of law and on the assumed ability of the courts to tell 'questions of law' apart from politics as per equally standard accounts of, for want of a better term, 'legal positivism.'

The standard account has, of course, been criticised from several different angles. Martin Loughlin, to take one prominent critic, claims that rights adjudication is intrinsically political because it requires judges to 'reach a determination on the relative importance of conflicting social, political and cultural interests in circumstances in which there is no objective—or even consensual—answer'.[41] In this critical version of the standard account, rights

---

[40] See however Allan R. Brewer-Carías, *Constitutional Courts as Positive Legislators. A Comparative Law Study* (Cambridge: Cambridge University Press, 2011).

[41] Martin Loughlin, *The Idea of Public Law* (Oxford: Oxford University Press, 2003), p. 129.

represent conflicting interests, and resolving disputes on conflicting interests will make rights adjudication necessarily political, as well. So the political nature of adjudication is dependent on the conflictual nature of the interests represented by the rights that the courts must adjudicate on.

The emphasis in Lefort's notion of rights is slightly different. What is at stake is not so much the conflicting nature of the interests that individual rights represent, although this may be relevant, too. More important is the inability to fix these interests – *any political interests* – into formal law.[42] According to the standard account, political interests, regardless of whether they are conflictual or not, can be stabilised into relatively fixed representations that can then be identified and isolated into 'questions of law', that is, into clearly delimited issues that the courts have the privilege to adjudicate on. So, for example, as a right, the freedom of expression as articulated in Article 10 ECHR would constitute a relatively stable set of circumstances that could time and again be adjudicated on in a more or less uniform way. But in Lefort's meaning, the existence and scope of such rights can always be contested with either new interpretations of the same right in question or even new rights.

The freedom of expression, to stick with our example, is, of course, always open to new interpretations that may clarify what falls under the protection of the right and what doesn't. There is an abundance of Strasbourg case law on Article 10 ECHR and on the 'limits of acceptable criticism' where the scope of the right is continuously redrawn even if the shifts may appear small.[43] The Lefortian point here is that this is not so much a consequence of the 'penumbral' quality of 'open-textured' human rights law more specifically, but the *contestability of all rights*.

Moreover, the freedom of expression can in similar situations be challenged by entirely new rights such as, for example, a right to be protected from incitement to ethnic, racial or religious hatred when the exercise of the freedom of expression compromises such protection. Strictly speaking no such 'right to protection from the abuse of a right', of course, exists in the ECHR framework unless one is directly affected as the protected 'victim' of hate speech. But it can be construed from, for example, Article 17 ECHR that prohibits the use of Convention rights – the freedom of expression, for instance – against the core values embedded in the Convention itself. For Lefort, the ways in which a new right is legally construed would be of

---

[42] See e.g. Bonnie Honig, *Political Theory and the Displacement of Politics* (Ithaca, NY: Cornell University Press, 1993), pp. 15–16.

[43] See e.g. Tarlach McGonagle in collaboration with Marie McGonagle and Ronan Ó Fathaigh, *Freedom of Expression and Defamation. A Study of the Case Law of the European Court of Human Rights*, ed. Onur Andreotti (Strasbourg: Council of Europe, 2016).

secondary importance. What is central is whether, to what extent, and how the argument made in favour of such a right is *effective* in the individual political contestation that is being staged.

So for Lefort, the factual and individual actionability of rights trumps the fixed stability that their legal formalisation might suggest. Any right seemingly fixed into law can always be contested with either a new right or with a reinterpretation of an existing one. The contestable quality of all rights accounts for what Abensour called the 'whirlwind of rights' that makes it impossible for the judiciary to limit itself to the ideal of the rule of law that the courts are thought to embody. Rights understood in this way always point to a regime of 'savage democracy' that goes beyond the formal limits of the *état de droit*. And they also outline a democratic role for the judiciary that goes beyond standard accounts drawn from any separation of powers doctrine.

A Balance of Terror in a Savage Democracy

This democratic role is not, I would finally argue, merely theory. The increased 'activism' of courts, both national and transnational, has been well documented.[44] In the latest wave of activism, the courts themselves have not been the main agents of the development. Two background phenomena can be identified.

First, as modern societies have brought ever new areas of human and social life under the regulation of legal norms, the scope of the judiciary's decision-making powers has correspondingly grown.[45] But even more importantly, the priority given to transnational instruments in national jurisdictions, especially instruments like the ECHR bearing relevance to basic and human rights, as well as the corresponding Strasbourg jurisprudence, has transformed the face of judicial decision-making more or less completely.[46] We have come far from the hypothetical model of a 'syllogism' that the judicial profession has traditionally entertained as the ideal model of disinterested legal reasoning.

---

[44] E.g. Louis Pereira Coutinho, Massimo La Torre, and Steven D. Smith, *Judicial Activism. An Interdisciplinary Approach to the American and European Experiences* (Dordrecht: Springer, 2015), and Mark Dawson, Bruno De Witte, and Elise Muir (eds.), *Judicial Activism at the European Court of Justice* (Cheltenham: Edward Elgar, 2013).

[45] E.g. Alec Stone Sweet, *Governing With Judges. Constitutional Politics in Europe* (Oxford: Oxford University Press, 2000).

[46] E.g. Miguel Maduro, Kaarlo Tuori, and Suvi Sankari (eds.), *Transnational Law. Rethinking European Law and Legal Thinking* (Cambridge: Cambridge University Press, 2014).

At the same time, the political framework within which the judiciary exercises its powers has changed. Since September 2001, the political balance that a traditional tripartite separation of powers is intended to establish has changed due to increases in the authority of the executive.[47] These changes are related to the more general phenomenon of 'emergency politics'.[48]

If we understand the separation of powers[49] to include an interbranch limitation of the use of powers in accordance with a 'checks and balances'[50] formulation, that is, as not merely a constitutional division of labour, but as an attempt to prevent the concentration of power into the hands of one government branch or another,[51] then it is important to keep in mind that the limiting effect of the separation goes beyond explicit interventions like, for example, instances in which the courts have struck down primary legislation in judicial or constitutional review. Most research into these interbranch relations will focus either on the norms of competence that define the constitutional powers available, or the case law that represents the singular occurrences in which those powers have been exercised. But there is a third perspective somewhere between the two mentioned. The intervention implied in the norms of competence includes a *potentiality* that creates stability through mutual deterrence as a 'balance of terror'. The factual ability of the judiciary to intervene in the activities of the legislature or the executive functions as a restraint even if the intervention suggested by the norm of competence is seldom actualised.

In the contemporary political climate, the 'balance of terror' of a traditional separation of powers with its 'checks and balances' has morphed into executive-driven forms of government where the ability of a democratically elected legislature to scrutinise and 'deter' the executive has weakened. As

---

[47] E.g. John E. Owens and Riccardo Pelizzo (eds.), *The 'War on Terror' and the Growth of Executive Power? A Comparative Analysis* (Abingdon: Routledge, 2010). On the 'unbalanced' European executive, see Deirdre Curtin, *Executive Power of the European Union. Law, Practices, and the Living Constitution* (Oxford: Oxford University Press, 2010).

[48] E.g. Bonnie Honig, *Emergency Politics. Paradox, Law, Democracy* (Princeton, NJ: Princeton University Press, 2009).

[49] There is an abundance of literature that problematises this admittedly simplified version of separated powers that I'm using here. See e.g. Christoph Möllers, *The Three Branches. A Comparative Model of Separation of Powers* (Oxford: Oxford University Press, 2013).

[50] The formulation is often accredited to the 'Federalists,' but the expression is, in fact, from John Adams. John Adams, *A Defence of the Constitutions of Government of the United States of America* (New York, NY: Da Capo Press, 1971).

[51] For this 'classical' view, see e.g. Charles de Secondat baron de Montesquieu, *The Spirit of the Laws*, trans. Anne M. Cohler, Basia Carolyn Miller, and Harold Samuel Stone (Cambridge: Cambridge University Press, 1989), p. 157.

a result, the *relative position* of the judiciary in the *trias politica* will have changed, too. Factual power positions in such separations are always relational in the sense that changes between two branches will always affect the third. Consequently, as the relationship between the executive and the legislature has changed in favour of the former, the judiciary will have to rethink its democratic role – or at least it has the opportunity to do so – and try to address the imbalance. Lefort's agonistic definition of rights in a 'savage democracy' provides one theoretical framework for explaining how such a democratic role works.

2

Public Space, Public Time: Constitution and the Relay of Authority in Arendt's *On Revolution*

Emily Zakin

either they were founders and, consequently, would become ancestors, or they had failed.

– Hannah Arendt[1]

They never let all of us be Americans.

– Amiri Baraka[2]

Introduction

In October 2013, the US federal government shut down for two weeks as a result of Congressional failure to pass legislation authorising funding for the new fiscal year. During that time, most federal employees were furloughed, and most government services discontinued. At issue was the Affordable Care Act (colloquially called Obamacare), President Obama's signature legislative achievement designed to bring the United States closer to universal health care. The Republican-controlled House of Representatives attempted to use the appropriations bill as leverage to defer and defund the ACA. A faction of the Republican party known as the Tea Party was the strongest proponent of the shutdown, arguing that health care reform was un-American and unconstitutional. At their most extreme, the Tea Partiers' claim to be and to speak for 'real Americans' was contradictorily coupled with expressions of allegiance to the principles of

---

[1] Hannah Arendt, *On Revolution* (New York: Viking, 1990), p. 203.
[2] Amiri Baraka, 'The Original Terrorists', *Portside*, October 17, 2013. Available at https://portside.org/2013-10-17/original-terrorists (accessed 25 August 2019).

43

Confederate secessionism.[3] A number of public intellectuals recognised at
the time the resonances with the American Civil War. Ta-Nehisi Coates
called the Tea Party protests unpatriotic and treasonous, an attempt to
undo 'the Union itself' by tearing at the fabric of our common bonds.[4]
Paul Krugman wrote on his *New York Times* blog: 'One irony here is that at
this point it's the liberals who believe in America, while the conservatives
don't.'[5] And as Amiri Baraka, a prominent African American poet, acerbi-
cally put it in his poem about the shutdown, 'They never let all of us be
Americans.' Published on the last day of the shutdown, Baraka's poem 'The
Original Terrorists' draws a link between the contemporary pathologies of
the Republican Party in the United States and the history of white supremacy, white racism and slavery. Implicit and entangled in the constitutional
claims surrounding Obamacare was the force of white identitarianism, the
exclusionary rhetoric of 'real Americans' that aimed to withhold the status
of 'American' from a portion of the citizenry.

In this paper, I will develop Hannah Arendt's understanding of the entwine-
ment of constitutional space and time. A constitution is for Arendt both a
durable objective thing in the public realm and a temporal relay between
founding and renewal. The objectivity and temporality of the American Constitution offers a conceptual pathway to think about its legacies of exclusion
and possibilities for transformation. These reside, I argue, in the relation of
founder to heir, and thus in the politics of intergenerational address that
forms and reforms a constitutional community across time. Although Arendt
fails to grapple with the American Constitution's foundational rootedness in
white supremacy, her constitutional theory nonetheless elucidates both the
possibilities for expanding the claims of civic inheritance and the persistence
of white identitarianism that lays claim to the image of real America and the
right to be or determine its legitimate heirs.

---

[3] The secessionist talk that metastasised in the US when there was a Black Democrat in office
as US President has quieted; those who believe in their exclusive claim to rightful American
descent are re-focused on the denial of others' access to citizenship. The federal government
shut down again in 2018–19, precipitated by President Trump's attempt to use the threat of
a veto of federal budget legislation as leverage to fund a wall at the US-Mexico border. The
2019 Republican led shutdown sought to re-literalise *nomos* as wall, by fixing rigid material
boundaries to immigration.

[4] Ta-Nehisi Coates, 'What this Cruel War was Over', *The Atlantic*, October 15, 2013. Available at https://www.theatlantic.com/politics/archive/2013/10/what-this-cruel-war-was-
over/280559/ (accessed 25 August 2019).

[5] Paul Krugman, 'The War on the Poor is a War on You-Know-Who', *The New York Times*,
October 11, 2013. Available at https://krugman.blogs.nytimes.com/2013/10/11/the-war-
on-the-poor-is-a-war-on-you-know-who/ (accessed 25 August 2019).

Constitution as Public Thing

Hannah Arendt's *On Revolution* illuminates the ways appeals to constitutional authority also make claims on who is addressed, inviting some and disinviting others into political community. In *On Revolution*, Arendt attributes the fundamental predicament of modern politics, its volatility and disintegration, to 'the progressive loss of authority of all inherited political structures', itself preceded by 'the loss of tradition' which had forged and sustained a common world in continuity with past and future.[6] In a secularising age that no longer has recourse to a transcendent ground, to ask about the source of authority for a body politic seems to lead to either an infinite regress or a vicious circle.[7] The apparent need for a higher law to anchor and legitimate a new political form led the French revolutionaries on a quest for the absolute, an absolute they found in the 'deification of the people',[8] whose will replaced the divine as the source of law and became sacralised itself.[9] The French Constitution of 1791, caught in the demand for origin, Arendt recounts, underwent a 'tragic fate' and 'remained a piece of paper', whose 'authority was shattered'.[10] The American revolutionaries, by contrast, evaded the vicious circle and resolved the problem of establishing authority in the absence of either tradition or transcendence, even as the American Constitution is silent on the source of its own 'ultimate authority'.[11] On Arendt's account, their key insight was that power and law have separate sources, and that power does

---

[6] Arendt, *On Revolution*, p. 117.

[7] Arendt sums up 'Sieyès's vicious circle' in the following way: 'those who get together to constitute a new government are themselves unconstitutional, that is, they have no authority to do what they have set out to achieve. The vicious circle in legislating is present not in ordinary lawmaking, but in laying down the fundamental law, the law of the land or the constitution which, from then on, is supposed to incarnate the "higher law" from which all laws ultimately derive their authority' (Arendt, *On Revolution*, pp. 183–4). Arendt argues that Sieyès cannot resolve 'the perplexities of foundation' (Arendt, *On Revolution*, p. 164) because the split between *pouvoir constituant* and *pouvoir constitué* strands the nation in the state of nature, even as its will anchors both power and law. Constitution making power can only replace 'monarchy, or one-man rule, with democracy, or rule by the majority' (Arendt, *On Revolution*, p. 164). It cannot establish a republic.

[8] Arendt, *On Revolution*, p. 183.

[9] 'Theoretically, the deification of the people in the French Revolution was the inevitable consequence of the attempt to derive both law and power from the selfsame source' (Arendt, *On Revolution*, p. 183).

[10] Arendt, *On Revolution*, p. 125.

[11] Arendt, *On Revolution*, p. 194. Arendt does not think that reason or self-evident truth is doing the heavy lifting it claims to, but she also writes that the legitimacy of the Constitution derives from the Preamble to the Declaration of Independence as its 'sole source of authority' (Arendt, *On Revolution*, p. 193).

not go all the way down.[12] This means the authority of law does not emanate directly from the power of the people but rather makes possible their political (artificial) equality. In distinguishing authority from power (as I will discuss further below), Arendt thereby rejects the concept of constituent power, the idea of the people as the source of (constituted) law, that law proceeds from the will of the people.[13]

Arendt praises the American framers for recognising that 'the seat of power to them was the people, but the source of law was to become the Constitution, a written document, an endurable objective thing'[14] that takes on an independent existence in the world separate from the act[15] (or work) that brought it into being. As she elaborates, 'the great significance attributed . . . to the constitutions as written documents testifies to their elementary objective, worldly character'.[16] As Bonnie Honig demonstrates in *Public Things: Democracy in Disrepair*, Arendt 'could not have made clearer her appreciation of things to worldly existence and indeed to reality itself'.[17] Public things, Honig writes, are 'world-stabilizing'[18] and even 'the infrastructure of secular immortality'.[19] By returning our attention 'to the *res* of *res publica*',[20] to the public things that anchor, orient, integrate and attach human relations, and around which 'collectivities may constellate'[21] Honig helps us to see how any 'we' in Arendt circulates through worldly intermediaries.

The success of the American Revolution in constituting a new authority is credited by Arendt to both 'the act of foundation itself',[22] which 'occurred in broad daylight' rather than outside of memory or shrouded in legend,[23] and to

---

[12] 'The American revolutionary insistence on the distinction between a republic and a democracy . . . hinges on the radical separation of law and power, with clearly recognized different origins, different legitimations, and different spheres of application' (Arendt, *On Revolution*, p. 166).

[13] On Arendt's view, a constitution 'is no more the expression of a national will or subject to the will of a majority than a building is the expression of the will of its architect or subject to the will of its inhabitants' (Arendt, *On Revolution*, p. 164).

[14] Arendt, *On Revolution*, p. 157.

[15] The act of foundation is of course many acts, including meeting, talking, promising, assembling, deliberating, writing.

[16] Arendt, *On Revolution*, p. 164.

[17] Bonnie Honig, *Public Things: Democracy in Disrepair* (New York: Fordham University Press, 2017), p. 1.

[18] Honig, *Public Things*, p. 2.

[19] Honig, *Public Things*, p. 42.

[20] Honig, *Public Things*, p. 13.

[21] Honig, *Public Things*, p. 6.

[22] Arendt, *On Revolution*, p. 196.

[23] Arendt, *On Revolution*, p. 204.

the existence of a written constitutional document, an objective, worldly thing with an independent life of its own. The American founding event, in Arendt's view, was not an act of (Rousseauean) identification, but an appeal to future generations to sustain a temporal loop that would confer the status of founders on the framers by holding past and future together. In recognising that either they 'would become ancestors, or they had failed',[24] the American founders invoke the recursive temporality of the future anterior. Put another way, we could say that either their initiative would be augmented, and their document revised, or they would not have founded. In this light we can see the written constitution as a worldly in-between that stabilises public space by framing a body politic in which people's plurality, action and power can flourish, and that conserves enduring public time by appealing to its own heirs, providing a shared opening into the world that is sturdy enough to sustain conflicting interpretations, heterogenous points of view, dissent and disagreement. The simultaneous independence and interconnection of the act of founding and the worldly thing, the deed and the document, authorises a space of appearances and a locus of temporality that outlasts individuals.

Promising and Pre-constituted Bodies

Chapter 5 of *On Revolution* is a puzzling and difficult one.[25] The preceding chapter concludes with the claim that 'the chief problem of American Revolution, once this [royal] source of authority had been severed from the colonial body politic in the New World, turned out to be the establishment and foundation *not of power but of authority*'.[26] Arendt associates power with the spontaneity of beginning, but authority with the stability of lasting worldly structures. Power, for Arendt, is ephemeral, existing only in its actualisation, whereas authority endures in mediating institutions. Both the spontaneity of power and the endurance of authority are necessary to sustain a political realm of public freedom. If power and authority are so distinguished,

---

[24] Arendt, *On Revolution*, p. 203.

[25] Other commentators have addressed Arendt's interpretation of the 'Preamble' to the *Declaration of Independence* which opens by declaring 'We hold these truths to be self-evident . . .' (Arendt, *On Revolution*, pp. 192–93). I will here leave aside Arendt's elucidation of the paradoxical power of this declaration, combining a performative promise with a self-evident absolute, and focus instead on the bond between event and document. See Jacques Derrida, 'Declarations of Independence', in Jacques Derrida, *Negotiations: Interventions and Interviews, 1971-2001*, trans. Elizabeth G. Rottenberg (Stanford: Stanford University Press, 2002), pp. 46–54, and Bonnie Honig, 'Declarations of Independence: Arendt and Derrida on the Problem of Founding a Republic', *The American Political Science Review* 85:1 (1991), pp. 97–113.

[26] Arendt, *On Revolution*, p. 178, my italics.

on what basis is the Constitution's own authority established? In Chapter 4, Arendt had noted both that 'the great good fortune of the American Revolution was the people of the colonies, prior to their conflict with England, were organized in self-governing bodies'[27] and that the Pilgrims who drew up the Mayflower Compact did so solely based on the power of 'mutual promise' to 'combine themselves together into a "civil Body Politick"'.[28]

One possible explanation Arendt gives in Chapter 4 for the legitimate foundation of constitutional authority is that the American constitutional delegates derived their authority to determine or constitute law and government from already established pre-constituted bodies, or, as she cites Madison, 'subordinate authorities',[29] and thus that authority was received 'from below'.[30] This depiction of already organised political units supports and exemplifies Arendt's narrative of political power as constituted (conventional, artificial) power,[31] and it enables her to consider the Americans as already genuinely political actors embedded in working institutions and able to join together out of (at least potentially) interlocking shared political spaces. The pre-existing sites for generating power mean that 'the revolution . . . did not throw them into a state of nature', into a formless pre-political void.[32] What Arendt calls 'authority from below' emerges not from a national will, the *will* of the *people* (as a singular nation), but from the political engagement of people (in the plural) acting in concert from dispersed institutional loci and recognised public spaces. These pre-constituted bodies might explain the confidence of the Americans' claims to political rights (against royal authority), and the liberatory movement of revolution, but they cannot explain the alchemy that transmutes liberation into freedom and action into new authority. They don't solve the conceptual conundrum of foundation.

Arendt also writes in Chapter 4 that

> binding and promising, combining and covenanting are the means by which power is kept in existence; where and when men succeed in keeping intact the power which sprang up between them during the course of any particular act or deed, they are already in the process of foundation, of constituting a stable worldly structure to house, as it were, their combined power of action.[33]

---

[27] Arendt, *On Revolution*, p. 165.

[28] Arendt, *On Revolution*, p. 167.

[29] Arendt, *On Revolution*, p. 165.

[30] Arendt, *On Revolution*, p. 166.

[31] She distinguishes power from 'pre-political natural force' which she takes to be violence (Arendt, *On Revolution*, p. 181).

[32] Arendt, *On Revolution*, p. 165.

[33] Arendt, *On Revolution*, p. 175.

This seems to suggest another explanation, that promising is the source not only of power[34] but also of lasting authority, although this would mean that power and authority do share a single lineage. But just a few pages later Arendt retracts the suggestion:

> while power, rooted in a people that had bound itself by mutual promises and lived in bodies constituted by compact, was enough 'to go through a revolution' . . . it was by no means enough to establish a 'perpetual union,' that is, to found a new authority[35]

Power for Arendt is ephemeral: it 'comes into being only if and when men join themselves together for the purpose of action, and it will disappear when, for whatever reason, they disperse and desert one another'.[36] Power exists in the present; on its own, it lacks duration. The power of covenant is thus not capable of establishing the authority of durable political institutions. As with the idea of pre-constituted bodies, the power of mutual promising is sufficient for revolution but insufficient for founding a republic or assuring its perpetuity.[37] Neither the fortunate contingency of pre-constituted bodies nor the power of promising can resolve the question of authority.

A central issue in founding and sustaining a republic is what Arendt calls 'world-building',[38] where the world is understood as the shared public space that sustains human relationships, the 'in-between space by which men are mutually related'.[39] The human world, Arendt writes in *The Human Condition*, 'depends for its reality and its continued existence, first, upon the presence of others who have seen and heard and will remember, and second, on the transformation of the intangible into the tangibility of things.'[40] Whereas power is aligned with the performative and virtuosic qualities of action, and thus also with action's ephemeral actualisation, constitutional authority is aligned with worldly structures that endure and maintain jurisdiction through time. Intrinsic to founding is a principle of durability or continuity, a temporal logic that appeals to future actions and re-activations. In the case

---

[34] She writes that 'power came into being when and where people would get together and bind themselves through promises, covenants, and mutual pledges' (Arendt, *On Revolution*, p. 181).

[35] Arendt, *On Revolution*, p. 182.

[36] Arendt, *On Revolution*, p. 175.

[37] Arendt, *On Revolution*, p. 182.

[38] Arendt, *On Revolution*, p. 175.

[39] Arendt, *On Revolution*, p. 175.

[40] Hannah Arendt, *The Human Condition* (Chicago: University of Chicago Press, 1998), p. 95.

of political world-building,[41] that appeal is made not (only) to our own future selves, but to future others who are invited into political community with us, thereby sharing a common world across generations.[42] But this appeal can only be transmitted through the tangible, material manifestations that reify words and actions into institutions and documents that remain in the world. The successful constitution of a political body rests on this element of temporal durability and continuity. A city is not a city if it dissolves itself from one generation to the next, if it vanishes with the vicissitudes of natal action. This commitment to the time of authority contributes to Arendt's dismissal of the force of political identity (the idea of a people)[43] and the purported necessity for a unified political will.[44] In rejecting the idea that power can become authority, Arendt out-sources authority to some*thing* that detaches itself from human actors and action and becomes part of the durable world, while still calling forth re-activations.

Identity, Will and Power

Arendt's account of founding a body politic is developed against the one offered by Rousseau (and Sieyès in his wake) where the power of the people, or the General Will, is said to provide the foundation of legitimate government. Arendt rejects Rousseau's version of the social contract, arguing that the attribution of a will to a collectivity converts a plurality of persons into a monolith, constructing 'the people' as a singular subject. Not only does Rousseau absolutise the people, but the insistence on the unity of their collective will displaces the nucleus of 'the future political body' away from 'the worldly institutions which this people had in common'[45] and on to the people themselves. By collapsing power and authority into one another,

---

[41] In *On Revolution*, Arendt equivocates on the relation between promising and world-building – while she says promising carries an 'element' of world-building, she phrases this in a way that makes promising and world-building analogous but not identical as practices of binding. Promising and world-building are parallel practices primarily in their orientation to the future: 'There is an element of the world-building capacity of man in the human faculty of making and keeping promises. Just as promises and agreements deal with the future and provide stability in the ocean of future uncertainty where the unpredictable may break in from all sides, so the constituting, founding, and world-building capacities of man concern always not so much ourselves and our own time on earth as our "successor," and "posterities"' (Arendt, *On Revolution*, p. 175).

[42] Arendt, *The Human Condition*, p. 55.

[43] The nation is either a 'fiction' or an 'absolute' (Arendt, *On Revolution*, p. 166).

[44] This is the basis of her criticism of Sieyès's theory of constituent power (Arendt, *On Revolution*, pp. 162, 164, 184).

[45] Arendt, *On Revolution*, p. 76.

Rousseau's contract destabilises itself since it is always vulnerable to a transitory and volatile will. [46]

Arendt distinguishes two different, and even 'mutually exclusive'[47] senses of social contract, which she claims have nothing in common other than a 'shared and misleading name'.[48] One of these is the self-constitution of society through a mutual bond 'between individual persons',[49] and the other is the contract between a people and a ruler that gives birth to a legitimate government. Even as she derides the second contract between society and its ruler as 'national' and 'absolute', Arendt's own account of the first 'mutual contract' bears, as Margaret Canovan has noted, 'striking similarities' with Rousseau.[50] In particular, we can, following Canovan, point to the distinction both Arendt and Rousseau make between natural man and artificial citizen, and to the role of covenanting in their accounts of political founding. For Arendt, as for Rousseau, political power and political freedom (if not, for Arendt, political identity) are conventional, not given by nature, and they are constituted by acts of consent.

Despite these points of shared contact, there is, as Canovan notes, a 'vital difference' between Arendt and Rousseau in their stance toward human plurality.[51] Where Rousseau aims to vanquish multiplicity by conceiving of the people as a united body with a single will and conceiving of the General Will as the ground of political community, Arendt insists on human plurality: 'not man but men inhabit the earth and form a world between them'.[52] In *The Social Contract*, Rousseau distinguishes between an 'aggregation' (of private and non-social individuals) and an 'association' or collective body;[53] only a people, and not a simple collection of private wills, can establish a body politic. The associative act that generates a people, producing unity out of multiplicity, forms a new 'common self' with a life and a will of its own, capable

---

[46] 'The so-called will of a multitude (if this is to be more than a legal fiction) is ever-changing by definition, and a structure built on it as its foundation is built on quicksand' (Arendt, *On Revolution*, p. 154).

[47] Arendt, *On Revolution*, p. 170.

[48] Arendt, *On Revolution*, p. 169.

[49] Arendt, *On Revolution*, p. 169.

[50] Margaret Canovan, 'Arendt, Rousseau, and Human Plurality in Politics', *The Journal of Politics* 45:2 (1983), pp. 286–302, at p. 287.

[51] Canovan, 'Arendt, Rousseau, and Human Plurality,' p. 290.

[52] Arendt, *On Revolution*, p. 175.

[53] Jean-Jacques Rousseau, *On the Social Contract*, in Jean-Jacques Rousseau, *Basic Political Writings*, trans. and ed. Donald A. Cress (Indianapolis: Hackett, 1987), pp. 141–227, at p. 147.

of collective self-determination.[54] Identity, and with it the power of joint will, is thus the first convention, and 'the act whereby a people is a people . . . is the true foundation of society.'[55] Only when a society with a distinctive form of life has emerged out of the state of nature, that is only when a single body with a single will has been formed, can a lawful government be created from the exercise of their general will.[56] Rousseau's General Will, in Arendt's view, does away with the dynamics of mediation, the in-between-ness of worldly relations. In shifting the focus from world to will, from what is tangible to what is invisible, it is inevitably also a shift from the public realm to interior reflection, a move that, Arendt claims, not only depoliticises but also makes enemies of us all.[57]

Arendt and Rousseau agree that power emerges from, and is established by, the people (differently construed as singular or plural), and that political associations are conventional, not natural.[58] But where Rousseau funnels power into law via the will, anchored in the nation, Arendt distinguishes the 'origin of power' from the 'source of law'[59] claiming that power and law require separate lineages and that willing is not the source of law. Whereas Rousseau's conception of the state as rooted in democratic sovereignty homogenises the will, converting plurality into singularity, a many into a one, for Arendt, the mutual contract that generates community is not a contract to be a people in the singular, but acts of promising that both presuppose and foster a plurality

---

[54] Rousseau, *On the Social Contract*, p. 148.

[55] Rousseau, *On the Social Contract*, p. 147.

[56] I am here setting aside another, distinctively Rousseauean, paradox of foundation: how the people can come into being without the laws that make their existence possible.

[57] Arendt understands Rousseau's conception of political identity to rely on 'the unifying power of the common national enemy' (Arendt, *On Revolution*, p. 77) who generates a sense of national unity. But, she adds, an external enemy is only useful in foreign affairs, and Rousseau had to go further in order to find an enemy that could provide the political identity, the oneness, necessary (in his view) for domestic politics. To 'discover a unifying principle within the nation itself' he needed an internal enemy, and he found this 'within the breast of each citizen, namely, in his particular will' (Arendt, *On Revolution*, p. 78). The shared antagonist of the people is each person's own (hidden, unseen, concealed) particularity, and true citizenship thus emerges only through the relentless, limitless vigilance against the self's own 'innermost motives' (Arendt, *On Revolution*, p. 97), a constant suspicion that recoils into a frenzied introspection.

[58] When Arendt attributes to Rousseau the revolutionary understanding of *le peuple* as a natural force, this is not quite right. Insofar as the people recognise themselves as a nation (conscious of their enemies and collectively organised) they are not wholly unconstituted. The nation is the social edge between nature and law, the willful anchor of the law. While not natural, the social body and its power nonetheless is, and Rousseau takes it to be, pre-political.

[59] Arendt, *On Revolution*, p. 182.

of perspectives, reciprocity and equality.[60] In the American colonial case, as we saw above, the people acted through a disparate set of pre-constituted political bodies and the 'American concept of people [is] identified with a multitude of voices',[61] with a plurality rather than a unity. What obviates the apparent need for homogeneity and singularity, for a nation conceived of as 'a body driven by one will'[62] is, Arendt claims, the 'joint effort'[63] and shared purpose[64] of political action, and in this emerges a truer sense of power as people acting in concert with and among equals. Put another way, for Arendt the act of becoming a people is not a necessary and preliminary stage of identity formation, prior to political existence, but an ongoing practice. Political identity does not reign sovereign over political form; instead, political form provides a space within which people can perpetually re-constitute themselves and create new forms of power.

Roman Founding and Greek Isonomy

As should be clear from her critique of Rousseau, Arendt distances her understanding of political community and collective action from the concept of democracy and its reliance on collective identity and rule of the people.[65] As she says about the Greek city-states, 'the *polis* was supposed to be an isonomy, not a democracy'.[66] Isonomy doesn't presuppose a collective political subject with a singular will. If human beings are not by nature equal, we need 'an artificial institution, the *polis*, which by virtue of its *nomos* would make them equal'.[67] *Nomos* is here understood as the boundary of law that, with the creation of a public realm, also establishes artificial equality among citizens.[68] Only in the (conventional and artificial) political space, in the presence of others, is there is an 'interconnection of freedom and equality'.[69] Isonomy provides a shared space of appearance but not a shared identity; the public space of speech and action itself is what is held in common.

---

[60] Arendt, *On Revolution*, p. 170.

[61] Arendt, *On Revolution*, p. 93.

[62] Arendt, *On Revolution*, p. 76.

[63] Arendt, *On Revolution*, p. 174.

[64] Arendt, *On Revolution*, p. 175.

[65] Arendt rejects both the 'popular' part and the 'sovereignty' part of popular sovereignty.

[66] 'The word "democracy" . . . was originally coined by those who were opposed to isonomy and who meant to say: What you say is "no-rule" is in fact only another kind of rulership; it is the worst form of government, rule by the demos' (Arendt, *On Revolution*, p. 30).

[67] Arendt, *On Revolution*, pp. 30–31.

[68] Arendt, *On Revolution*, p. 31.

[69] Arendt, *On Revolution*, p. 31.

Despite the modern breakdown of the Roman trinity of religion, tradition and authority, Arendt identifies a kind of bridge to Rome in the constitutive moments of the American Revolution, a Roman lineage implicit less in the founders' self-conception, than in their experience. The Americans followed the Roman model, not by adherence to Roman tradition, but insofar as they were inspired by an experience that resonated with their own, 'a dimension which had not been handed down by tradition' at all,[70] namely the experience of political action itself.[71] Rome symbolises, for Arendt, a form of political community vitally bound to its past, where the world is shared not only between cohabitants but between previous and future generations. The American founders, Arendt claims, had inherited as part of their schooling, 'two foundation legends' – 'the exodus of Israeli tribes' and the founding of Rome, whose contrast maps onto two different conceptions of legislation, one as lawmaking (i.e., giving commandments), and the other as alliance, perpetually regenerated through treaties that augment and re-found the original event. Unlike a commandment that emanates from a transcendent realm, Roman law does not so much command obedience as bind its citizens back to the beginning of Roman history and the foundation of eternity,[72] sustaining both the expansion of spatial jurisdiction and persistence through time.[73] The eternal city of the Romans is a worldly and not an otherworldly eternity.

Arendt emphasises that in contrast to the Greek idea of *nomos*, Roman law or *lex* is not conceived of as a wall but as a link to the past that makes further alliances possible; it is primarily *temporal* and not *spatial*. Unlike the Greek *nomos*, Roman *lex* acts as a bond and not a boundary; it establishes relationships rather than demarcates borders. In their connection to the past, and anticipation of the future, the Romans, Arendt claims in 'What is Authority?' had a genuinely political, as opposed to philosophical or technical, experience of authority, one that makes clear the distinction between authority, on the one hand, and on the other hand both persuasion ('through arguments') which presupposes equality and is directed toward one's fellow citizens, and coercion ('by force') which is tyrannical. Arendt further distinguishes political authority from expertise.[74] Authority, in this light, is neither tyranny nor

---

[70] Arendt, *On Revolution*, p. 197.
[71] Arendt's point here is that the practical experience of acting and initiating can bypass the conceptual conundrum of beginning: 'The very concept of Roman authority suggests that the act of foundation inevitably develops its own stability and permanence' (Arendt, *On Revolution*, p. 202).
[72] Arendt, *On Revolution*, p. 198.
[73] Arendt, *On Revolution*, p. 189.
[74] Hannah Arendt, 'What is Authority?' in Hannah Arendt, *Between Past and Future* (New York: Penguin Books, 2006), pp. 91–141, at p. 93.

equality nor expertise but a kind of recognition or respect on the part of those who find themselves obligated or tied back to an ancestral event. It issues in confirmation rather than command or coercion.

Arendt writes that 'authority, in contradistinction to power (*potestas*), had its roots in the past, but this past was no less present in the actual life of the city than the power and strength of the living'.[75] Authority, in other words, is not obscure and invisible, but concrete and tangible. Arendt gives the Roman experience of political authority the image of an inverted pyramid: directed toward its peak, which reaches 'into the depth of the earthly past',[76] the time of authority is recursive. The political experience of authority lies in this sense of being tied back and obligated to the legendary act of foundation,[77] held to the claim for remembrance and re-activation, the perseverance of the past in the present, and the past's dependence on the present: 'For *auctoritas*, whose etymological root is *augere*, to augment and increase, depended upon the vitality of the spirit of foundation',[78] the continuity of a 'principle established in the beginning'[79] that is transmitted and carried forward through augmentation. In this recursive temporality, Roman authority is 'relative by definition' and needs 'no absolute source'.[80]

Event and Document

Arendt highlights the duality of the meaning of the word 'constitution' which can have two distinct senses: the act of constituting, on the one hand, and the constitution as a written document on the other.[81] In Arendt's account of authority, it is the interchange between the act of founding (with its temporal arc of anticipated remembrance) and the written constitution (with its objective, worldly qualities) that short-circuits the conundrum of origin (the search for an absolute or transcendent source of law) and withstands the theological appeal to the will of the people. The extraordinary moment is not a higher law, or a transcendent absolute, or an immortal legislator, or the power of the people, or even mutual promising, but 'the extraordinary capacity to look upon yesterday with the eyes of centuries to come'.[82] In this way, Arendt envisages the American Constitution as following 'the great

[75] Arendt, 'What is Authority?', p. 122.
[76] Arendt, 'What is Authority?', p. 124.
[77] Arendt, 'What is Authority?', p. 121.
[78] Arendt, *On Revolution*, p. 201.
[79] Arendt, *On Revolution*, p. 201.
[80] Arendt, *On Revolution*, p. 189.
[81] Arendt, *On Revolution*, p. 203. See also Arendt, *On Revolution*, p. 145.
[82] Arendt, *On Revolution*, p. 198.

Roman model'[83] which vests authority in 'the vitality of the spirit of foundation',[84] a temporal event rather than a transcendent anchor. With a distinctively Roman intuition of authority, the Americans sought a 'lasting institution,' even, she writes, an 'Eternal City',[85] by appealing to 'the authority which the act of foundation carried within itself'.[86] They are Roman in connecting foundation to preservation and revolutionary newness to 'conservative care',[87] so that 'permanence and change were tied together'.[88]

In the idea of 'binding themselves back to a beginning',[89] Arendt links revolution and constitution, arguing that revolution's essence is 'the foundation of a body politic which guarantees the space where freedom can appear'[90] and enables future generations to carry over the revolutionary spirit in their own performance of public freedom.[91] Where there is a successful constitution, the two meanings (the act and the document) become inseparable in an authoritative boomerang between a founding event available to be remembered and a shared object available for augmentation, interpretation and differing perspectives. Authority emanates from the act of foundation itself,[92] as it lives on in memory and survives the transience of human power, only when the act is coupled with its augmentation. Consonant with the Roman concept of foundation, Arendt considers that 'the very authority of the American Constitution resides in its inherent capacity to be amended and augmented'.[93] The constitution is binding in the sense of relying for its own preservation on transmission and transformation, and Arendt re-situates constitutional 'worship'[94] in this context of intergenerational transmission and trans-temporal community.

Who Inherits?

Who are (or will have been) the American people? Despite Arendt's attention to the way that later actions shape and convene earlier ones, *On Revolution* is curiously reticent about civil war generally, and the American Civil War

---

[83] Arendt, *On Revolution*, p. 199.
[84] Arendt, *On Revolution*, p. 201.
[85] Arendt, *On Revolution*, p. 229.
[86] Arendt, *On Revolution*, p. 199.
[87] Arendt, *On Revolution*, p. 202.
[88] Arendt, *On Revolution*, p. 201.
[89] Arendt, *On Revolution*, p. 198.
[90] Arendt, *On Revolution*, p. 125.
[91] Arendt, *On Revolution*, p. 126.
[92] The 'act of foundation' is the 'foundation of authority' (Arendt, *On Revolution*, p. 204).
[93] Arendt, *On Revolution*, p. 202.
[94] Notably, Arendt is not concerned with anything like 'original intent' which would reside within the interior meaning of the author rather than in the publicly available letter.

in particular. Chapter One makes a brief reference to Aristotle's understanding that friendship between citizens is the 'most reliable safeguard' against 'factional strife',[95] but no mention is made of constitutional crisis when Arendt mourns the 'lost treasure' of the American Revolution. Even as she identifies slavery as 'the primordial crime upon which the fabric of American society rested',[96] Arendt is evasive about the imbrication of the institution of American slavery with the revolutionary cause, the Constitution's delineation of the American people, and the balance of powers between the states. And while Arendt is notoriously vocal about the segregationist crises in her own time, *On Revolution* does not link the fracture of political space and the divisions of racism to founding acts.[97]

Partly this is because, even aside from her dismissal of the social question, Arendt takes the limit or negative of power (limited government as a way of protecting individual rights) to be secondary to the creation of political space that secures the right to be a citizen. Arendt considers the Bill of Rights, with its list of civil liberties, to be merely a 'necessary supplement' to the primary act of establishing a public realm of freedom and 'the creation of a new power'.[98] What Arendt sees as the 'new system of power'[99] is the generation and stabilisation of power both through its separation and distribution among the various branches of government[100] and through 'the balancing of power between the federal and the state governments'.[101] This 'new' power is premised on its own divisibility and diffusion among a plurality of locales rather than on the 'indivisibility of power'.[102] Arendt applauds the federal structure for its erosion of sovereignty, and for forging a power principle 'strong enough to found a perpetual union',[103] but she blithely passes over the remnants of state sovereignty thereby secured. American federalism is founded on a balance of power that keeps sovereignty vested in individual states and allowed slavery to continue.

[95] Arendt, *On Revolution*, p. 34.

[96] Arendt, *On Revolution*, p. 71.

[97] See especially Kathryn Gines, *Hannah Arendt and the Negro Question* (Bloomington: Indiana University Press, 2014). Gines argues that Arendt dismisses 'racialized slavery as a "social question"' (Gines, p. 62), in line with her distinction between the political and the social. As Gines cites Arendt from *On Revolution*: 'the absence of the *social question* from the American scene was, after all, quite deceptive, and that abject and degrading misery was present everywhere in the form of slavery and Negro labor' (Gines, p. 62 (her italics), citing Arendt, *On Revolution*, p. 70).

[98] Arendt, *On Revolution*, p. 149.

[99] Arendt, *On Revolution*, p. 147.

[100] Arendt, *On Revolution*, pp. 267–8.

[101] Arendt, *On Revolution*, p. 152.

[102] Arendt, *On Revolution*, p. 153.

[103] Arendt, *On Revolution*, p. 154.

Arendt is thus less than acute in recognising the way the multiplicity of internal commonwealths (the federal structure) is a key feature of American identitarianism, providing a pathway for people in the plural to self-identify as pluralities of peoples. Even as a nominal national identity is asserted, the title to it results in ever more radicalised (and racialised) attempts to claim exclusive right to be recognised as the true and only legitimate descendants, to refuse to recognise as fellow inheritors those taken to be ersatz Americans or insufficiently attuned to the original spirit of the people.

Arendt's account of constitutional authority might nonetheless provide a resource for thinking about the perils of secessionism, Balkanisation, hyper-partisanship, and the resurgence of ethnic nationalism. Arendt recognises that the idea of a 'people' can lead to a destabilising hyper-particularisation dissolvent of unity and incapable of holding any joint action together, and that the logic of collective willing can lead to a pursuit of identity that just as easily contracts the boundaries of 'we' as expands them. The history of American secessionism, past and present, reveals the ways in which the 'people' is susceptible to this factionalisation of the 'we', intensifying internal antagonisms within constitutional borders. As noted above, this centrifugal logic of splintering was on full display during the 2013 Republican-led shutdown of the American government in the midst of Obama's presidency.

In a political context of resurgent tribalism, it is perhaps not surprising that no less a staunch cosmopolitan than Martha Nussbaum has recently endorsed the cultivation of patriotism and affective allegiance toward one's fellow citizens as an antidote to the extremes of internal antagonism.[104] Advocating in a Renanian vein[105] for a 'narrative of the nation',[106] Nussbaum

---

[104] Martha C. Nussbaum, 'Teaching Patriotism: Love and Critical Freedom', in Martha C. Nussbaum, *Political Emotions: Why Love Matters for Justice* (Cambridge: Harvard University Press, 2013), pp. 204–256. This is a striking reversal from earlier work which claimed, for instance, that 'to give support to nationalist sentiments subverts, ultimately, even the values that hold a nation together, because it substitutes a colorful idol for the substantive universal values of justice and right'. See Martha C. Nussbaum, 'Patriotism and Cosmopolitanism', in Martha C. Nussbaum, *For Love of Country?*, ed. Joshua Cohen (Boston: Beacon Press, 1996), pp. 2–17, at p. 5.

[105] Ernest Renan, 'What is a Nation?', in Stuart Woolf (ed.), *Nationalism in Europe: 1815 to the Present* (New York: Routledge, 1995), pp. 48–60. Renan defends the idea of nation as a community of memory and forgetting, bound if not quite by a principle of identity, then by attachments and identifications. Renan makes explicit the temporal dimension of national identity in 'the desire to live together, the will to continue to value the heritage that has been received in common' (Renan, 'What Is a Nation?', p. 58).

[106] Nussbaum, 'Teaching Patriotism', p. 229.

cites Lincoln's Gettysburg Address, which returns to the founding act and is accompanied by an invocation of the people, as a call for a renewed commitment to American principles that link the memory of founding with a crucial moment of re-activation or re-founding[107] and does so through reliance on an emotionally compelling appeal to the nation as nation: a single people. Nussbaum also cites MLK's 'I Have a Dream' speech which describes the founding documents as 'a promissory note to which every American was to fall heir'.[108] In both cases, Nussbaum highlights the way that the relay of re-activation summons an idea of the American people. The speeches are simultaneously claims for the durability of the union, acts of political renewal, and appeals for inclusive identification.[109]

Nussbaum's wager or hope is that appeal to American ideals might provide a counter-weight to exclusionary policies and open up the nation, rather than close it down. Can patriotism or national identity provide a bulwark against tribal identity? The Arendtian logic of authority, the relay between constitution and augmentation I have depicted above, can perhaps illuminate the distinction between those (white ethnonationalists) who appeal to a substantively shared identity and an unchanging original intent in order to stake their claim as sole heirs, and those (civic nationalists) who stake their inheritance claims, within the midst of the written document's self-divisions and the founding act's fault lines and occlusions, on a re-articulated, augmenting vision of the constituting address (and its addressees). Remembering that for Arendt equality is 'not natural but political',[110] and that *nomos* always has a 'spatial significance'[111] that delimits its jurisdiction, a range 'within which defined power may be legitimately exercised',[112] it seems clear that any invocation to a 'who' (the addressees of a constitution) for Arendt cannot be universal. But insofar as a constitution is open to, and even dependent on, its own regeneration, renewal and reparation, this 'who' is temporally mobile and cannot be circumscribed in advance. The founders could not anticipate the descendants to whom they were appealing, who would be bound by their document.

---

[107] Nussbaum notes that in the Gettysburg Address, Lincoln refers to the Declaration of Independence and omits the Constitution 'with its protection for slavery' (Nussbaum, 'Teaching Patriotism', p. 231).

[108] Nussbaum, 'Teaching Patriotism', p. 236.

[109] Nussbaum is not alone in re-thinking the value of so-called civic nationalism in response to an era of domestic strife and rising ethnonationalism.

[110] Arendt, *On Revolution*, p. 278.

[111] Arendt, *On Revolution*, p. 275.

[112] Arendt, *On Revolution*, pp. 186–7.

Still, I am reluctant to identify Arendt's constitutionalism with civic nationalism and its reversion to identity.[113] Arendt is neither a cosmopolitan nor a nationalist – the founder/successor relation she depicts in the authoritative relays of shared inheritance moves through public space and public time, not through collective identity. Even as the event of founding recedes into the past, it animates the written document and takes on an authoritative aura that reverberates and is transmitted to future generations who take themselves to be bound back to it. And even as the written document takes on the objective weight of thinghood, it remains entangled with both the constitutive founding act that brings it into being and the anticipated future acts that will keep it intact by renewing it. The appeal or claim to authority works in both directions (to have been an ancestor and to be recognised as a descendant).

On Revolution addresses what appears to be the central conundrum of legitimacy, the question of how 'to found a new authority . . . sufficient to assure perpetuity, that is, to bestow upon the affairs of men that measure of stability without which they would be unable to build a world for their posterity'.[114] On Arendt's account, for revolutionary founding to evade the twin dangers of a vicious circle or appeal to an absolute, and to succeed in the constitution of a political body, it must enact and invoke both a worldly and a temporal component, setting in motion an exchange between political space and political time. Legitimacy comes neither from the transcendence of divinity nor from the immanence of human power, but from the past and from the future.[115] There is no space of appearances without a temporal dimension that anchors it to ancestors and posterities. Constitutional authority in Arendt emanates from the reverberations and relays between the act of foundation and the document as a worldly thing, and between past and future, sustaining the political life of a community in a temporal arc and an objective artifact.

---

[113] While, as I have been arguing, Arendtian isonomy or civic equality is formed through shared political space and intergenerational time, its invitation to renewed action keeps the boundaries of identity (and citizenship) open. Civic nationalism often presents as an expectation for assimilation that, even while it accommodates or integrates outsiders, carries with it implicit demands for commitment or renunciation (as can be seen, for instance in accusations of 'dual loyalty' sometimes made to those deemed insufficiently to belong).

[114] Arendt, *On Revolution*, p. 182.

[115] On this point, see also Hanna Lukkari's contribution in this volume.

3

Are There Inherent Limits to Constitutional Amendment? An Analysis of Carl Schmitt's Argument

Lars Vinx

Limits to Amendment and Democratic Legitimacy

An increasing number of democratic constitutions contain provisions that cannot be amended at all.[1] Let us call such constitutional provisions 'strongly entrenched', to distinguish them from constitutional provisions that are protected from change by a mere supermajoritarian requirement or some other special procedural hurdle. If a constitution contains strongly entrenched provisions, it will become possible for procedurally valid constitutional amendments to be unconstitutional, as a result of a material violation of a strongly entrenched constitutional provision.[2] Where strongly entrenched constitutional provisions exist, they are often enforced by supreme or constitutional courts.[3]

The evidence on the effectiveness of strong constitutional entrenchment in protecting democratic constitutionality is mixed. Judicial enforcement of limits to constitutional amendment has at times played a positive role in the constitutional politics of democratic states. The Indian Supreme Court's

---

[1] Yaniv Roznai, 'Unconstitutional Constitutional Amendments – The Migration and Success of a Constitutional Idea', *American Journal of Comparative Law* 61:3 (2013), pp. 657–719. See also Yaniv Roznai, *Unconstitutional Constitutional Amendments: The Limits of Amendment Powers* (Oxford: Oxford University Press, 2017).

[2] See Richard Albert, 'Unconstitutional Amendments', Canadian Journal of Law and Jurisprudence 22:1 (2009), pp. 5–47, and Gary Jeffrey Jacobsohn, *Constitutional Identity* (Cambridge, MA: Harvard University Press, 2009).

[3] See Kemal Gözler, *Judicial Review of Constitutional Amendments. A Comparative Study* (Bursa: Ekin Press, 2008), Gary Jeffrey Jacobsohn, 'An Unconstitutional Constitution? A Comparative Perspective', *International Journal of Constitutional Law* 4:3 (2006), pp. 460–487, and Sudhir Krishnaswamy, *Democracy and Constitutionalism in India. A Study of the Basic Structure Doctrine* (New Delhi: Oxford University Press, 2010).

basic structure doctrine, for instance, helped to pull the country back from the brink of dictatorship.[4] But strong constitutional entrenchment was incapable, in some more recent cases, to prevent democratic backsliding.[5] At any rate, the question of the effectiveness of material limits to amendment in preventing undesirable constitutional change towards populist authoritarianism will become relevant only once we are able to answer a prior question of justification.

In the context of democratic constitutionalism, strongly entrenched constitutional provisions give rise to an obvious question of legitimacy. To judicially enforce constitutional rights against a democratic majority, it is often argued, violates the principle of democratic equality, since a small group of unelected judges may come to define the meaning of the constitution in a way that conflicts with the will of the people. Such restrictions of democracy may be justifiable on pragmatic grounds in troubled democratic polities where a respect for rights is not firmly embedded in political culture. But they must be illegitimate in well-established democracies, where the guardianship of the constitution can and should be entrusted to the people themselves or to their elected representatives.[6] If this general critique of formal constitutionalism is sound, then it must clearly be even more illegitimate to impose material limits, limits that cannot be overcome at all, on the process of constitutional amendment.[7] Amendments, to be duly passed, often require a supermajority of members of parliament and sometimes approval in a popular referendum. Fulfilment of the conditions for a valid amendment would appear to indicate the will of the people much more clearly than an ordinary legislative majority.

---

[4] Granville Austin, *Working a Democratic Constitution: A History of the Indian Experience* (New Delhi: Oxford University Press, 2003).

[5] One prominent example is Turkey. See Andrew Arato, *Post Sovereign Constitution Making: Learning and Legitimacy* (Oxford: Oxford University Press, 2016), pp. 223–268, and Gülşen Seven and Lars Vinx, 'The Hegemonic Preservation Thesis Revisited: The Example of Turkey', *Hague Journal on the Rule of Law* 9:1 (2017), pp. 45–82.

[6] See Jeremy Waldron, *Law and Disagreement* (Oxford: Oxford University Press, 1999) as well as Jeremy Waldron, 'The Core of the Case Against Judicial Review', *Yale Law Journal* 115:6 (2006), pp. 1348–1406, Mark Tushnet, *Taking the Constitution Away from the Courts* (Princeton, NJ: Princeton University Press, 2000), Larry D. Kramer, *The People Themselves. Popular Constitutionalism and Judicial Review* (New York: Oxford University Press, 2004), and Richard Bellamy, *Political Constitutionalism. A Republican Defense of the Constitutionality of Democracy* (Cambridge: Cambridge University Press, 2007).

[7] See John R. Vile, 'The Case Against Implicit Limits on the Constitutional Amending Process', in Sanford Levinson (ed.), *Responding to Imperfection. The Theory and Practice of Constitutional Amendment* (Princeton, NJ: Princeton University Press, 1995), pp. 191–214 and Melissa Schwartzberg, *Democracy and Legal Change* (New York: Cambridge University Press, 2007).

Strong constitutional entrenchment, then, is an even more blatant affront to the will of the people than ordinary constitutional entrenchment.[8]

Despite these objections, several notable authors have defended the claim that material limits to constitutional amendment need not be democratically illegitimate – and even that such limits are inherent in any liberal and democratic constitution, whether explicitly expressed in the constitutional text or not.[9] In this paper, I will offer a reconstruction of the most elaborate and influential defence of that view: Carl Schmitt's argument for inherent limitations of the power of amendment under the Weimar Constitution.[10] I will argue that

---

[8] Schwartzberg, *Democracy and Legal Change*, pp. 184–189.

[9] See Walter F. Murphy, 'An Ordering of Constitutional Values', *Southern California Law Review* 53 (1979–1980), pp. 703–760, Jeff Rosen, 'Was the Flag Burning Amendment Unconstitutional?', *Yale Law Journal* 100:4 (1991), pp. 1073–1092, Samuel Freeman, 'Original Meaning, Democratic Interpretation, and the Constitution', *Philosophy and Public Affairs* 21:1 (1992), pp. 3–42 as well as Samuel Freeman, 'Political Liberalism and the Possibility of a Just Democratic Constitution', *Chicago-Kent Law Review* 69:3 (1994), pp. 619–668, John Rawls, *Political Liberalism* (New York: Columbia University Press, 1996), pp. 237–240, and Luigi Ferrajoli, 'The Normative Paradigm of Constitutional Democracy', *Res Publica* 17:4 (2011), pp. 355–367.

[10] For discussion of Schmitt's argument for inherent limits to amendment see Margit Kraft-Fuchs, 'Prinzipielle Bemerkungen zu Carl Schmitts Verfassungslehre', *Zeitschrift für öffentliches Recht* 9 (1930), pp. 511–541, Horst Ehmke, *Grenzen der Verfassungsänderung* (Berlin: Duncker & Humblot, 1953), pp. 33–53, Dieter Conrad, 'Limitation of Amendment Procedures and the Constituent Power', in Dieter Conrad, *Zwischen den Traditionen. Probleme des Verfassungsrechts und der Rechtskultur in Indien und Pakistan* (Stuttgart: Franz Steiner Verlag, 1999), pp. 47–85, Joel I. Colon-Rios, *Weak Constitutionalism. Democratic Legitimacy and the Question of Constituent Power* (Abingdon: Routledge, 2012), pp. 126–151. Schmitt is often credited with (and took credit for) the explicit introduction of limits to amendment in the German Basic Law of 1949. See Jan-Werner Müller, *A Dangerous Mind. Carl Schmitt in Post-War European Thought* (New Haven and London: Yale University Press, 2003), pp. 63–75, Gregory H. Fox and Georg Nolte, 'Intolerant Democracies', *Harvard International Law Journal* 36:1 (1995), pp. 1–70, at pp. 18–20, Volker Neumann, *Carl Schmitt als Jurist* (Tübingen: Mohr Siebeck, 2015), pp. 110–118, and Carl Schmitt, *Verfassungsrechtliche Aufsätze aus den Jahren 1924-1954. Materialien zu einer Verfassungslehre* (Berlin: Duncker & Humblot, 1958), pp. 345–6. Schmitt's argument, moreover, animates the German Federal Constitutional Court's reasoning in the *Maastricht* and *Lisbon* decisions. See Robert C. Van Ooyen, *Die Staatstheorie des Bundesverfassungsgerichts und Europa. Von Solange über Maastricht zu Europa* (Baden-Baden: Nomos, 2010), pp. 23–37, and Lars Vinx, 'The Incoherence of Strong Popular Sovereignty', *International Journal of Constitutional Law* 11:1 (2013), pp. 101–124. Schmitt's argument has been invoked by several constitutional or supreme courts reviewing constitutional amendments. See Joel I. Colon-Rios, 'Carl Schmitt and Constituent Power in Latin American Courts', *Constellations* 18:3 (2011), pp. 365–388, and Richard Stacey, 'Constituent Power and Carl Schmitt's Theory of Constitution in Kenya's Constitution-Making Process', *International Journal of Constitutional Law* 9:3–4 (2011), pp. 587–614. The most elaborate recent attempt to theorise and justify limits to amendment takes its cues from Schmitt's approach. See Roznai, *Unconstitutional Constitutional Amendments*, pp. 105–134.

Schmitt presents a plausible case for the view that constitutional entrenchment in its ordinary, supermajoritarian form can be democratically legitimate only where it protects inherent limits to constitutional amendment. Any general defence of the legitimacy of constitutional entrenchment and judicial review must therefore stand and fall with the claim that there are inherent limits to amendment in every democratic constitution.

The Insufficiency of the Relative Concept of Constitution

Schmitt built his argument for inherent limits of constitutional amendment on a *reductio ad absurdum* of the standard interpretation of the Weimar Constitution's amendment clause. Article 76 of the Weimar Constitution determined that the constitution was to be amended by 'way of legislation', with the approval of two-thirds of the members of parliament present and voting. The text of the Weimar Constitution did not contain any eternity-clauses. Most interpreters of the Weimar Constitution concluded that there were no material limits to constitutional amendment.[11] In this orthodox approach to the amendment clause of the Weimar Constitution, the constitutional quality of a constitutional law was seen to consist exclusively in the fact that its enactment, repeal, or amendment required the use of a special procedure of legislation. The constitution was regarded simply as the set of constitutional laws, a set that was held to contain all and only the legal norms that, at any point in time, happened to be under the protection of the supermajoritarian requirement of Article 76.

Schmitt argued that such an understanding of the constitution – he calls it the 'relative concept of constitution' – is highly counter-intuitive.[12] Take the following example: the Weimar Constitution determined, in its first Article, that 'the German *Reich* is a republic'. It also determined, in Article 129, that public servants have a right to access their personnel files. Intuitively, the first provision is much more fundamental than the second. We would expect

---

[11] See Richard Thoma, 'Die Funktionen der Staatsgewalt: Grundbegriffe und Grundsätze', in Gerhard Anschütz and Richard Thoma (eds.), *Handbuch des deutschen Staatsrechts*, vol. 2 (Tübingen: Mohr Siebeck, 1932), pp. 108–159, at pp. 153–157, and Gerhard Anschütz, *Die Verfassung des deutschen Reiches vom 11. August 1919*, 4th edn. (Berlin: Georg Stilke, 1933), p. 401. Schmitt's claim that there were limits to amendment was supported by some other Weimar-era authors. See for example Karl Loewenstein, *Erscheinungsformen der Verfassungsänderung. Verfassungsrechtliche Untersuchungen zu Artikel 76 der Reichsverfassung* (Tübingen: Mohr Siebeck, 1931), pp. 305–308, and Gerhard Leibholz, *Die Gleichheit vor dem Gesetz. Eine Studie auf rechtsvergleichender und rechtsphilosophischer Grundlage*, 2nd edn. (München: C.H. Beck, 1959), p. 124.

[12] Carl Schmitt, *Constitutional Theory*, trans. Jeffrey Seitzer (Durham, NC: Duke University Press, 2008), pp. 67–74.

to find a provision determining the form of state in a written constitution. The provision in Article 129, by contrast, is clearly inessential. It could have been left out without any impairment to the functioning or basic character of the constitution. The orthodox view lacked the resources to recognise the seeming difference in material importance between the two provisions.[13]

A constitution is normally taken to be a kind of fundamental law. It is supposed to determine the basic structure of the state and to lay down the rules according to which its main organs are to function. In a liberal understanding, the constitution is also to determine the limits of state power over the individual. That constitutional norms which are fundamental in one of these two senses are often protected by the procedural requirement of a supermajority, Schmitt argues, should be regarded as a reflection of their intrinsic importance. What makes a constitutional law fundamental is not the fact that it happens to be protected by a procedural barrier. Rather, the protection by the procedural barrier is justified only on the condition that the norms that it protects are indeed materially fundamental, even apart from the procedural means employed to protect them.[14] If we find this intuition compelling, we are forced to conclude that there must be some criterion for the constitutionality of a norm other than the purely procedural criterion derived from Article 76, one that is based on the importance of the norm's material content.

This intuition, however plausible, does not suffice to show that there are inherent limits to constitutional amendment. The view that the norms that are justifiably protected by the requirement of a supermajority are so protected in virtue of their intrinsic constitutional significance suggests that it would be wrong to use the amendment procedure to abolish those norms. But it does not by itself entail that it would be illegal to do so. A proponent of the orthodox interpretation of the Weimar Constitution might agree with Schmitt that a constitutional provision protecting a basic individual right, like the right to free expression, is fundamental in a democracy, in a political or moral sense, while the protection of a public servant's entitlement to see the personnel file is not. He or she might very well agree, moreover, that a constitutional amendment that abrogates the right to free expression would disfigure the constitution and undermine its democratic character. But he or she might nevertheless coherently deny that this entails that an amendment abrogating the right to free expression would be legally invalid.

[13] Schmitt, *Constitutional Theory*, pp. 67–68.
[14] Schmitt, *Constitutional Theory*, pp. 72–74.

Constitutional scholars are not entitled to read limitations to amendment into the constitution without any textual basis. To do so confuses the scholarly authority of legal scholars with the legislative authority of a constituent power. It is not hard, moreover, to think of normative reasons for why a constituent assembly should refrain from imposing explicit material limits to amendment, in the form of explicit eternity-clauses. Even someone who held that constitutional amendments with this or that content would disfigure the constitution or undermine its basic character or identity might nevertheless reasonably take the view that the concrete textual expression of fundamental constitutional principles ought to be open to adaptive revision by amendment. Since such adaptive revision would be ruled out by eternity-clauses, it is preferable, one might conclude, to make do with a mere procedural protection of materially fundamental constitutional norms, even if that raises the theoretical possibility of legally valid constitutional amendments that disfigure the constitution.

Schmitt's argument so far also suffers from a problem of fit. As we have seen, Schmitt observed that the Weimar Constitution contained provisions that were not materially fundamental, such as the right of public servants to see their personnel files. The most obvious response to this problem, of course, would have been to argue that norms the content of which was not intrinsically fundamental ought not to have been included in the constitution. Schmitt indeed argued, in his constitutional writings, that it had been a mistake for the constituent assembly to extend constitutional protection to norms that, in his view, were not intrinsically fundamental.[15] But the claim that it had been a mistake for the constituent assembly to extend constitutional protection to norms that he judged to be non-fundamental was clearly no more than an argument *de lege ferenda*. If Schmitt had claimed, on the other hand, that the procedural hurdle imposed by article 76 protected only a subset of the norms included in the text of the constitution, he would have put himself into an open and direct conflict with the constitutional text.

The only possible way – in the context of an interpretation of the Weimar Constitution – for Schmitt to draw a distinction between materially fundamental constitutional norms and constitutional norms not materially fundamental was to elevate the former to the status of inherent limits to constitutional amendment. Schmitt thus needed to explain why we are compelled – as a matter of general democratic-constitutional theory – to presume that the material fundamentality of a constitutional norm implies that we can take it to enjoy heightened legal protection against change, that is, that we are justified to regard it as an inherent legal limit to the power of amendment. Let us now consider how Schmitt tried to meet this challenge.

---

[15] Schmitt, *Constitutional Theory*, pp. 84–88.

The Principle of Equal Chance and the Argument from Militant Democracy

Schmitt's attempt to fill the gap between his criticism of the relative concept of constitution and his claim that there are inherent limits to amendment in any democratic constitution takes the form of an analysis of the conditions of the legitimacy of what Schmitt calls the 'legislative state', which is developed most extensively in *Legality and Legitimacy*.[16]

Schmitt's use of the term 'legislative state' refers, roughly, to a parliamentary democracy with a purely procedural constitution, of the sort advocated by contemporary political constitutionalists. The democratic theory of Hans Kelsen is the most prominent Weimar-era theoretical account of the legislative state.[17] In *Legality and Legitimacy*, Schmitt sets out to contest the claim that the Weimar Constitution can be understood as the constitution of a legislative state. His argument starts out from the general assumption that every state must make a claim to legitimate authority. And any such claim to legitimate authority, including that raised by the legislative state, Schmitt goes on to argue, must make an appeal to some 'substantive principle of justice' that serves to legitimate the state's decision making.[18]

Schmitt holds that the principle of the legitimacy of a legislative state cannot be output-oriented. Proponents of the legislative state understand legality as the expression of the present will of the majority of democratically elected legislators. Whatever that majority decides (or decides to acquiesce in) is supposed to be binding, for the time being, irrespective of the content of the decision.[19] The legitimacy of the rulings taken by a pure legislative state, therefore, cannot be explained in instrumental terms, for instance by claiming that such a state is likely (or more likely than some other state) to make choices which are held to be substantively correct on procedure-independent grounds. Rather, the legislative state's principle of legitimacy must relate to some outcome-independent moral quality of purely majoritarian democratic decision making.

---

[16] Carl Schmitt, *Legality and Legitimacy*, trans. Jeffrey Seitzer (Durham, NC: Duke University Press, 2004), pp. 3–26.

[17] Hans Kelsen, *The Essence and Value of Democracy*, ed. Nadia Urbinati and Carlo Invernizzi-Accetti, trans. Brian Graf (Lanham, MD: Rowman&Littlefield, 2013). For discussion of Kelsen's theory of democracy see Sandrine Baume, *Hans Kelsen and the Case for Democracy* (Colchester: ECPR Press, 2012) and Lars Vinx, *Hans Kelsen's Pure Theory of Law. Legality and Legitimacy* (Oxford: Oxford University Press, 2007), pp. 101–144.

[18] Schmitt, *Legality and Legitimacy*, p. 28.

[19] Schmitt, *Legality and Legitimacy*, pp. 23–26.

Schmitt puts forward the proposal that the legislative state is legitimised by adherence to a principle of equal chance that expresses the political equality of democratic citizens as participants in the political process. Schmitt defines it as 'the principle that there must be an absolutely equal chance for all conceivable opinions, tendencies, and movements to reach a majority' and for the political goals associated with those 'opinions, tendencies, and movements' to come to be realised through legislative activity.[20] Of course, the claim here is not that the state must somehow ensure that every political opinion, tendency, or movement, even one that lacks significant support among citizens, be as likely as any other to win political power. What the principle demands is that no political opinion or movement be deprived of an equal opportunity to compete for electoral support.

The principle of equal chance requires that all citizens enjoy equal rights of political participation as individuals and that their individual votes be given equal weight in determining the outcome. Schmitt puts emphasis on the idea that this requirement can only be met if the procedural rules that determine how elections are to take place are stable and are not constantly tampered with by current legislative majorities.[21] In addition, the principle demands that individuals must be free to associate in political parties to pursue their political goals and that political parties have equal access to the process of democratic competition for the electorate's support. Note that the principle, as Schmitt describes it, implies that there must be no constitutional entrenchment and, *a fortiori*, no material limits of amendment. The demand that all political groups are to have an equal chance to reach a majority and thus to realise their political goals rules out procedural hurdles that disfavour certain legislative outcomes, as well as material limits of amendment that altogether block the realisation of certain political aims.

Imagine, then, that you live in a legislative state and are a member of a group or party that is currently out of power and thus subject to the decisions of a politically hostile majority. Why should you or your group acknowledge a duty to respect decisions, at least for the time being, which you may hold to be wrong, instead of contesting them illegally or even violently?[22] Part of the answer must, of course, be that the decisions in question were taken through a procedure that afforded you and your group an equal chance to win political power and to make your view prevail. You and your group participated as political equals in the process of decision-making that led to the decisions that you now reject as misguided. But this, Schmitt plausibly suggests, cannot

[20] Schmitt, *Legality and Legitimacy*, p. 28.
[21] Schmitt, *Legality and Legitimacy*, pp. 35–36.
[22] Schmitt, *Legality and Legitimacy*, pp. 29–30.

suffice to legitimate the decisions in question. The principle of equal chance, under any plausible reading, must be forward-looking as well as backwards-looking. You can be bound, for the time being, to respect decisions taken by a politically hostile present majority only on the further condition that you continue to enjoy an equal chance to win power or to become part of a legislative majority in the future, so as to reverse any presently existing law that you consider to be substantively wrong.[23]

Schmitt argues that this forward-looking character of the principle of equal chance renders its operation in political practice highly fragile. To see how, note that the forward-looking character of the principle can lead to tension with a purely procedural understanding of democracy. It clearly implies that all decisions that impair or restrict the future application of the principle must be illegitimate, from the point of view of those whose future equal chance is impaired, even if the procedural genesis of the decisions in question honoured the principle of equal chance. It follows that a proponent of the principle of equal chance must reject the claim that any decision created by democratic procedure would have to be regarded as legitimate. The principle of equal chance, in its forward-looking aspect, forbids any decision with a material content that restricts or undercuts the future operation of the principle.

It would be a violation of the principle of equal chance, for instance, for the current majority to enact a law that disenfranchises a part of the citizenry in order to make it less likely that it will lose power in a future election. It would also be a violation of the principle for the current majority to introduce new procedures of decision making that require qualified majorities, in the future, to overturn present decisions made by a simple majority. Of course, the problem is not limited to the sphere of legislative activity. There is a constant temptation for the majority to lean on its executive power to disadvantage its political opponents: even seemingly minor violations of the principle of equal chance – a little bit of gerrymandering here, some administrative pressure put on this or that critical newspaper there, some extra-time for the spokesperson of government on public television – may be very helpful in preserving one's status as a majority.[24]

The fact that every governing majority will likely be tempted to avail itself of that surplus of power suggests that the mere absence, at present, of decisions that openly violate the principle of equal chance, while clearly necessary, would not be enough for a current minority to be subject to a duty of deference. Once a majority begins to take legislative or administrative

---

[23] Schmitt, *Legality and Legitimacy*, p. 28 and p. 32.
[24] Schmitt, *Legality and Legitimacy*, pp. 31–33.

decisions that openly violate the principle of equal chance, it may well be too late for a minority to fight back, and to do so within the political process, with any prospect of success. Schmitt concludes that a current minority can be expected to adopt a posture of deference towards a current majority's decisions only if the minority has the assurance that the majority will continue to respect its political rights. Such assurance may be missing even where a current majority has not yet begun to violate the principle of equal chance. And absent a degree of trust, on the part of the minority, in the majority's continuing willingness to abide by the principle of equal chance, appeals to the principle addressed to the current minority will lack legitimating force.[25]

Though the principle of equal chance can be violated only by present majorities, the duty to preserve the underlying mutual trust that sustains the legitimating power of the principle falls on all political camps. Assurance that the principle of equal chance will continue to be respected can come to be undermined even by a minority that does not currently have the power to strip its political opponents of an equal chance. A current minority, for instance, might openly reject the principle and declare that it will discontinue its operation, should it ever win a majority in the future. Even where such goals are not openly declared, a minority's behaviour might provide strong reason to believe that it intends to permanently entrench itself in power if it was ever to gain the opportunity to do so through a democratic election. The trust that is required for the principle of equal chance to be operative, Schmitt concludes, must, therefore, be reciprocal. A current majority must also be able to trust a minority that the latter will respect the former's right to regain power under conditions of equality, should their roles come to be reversed. Absent that trust, it would be irrational for the current majority to extend the protection of the principle of equal chance to the current minority and to refrain from trying to entrench its position.[26]

The principle will be able to legitimate decisions to a current minority only where all political camps accept, and know that each other accepts, that a temporary majority must submit to certain constraints on its decision making; constraints that, or so it seems, could not be made legally enforceable – by introducing entrenched constitutional provisions or limits to amendment – without violating the principle of equal chance. This fragility, Schmitt thinks, will tend to make the principle of equal chance all but inapplicable in political environments characterised by non-trivial political conflict or disagreement.[27] Let us assume that an anti-democratic party has openly declared that it is

[25] Schmitt, *Legality and Legitimacy*, p. 33.
[26] Schmitt, *Legality and Legitimacy*, pp. 33–34.
[27] Schmitt, *Legality and Legitimacy*, pp. 33–36.

committed to the abolition of democracy, but that it will pursue this aim by legal means. Once it wins an election, the party is going to use its legislative majority to introduce one-party dictatorship. Up to that point, it is going to act in scrupulous conformity with the laws of the democratic polity. Is the party entitled to the protection of the principle of equal chance? Or would the current majority be justified in stopping its rise to power by denying it an equal chance?

Schmitt suggests that it would be wrong to extend the protection of the principle of equal chance to the anti-democratic party. A group that is currently in power, and thus temporarily commands the democratic process of legislation, can be expected to grant an equal chance to its adversaries only if it has reason to believe that it will be afforded an equal chance to regain power by its adversaries should it find itself out of power in the future. If faced with a party whose declared or proven aim it is to abolish democracy and to deny an equal chance to its opponents once it has taken power, the current majority, in Schmitt's view, would be justified to use its legislative power to stop the anti-democrats from taking over, by the use of measures of democratic militancy.[28] However, if the current majority refuses to apply the principle of equal chance on such grounds, it will no longer be able, as Schmitt also points out, to legitimate its decisions to the anti-democrats by way of appeal to the principle of equal chance. It will no longer be able to demand deference to its decisions from the anti-democrats by telling them that they continue to enjoy an equal chance to realise their political goals, since they no longer do.

Schmitt concludes that those forced to contend with a political movement aiming to abolish democracy by democratic means are faced with a dilemma: to treat the principle of equal chance as a supreme constitutional principle, one that must never be violated, would rob democracy of the power to defend itself against being abolished by democratic means. It would absurdly require a majority that is willing to respect the rules of the democratic game to allow these rules to be used for its own enslavement. If we take it, on the other hand, that a democracy might be justified in defending itself against being abolished by democratic means, we must abandon the view, Schmitt thinks, that the principle of equal chance is the fundamental ground of democratic legitimacy, since any exercise of democratic militancy would, in his view, constitute a clear violation of the principle of equal chance.[29] The only way to escape this dilemma, Schmitt thinks, is to reject the ideal of the legislative state, to reject any theory of democracy that accords supremacy

---

[28] Schmitt, *Legality and Legitimacy*, p. 33.
[29] Schmitt, *Legality and Legitimacy*, p. 30 and pp. 47–50.

to the principle of equal chance, and to replace it with an understanding of democracy based on substantive values or principles that are not themselves up for grabs in the democratic process.[30]

Assume, for the sake of argument, that some such alternative conception of democracy is available and that it is consequently constitutionally justifiable, under certain conditions, for a democratic state to engage in a practice of democracy militancy to prevent that conception from being abolished or undermined by democratic means.[31] It must then also be the case that there are material limits to constitutional amendment.[32] There could be no justification, in a democracy, for restricting rights to political participation with a view to preventing the realisation of some political goal unless the realisation of that goal was also constitutionally impermissible.

This argument from militant democracy forces a certain reading of procedural hurdles to amendment, as they apply to constitutional provisions that are essential to the indefinite continuation of free and fair democratic competition. Material limits to amendment could be textually expressed, in a written constitution, in the form of an amendment clause that protects constitutional norms by putting up special procedural hurdles to change, but that does not explicitly impose material limits to change. However, once we hold that measures of militant democracy are justifiable to protect at least some of the content of the constitution, it must be wrong to interpret the protection of that content by an amendment clause as merely instituting a supermajoritarian form of pure proceduralism.

If a supermajority of legislators was constitutionally permitted to change all constitutional norms in whichever way it pleased, it could not be justifiable to restrict rights of political participation in order to prevent a political

---

[30] My discussion here should not be taken to indicate approval of the view that Schmitt is to be regarded as a defender of Weimar democracy, as argued in Benjamin Schupmann, *Carl Schmitt's State and Constitutional Theory. A Critical Analysis* (Oxford: Oxford University Press, 2017). I take it that Schmitt's theory of constituent power is profoundly undemocratic. See Vinx, 'The Incoherence of Strong Popular Sovereignty' and Lars Vinx, 'Ernst-Wolfgang Böckenförde and the Politics of Constituent Power', *Jurisprudence* 10:1 (2019), pp. 15–38. My claim here is that Schmitt's attack on a proceduralist understanding of the Weimar Constitution in *Legality and Legitimacy* can be read in a fruitful way, if it is separated from the wider context of Schmitt's authoritarian and executive-centred understanding of popular sovereignty.

[31] For recent defences of militant democracy see Alexander Kirshner, *A Theory of Militant Democracy. The Ethics of Combating Political Extremism* (New Haven, CT: Yale University Press, 2014) and Bastiaan Rijpkema, *Militant Democracy. The Limits of Democratic Tolerance* (Abingdon: Routledge, 2018).

[32] See Carl Schmitt, *Der Hüter der Verfassung* (Berlin: Duncker & Humblot, 1931), pp. 112–113 and Schmitt, *Verfassungsrechtliche Aufsätze*, p. 345.

group from realising certain political goals in free and fair political competition. In a democracy, it must be permitted to advocate, under fair conditions, for any constitutional change that it is constitutionally permissible to bring about. If the realisation of some political goal, on the other hand, is rightly held to be constitutionally impermissible, even were it to take place in a perfectly democratic form, it is hard to see why it should make a difference whether the goal in question is to be realised through an ordinary act of legislation or by way of constitutional amendment. Once we admit to the justifiability of democratic militancy, it makes no sense, therefore, to hold that a constitution is open to be changed in any way whatsoever, but only through a special procedure of amendment.[33] Constitutional provisions that could be invoked to justify democratic militancy must be protected against formally valid exercises of the power of amendment, whether the constitution contains explicit eternity-clauses or not.

This line of argument suggests that constitutional entrenchment would ideally be employed only to protect inherent material limits to amendment. Ordinary constitutional entrenchment, as much as strong entrenchment by way of eternity-clauses, is an apparent violation of the principle of equal chance, as it seems to conflict with the requirement that every vote is to be given equal weight. A supermajoritarian requirement for constitutional change, as Schmitt points out, allows a past supermajority to hold future majorities hostage to its decisions, for as long as the future majorities fail to reach the supermajoritarian threshold. It accords disproportionate influence to those who want to hold on to an existing constitutional norm. Members of that group can get their way even if they have now turned into a minority.[34] This problem is aggravated if a constitution is first enacted by a simple majority vote of either the members of a constituent assembly or of the general electorate. In that case, a present majority of 51 per cent – perhaps one that has been formed through bargaining between special interests that fall far short, individually, of representing the bulk of the citizens – will have the power to thwart the ambitions of a significantly larger future majority so long as the latter falls short of the required threshold.[35]

If constitutional entrenchment violates the principle of equal chance, it must be incompatible with the ideal of democracy instantiated by the legislative state. Its justification, if there is any, must then lie elsewhere. The only plausible strategy to justify constitutional entrenchment, Schmitt argues, is to rely on some version of the view that there are core constitutional values

---

[33] Schmitt, *Legality and Legitimacy*, pp. 39–58.
[34] Schmitt, *Legality and Legitimacy*, pp. 51–53.
[35] Schmitt, *Legality and Legitimacy*, pp. 39–45.

that must be protected, even in a democracy, against an ordinary legislative majority.[36] But if that is true one must ask why the substance of those values should not also be protected against a legislative supermajority. Is the violation of the substance of a fundamental value any less objectionable if it is perpetrated by a very large instead of a small majority? The answer to this question must surely be no.[37]

At times, Schmitt gives this argument an almost Waldronian bent: if one did not trust a simple legislative majority, in a modern pluralistic party-state, to be sufficiently mindful of the fundamental identity of the constitution, there would seem to be no good reason to hold that a supermajority can be expected to do better. After all, even a coalition large enough to bring about constitutional change may, as much as an ordinary parliamentary majority, be nothing more than a circumstantial alliance based on horse-trading and the pursuit of narrowly sectional gain. Our options are either to trust simple majorities or to hold that there are limits to what a supermajority can permissibly do, even where the written constitution does not contain explicit limits to amendment. If one believes that it is justifiable to protect constitutional norms with supermajoritarian hurdles, Schmitt concludes, one must concede that there are material limits to constitutional amendment.[38] Thoroughgoing political constitutionalism, on the other hand, will have to eschew constitutional entrenchment. The only way to justify the latter is to adopt a constitutional vision that embraces substantive values which are shielded from wholesale abrogation through constitutional amendment. Limits to amendment and strong constitutionalism inevitably come as a package.

Further Questions

Let me summarise Schmitt's argument(s) for inherent limits to constitutional amendment. In *Legality and Legitimacy*, Schmitt convincingly argues that one must recognise that there are implied limits of amendment as soon as one endorses the legitimacy of militant democracy. Any constitutional principle, right, or value the protection of which might, under proper circumstances, come to justify democratic militancy must also constitute an inherent limit to amendment. There can be no justification for militant democracy unless there are political goals the pursuit and realisation of which through the democratic process is constitutionally impermissible, irrespective of the strength of legislative support. If the realisation of the goals in question was constitutionally permissible on the condition that it had the support of a supermajority, it

---

[36] Schmitt, *Legality and Legitimacy*, pp. 45–47.
[37] Schmitt, *Legality and Legitimacy*, p. 41.
[38] Schmitt, *Legality and Legitimacy*, pp. 47–51.

would have to be legal for the supporters of that goal to compete, on an equal footing, for that supermajority. And to avoid the conclusion that militant democracy could be justifiable, one would have to embrace the absurd view that democrats must allow democracy to be used for their own enslavement by fascists and other totalitarians.

More importantly, Schmitt offers strong reason to think that ordinary constitutional entrenchment through special procedural requirements can be legitimate only to protect inherent limits to constitutional amendment. There is no convincing rationale for such procedural hurdles on amendment that does not also entail that the provisions which they protect are, at least in their essence, protected from wholesale abrogation. Those who support a purely procedural conception of democratic legitimacy must altogether reject the justifiability of constitutional entrenchment, even in its weaker, procedural form. The only other option is to embrace an understanding of democracy based on substantive values. Such an approach will be committed to the conclusion that there are material limits to constitutional amendment, even where these are not explicitly expressed in the constitutional text.

These limits clearly must be legal if they are to offer a justification for measures of militant democracy. It would obviously make very little sense to hold that non-violent political activity is subject to legal restriction, if it pursues anti-democratic goals, and yet to deny that political decisions – be they legislative or executive – that implement those very same goals would have to be regarded as legally valid. The more general argument that procedural constitutional entrenchment, to be legitimate, must protect material limits to amendment yields a similar conclusion. Supermajoritarian requirements for constitutional change are clearly legal hurdles. If they are justified only because they protect underlying material limits to amendment, it makes no sense to deny that these underlying limits are legal limits.

Our presentation of Schmitt's argument for inherent limits of amendment has left one crucially important question unaddressed. How does one distinguish between constitutional norms that are materially fundamental, in a democracy, and thus shielded from wholesale abrogation by amendment, and constitutional norms that are not? Schmitt's own writings contain two different answers to that question. One is intimated, in *Legality and Legitimacy*, but eventually rejected by Schmitt himself: limits to amendment, in a democracy, must protect the indefinite continuation of the free and fair democratic competition that realises the value of the political equality of citizens.[39] Schmitt, as an opponent of parliamentary democracy, himself preferred a different way forward.[40] He argued,

---

[39] See Rijpkema, *Militant Democracy*, pp. 278–286, and Minkkinen's and Zakin's chapters in this collection.

[40] Schmitt, *Constitutional Theory*, pp. 125–135.

in his *Constitutional Theory*, that it is necessary to distinguish between the power of constitutional legislation under an amendment rule and the constituent power, and he claimed that it would be wrong to attribute constituent power to a parliamentary supermajority which is constitutionally authorised to engage in constitutional legislation. Once we draw this distinction, it becomes possible to conceive of the power of amendment as an inherently limited power even while making room for the idea that the material content of the constitution is fully at the discretion of the people as constituent power. Democracy is both inherently constitutional, in its constituted form, and inherently unbound, in its constituent form.

Let me close with the suggestion that this juxtaposition of unboundedness in constituent authority and boundedness in constituted government is not fully coherent. Schmitt's attempt to impose immovable restrictions on the constitutional legislator draws much of its plausibility from the danger that purely procedural majoritarianism will come to undermine the presuppositions of its own legitimacy. It is rather hard to see why such a danger – if it exists in the field of constitutionally organised politics – would not exist in the field of constituent power. Schmitt's way to deal with this challenge is to argue that those who disagree with a constituent decision are, in effect, to be regarded as enemies of the people.[41] Their dissent, in Schmitt's account of constitutional politics, does not fracture the unity of the people's will and it does not undermine the authority of that will over those who qualify as members of the constituent power. If values are infringed by a purely political exercise of constituent power, they must be values that are alien to the (true) people. Democracy, Schmitt claims, presupposes substantive homogeneity.[42]

The resulting overall constitutional vision fails because the benefits of constitutionalism cannot, in a pluralist society, be enjoyed in the shadow of a sovereign dictatorship tasked with the protection of substantive social homogeneity. Schmitt's way forward amounts to giving up on the promise of democracy, that is, on the open-ended collective self-government of a group of political equals. Schmitt's argument for inherent limits to amendment nevertheless deserves attention, if separated from the wider context of Schmitt's flawed theory of popular sovereignty. It illustrates why a coherent democratic constitutional theory will find it difficult to refuse to recognise inherent limits to constitutional amendment. It also suggests, *pace* Schmitt, that the legitimate purpose of such limits must be to protect the value of political equality, as it is realised in the indefinite continuation of free and fair political competition.

---

[41] See Vinx, 'Ernst-Wolfgang Böckenförde and the Politics of Constituent Power', and Brännström's chapter in this collection.

[42] Schmitt, *Constitutional Theory*, pp. 255–267.

Part 2

Popular Identity and its Others

4

The People: Ethnoracial Configurations, Old and New

Leila Brännström

Introduction

Radical right-wing parties that are primarily concerned with non-Western immigration and minorities of non-Western origin have been receiving considerable electoral support in Western and Northern Europe in recent years. The Swedish exponent of the 'anti-foreigner right'[1], the Sweden Democrats, currently supported by around 20 per cent of the electorate, is, among other things, championing a 'clarification' of the identity of 'the people' in the constitutional context. The party proposes that the Instrument of Government, which commences by stating that all public power in Sweden proceeds from the people, should begin with a narrative about 'Sweden as a country and the Swedes as a people' so as to 'eliminate any doubts about the identity of *the* people who are entitled to popular rule' [my emphasis].[2]

---

[1] The 'family' of parties that I label 'anti-foreigner right' has alternatively been categorised as 'right-wing populist', 'national populist', 'nationalist', 'ethnic nationalist', 'radical right' or 'the far right'. Labels including the adjective 'populist' seem inappropriate to me because, in Jens Rydgren's words, 'populism is not the most pertinent feature of this party family' ('Radical right-wing parties in Europe: What's populism got to do with it?' *Journal of Language and Politics*, 16:4 (2017), pp. 485–496, at 486). Rydgren's suggestion that these parties should be called ethnic nationalist does, in turn, fail to capture the way in which some of these parties construct their 'we' in civilisational rather than in ethnic national terms (see the articles referred to in footnote 4). Although the parties in question are right wing, their level of 'radicalism' regarding questions other than immigration and non-Western minorities vary. Since the most distinguishing feature of these parties' is that they oppose non-Western immigration and perceive the presence of minorities of non-Western origin in their countries as a problem, 'anti-foreigner right' seems appropriate. The choice of this term should, however, not be read as suggesting that minorities of non-Western origin would be 'foreign' to Western Europe – the term only reflects that the parties in question turn against what they see as foreign.

[2] Motion 2017/18:878 tabled by Jonas Millard et al, 2 October 2017. See also 'Folkstyre', 13 March 2019. Available at https://sd.se/our-politics/folkstyre/ (accessed 21 May 2019).

A follow-up question that is close at hand here is who exactly the party thinks belongs to, or could in the future belong to, the Swedish people. The Sweden Democratic answer to this question has its own peculiarities but bears family resemblances to how other anti-foreigner parties in Northern and Western Europe decide who belongs to the people of the land proper. This chapter will take the Sweden Democrat's ambition to fix the subject of popular sovereignty as the point of departure for discussing some of the ways in which the contemporary anti-foreigner political forces of Northern and Western Europe imagine 'the people' and identify their allies and enemies within and beyond state borders.

Why the specific focus on Northern and Western Europe? This is because of an argument made by Rogers Brubaker and others, which suggests that the anti-foreigner parties of this region – the most secularised region of the world and the most liberal one (at least according to its own self-understanding) – make a distinctive block because they do not draw the line between 'self' and 'other', between 'we' and 'them', along 'ethnic national' or 'white/non-white' lines but along a civilisational line in which 'our' side is secular and liberal, and the 'others' are religious and illiberal.[3]

To set the stage for an exploration of anti-foreigner right-wing parties' understanding of proper belonging, the chapter will start by looking at Carl Schmitt's ideas about political friendship, and more specifically the way he imagines the relationship between 'us' in a political and constitutional sense and 'the people' in national and ethnoracial[4] terms. The choice to begin with Schmitt is not arbitrary. His thoughts about the nature of the political association have found their way into the discourse of many radical right-wing parties of Western and Northern Europe, mainly via the French *Nouvelle Droite* (often referred to as the European New Right on account of its transnational impact).[5]

---

[3] Rogers Brubaker, 'Between Nationalism and Civilizationism: the European Populist Moment in Comparative Perspective', *Ethnic and Racial Studies* 40:8 (2017), pp. 1191–1226. See also e.g. Daphne Halikiopoulou, Steven Mock and Sofia Vasilopoulou, 'The Civic Zeitgeist: Nationalism and Liberal Values in the European Radical Right', *Nations and Nationalism* 19:1 (2013), pp. 107–127.

[4] Although 'race' and 'ethnicity' evoke different connotations, they overlap and have in the European context of the last century both worked through legible markers to differentiate and stratify groups of people of purportedly 'common origin'. Cf. Stuart Hall, 'Old and New Identities: Old and New Ethnicities', in Les Back and John Solomos (eds), *Theories of Race and Racism: A Reader* (London: Routledge, 2000), pp. 144–153. I will therefore not differentiate between the two, but instead use the term 'ethnoracial' (when not reiterating the language of others).

[5] About *Nouvelle Droite,* its transnational impact and Carl Schmitt's influence, see below.

In what follows, the main outlines of Schmitt's concept of the political will first be recalled, followed by an exploration of Schmitt's notion of friendship, and its affinities with and differences from ethnicity, nationality and race. Next, the chapter will chart how Schmitt's ideas have been utilised and tailored by the *Nouvelle Droite* and later picked up by a host of far right parties. The chapter will close by returning to the Sweden Democrats and their notion of Swedishness.

Schmitt's Concept of the Political

In *The Concept of the Political*[6] (1932, hereafter *The Concept*) Schmitt suggests that the distinction between friend and enemy is an independent criterion which can be used to distinguish what is political from what is not, similar to how the difference between the good and evil, the beautiful and the ugly and the profitable and the non-profitable can serve to identify moral, aesthetic and economic issues respectively.[7] The political in Schmitt's sense does not refer to particular spheres or kinds of activity, but to 'the intensity of an association or dissociation'.[8] Only 'the utmost degree of intensity' constitutes a political friend-enemy constellation and any kind of conflict – moral, economic, religious, etc. – becomes political if it reaches that level.[9] The political is, in short, the opposition between collectivities of people whose members are ready to defend – by armed struggle if necessary – the group and its established 'form of existence' against those who wish to negate their 'way of life'.[10] The political does, however, not refer to armed battle itself, which has its own technical, psychological and military laws, but to the specific 'mode of behavior', which follows from the ever-present possibility of armed conflict with concrete enemies.[11] Schmitt argues that because political

---

[6] Carl Schmitt, *The Concept of the Political*, trans. G. Schwab (Chicago: University of Chicago Press, 2007). 'Der Begriff des Politischen' originally appeared in 1927 as an essay in the *Archiv für Sozialwissenschaft und Sozialpolitik*. Schmitt then revised it for publication as a freestanding volume in 1932 as well as again in 1933, in an openly Nazified version that he chose not to reprint after the war. The revisions of the text and the possible sources of inspiration behind these revisions have been discussed by a number of scholars. See e.g. Samuel Moyn, 'Concepts of the Political in Twentieth-Century European Thought', in Jens Meierhenrich and Oliver Simons (eds), *The Oxford Handbook of Carl Schmitt* (Oxford: Oxford University Press, 2016), pp. 291–311, at 297–299; William E. Scheuermann, *Carl Schmitt: The End of Law* (Lanham: Rowman and Littlefield Publishers, 1995), pp. 225–237. Circumventing this discussion, this chapter will engage with the 1932-version of the text, which is the widespread and influential one.

[7] Schmitt, *The Concept of the Political*, p. 26.

[8] Schmitt, *The Concept of the Political*, p. 38.

[9] Schmitt, *The Concept of the Political*, p. 26, pp. 37–38.

[10] Schmitt, *The Concept of the Political*, pp. 27–28.

[11] Schmitt, *The Concept of the Political*, p. 37 and p. 34.

communities raise concrete existential questions about physical life, they transcend all other groupings to which a person might belong. If a political entity exists at all, it is always the primary, decisive and sovereign entity.[12]

Schmitt's definition appears to refer to the distinguishing criteria of political association, not necessarily to that of every political act, but he himself only speaks about the political in general terms and as a unitary phenomenon. It is not clear why the spectre of outright violence between groups would be the adequate criterion for identifying the political generally, and Schmitt does not offer any arguments to clarify that either. Instead, he insists that his concept is not normative and, in particular, does not favour war or militarism. It only refers to the realities of a world in which 'peoples [Ger. *die Völker*]' 'continue to group themselves according to the friend and enemy antithesis'.[13] The reference to how 'peoples' actually behave discloses some of the assumptions built into Schmitt's concept. Firstly, the political world inevitably consists of different peoples and not of individuals or of humanity as a unit: 'The political world is a pluriverse, not a universe'.[14] Secondly, the political manifests itself primarily in the relationship between states, that is to say, in the international arena.

Schmitt considers domestic politics in internally pacified states as political only in a secondary sense. Internal disputes and antagonisms become political in the primary sense only if they reach such levels of intensity that armed conflict and civil war become tangible possibilities.[15] Samuel Moyn, among others, has objected that Schmitt treats domestic antitheses and contrasts as something else and different than international politics, which means that his concept is unable to 'cut across the divide between international and domestic spheres'.[16] Ernst-Wolfgang Böckenförde, in contrast, has emphasised that for Schmitt domestic and international politics are connected because both take place in the shadow of open violence.[17] The possibility of an escalating friend-enemy grouping cannot be completely eliminated from within the state even if, 'the accomplishment of the state as

---

[12] Cf. Schmitt, *The Concept of the Political*, p. 38. See also pp. 43–44.

[13] Schmitt, *The Concept of the Political*, p. 28.

[14] Schmitt, *The Concept of the Political*, p. 53.

[15] Schmitt, *The Concept of the Political*, pp. 29–32.

[16] Moyn, 'Concepts of the Political in Twentieth-Century European Thought', pp. 296–297. See also Hasso Hofmann, *Legitimität gegen Legalität: Der Weg der politischen Philosophie Carl Schmitts* (Neuwied/Berlin: Luchterhand Verlag, 1964), pp. 114–115.

[17] Ernst-Wolfgang Böckenförde, 'The Concept of the Political: A Key to Understanding Carl Schmitt's Constitutional Theory', in Ernst-Wolfgang Böckenförde, Mirjam Künkler and Tine Stein (eds), *Constitutional and Political Theory: Selected Writings* (Oxford: Oxford University Press, 2017 [1988]), pp. 69–85, at 72.

a political unity is precisely to relativize all the antagonisms, tensions, and conflicts that arise within it'.[18]

In the new preface that Schmitt wrote for *The Concept* on the occasion of its republication in 1963, he asserted that he had not attempted to capture the essence of the political for all ages but instead to clarify how the concepts of the state and the political were related to those of war and enemy during the era of 'the classical European state', in which legal concepts were completely permeated by the state and presupposed the state as the model of political unity.[19] The publication, he suggested, had addressed constitutional and international lawyers and had concerned that which was between them, namely the internally peaceful state assumed in the *jus publicum Europaeum*.[20] He added that with the rise of revolutionary political ideologies with planetary ambitions and the emergence of new forms and methods of warfare, the era of statism [Ger. *Staatlichkeit*] was coming to an end and the phenomenon of enmity was changing character, prompting the question of the political to be asked anew.[21] He himself had in fact already made new forays into this question. Taking into account the fact that some powers radiated their culture, economy and influence beyond their boundaries, he had in a number of publications theorised the emerging global order as a struggle between a single empire and a number of *Grossräume* (spaces of politics functioning as restraining instruments against the universalism of a single *nomos*[22] of the earth).[23] He also had re-visited and re-elaborated – although in a 'sketchy' way – contemporary forms of hostility by focusing on the irregular, but politically motivated, fighter.[24] What Schmitt's afterword,

---

[18] Böckenförde, 'The Concept of the Political', p. 71. Hofmann links Schmitt's prioritisation of international politics to his preference for authoritarianism in the domestic sphere. Hofmann, *Legitimität gegen Legalität*, pp. 114–124.

[19] Carl Schmitt, 'Vorwort' in *Der Begriff des Politischen: Text von 1932 mit einem Vorwort und drei Corollarien* (Berlin: Duncker & Humblodt, 1963), pp. 9–19, at 10–11. We can recall here that Schmitt's whole inquiry into the concept of the political starts off with the proposition that the 'concept of the state presupposes the concept of the political'. Schmitt, *The Concept of the Political*, p. 19.

[20] Schmitt, 'Vorwort', pp. 12–13.

[21] Schmitt, 'Vorwort', p. 10, pp. 17–19.

[22] Schmitt contrasted the Greek word *nomos*, signifying a concrete spatial order, with *Gesetz*, a formal and abstract set of rules, which he associated with the normativism of nineteenth-century jurisprudence.

[23] See e.g. Carl Schmitt, 'Grossraum gegen Universalismus' in *Positionen und Begriffe im Kampf mit Weimar-Genf-Versailles, 1923–1939* (Berlin: Duncker & Humblot, 2014 [1939]), pp. 336–344.

[24] Carl Schmitt, *Theory of the Partisan: Intermediate Commentary on the Concept of the Political*, trans. G.L. Ulmen (New York: Telos Press Publishing, 2007 [1962]).

commentaries and re-workings suggest is that the concept of the political is not necessarily tied to the state as a form even if that is how Schmitt initially formulated it. Political friendship can take, and has historically taken, different forms.[25] What is non-negotiable in Schmitt's conceptualisation is the idea that political existence necessitates the imposition of a *border* between friends and enemies.[26]

The Substance of Friendship

In *The Concept*, Schmitt portrays the enemy in ethnoracial terms as 'existentially something different and alien' and thereby presents the potential for lethal conflict as the ultimate consequence of a fundamental difference as such.[27] It is, however, at the same time true that Schmitt argues that the enemy is the one, whoever he or she might be, who threatens and negates one's 'form of existence'.[28] Schmitt's rendering of the friend/enemy distinction thus oscillates between a 'naturalist' account emphasising inherent differences between peoples and a 'normative' account which focuses on one's own 'form of existence' and involves interpretations of what a community's way of life might mean in shifting historical circumstances and what might pose an existential threat to it.[29] 'Form of existence' is another way for Schmitt to speak about the substance of political friendship which according to him *can* be 'national, religious, cultural, social, class, or of any other type', but, he notes, apart from the case of the Federation of Soviet Socialist Republics, 'substance resides mostly today in a national similarity

---

[25] Cf. Schmitt, *The Concept of the Political*, p. 46.

[26] On the 'border' as the key for understanding Schmitt's thinking on sovereignty and the political, see Étienne Balibar, *We, the People of Europe? Reflections on Transnational Citizenship*, trans. J. Swenson (Princeton: Princeton University Press 2004), pp. 135–141.

[27] Schmitt, *The Concept of the Political*, p. 27. Taking this phrasing into account, Raphael Gross argues that Schmitt is referring to the Jews when he speaks of the political enemy. The references are encoded but can be unearthed by those who can read the antisemitic grammar of Schmitt's time. Raphael Gross, *Carl Schmitt and the Jews: The 'Jewish Question,' the Holocaust and German Legal Theory*, trans. J. Golb. (Madison: University of Wisconsin Press, 2007), pp. 177–178. See also Raphael Gross, 'The "True Enemy": Antisemitism in Carl Schmitt's Life and Work', in Jens Meierhenrich and Oliver Simons (eds), *The Oxford Handbook of Carl Schmitt* (Oxford: Oxford University Press, 2016), pp. 96–116. Although Gross is most probably right about the heavy presence of antisemitic tropes in Schmitt's Weimar-era texts, Schmitt's construction of the friend-enemy-relationship cannot be reduced to an expression of antisemitism.

[28] Schmitt, *The Concept of the Political*, p. 27.

[29] Cf. Hofmann, *Legalität gegen Legitimität*, pp. 137–141.

of the population'.[30] What exactly is Schmitt talking about when speaking of national similarity?

In the liberal/civic tradition, the nation refers to the body of citizens on a territory who are organised in the form of a state, which is their political expression.[31] 'The people' are thus defined with reference to the state, which means that nationality in this tradition presupposes already existing states and cannot give any clues about the basis of political community in the first place. The conservative notion of nationhood might, at first sight, seem to have more to offer here: nations are ethnic groups with political aspirations of autonomy.[32] Upon closer inspection, however, we see that this answer only shifts the question: what are ethnic groups and how do such groups emerge?

The dominant way in which 'ethnic groups' are defined in anthropology bears some striking similarities with Schmitt's notion of the political. In the late 1960s, Fredrik Barth famously suggested that an ethnic group is distinct by virtue of the *boundaries* that delimit the group from other groups and not the 'cultural stuff' that it encloses.[33] Thus, similar to political units in Schmitt's sense, ethnic groups are defined relationally, and the substantive criteria demarcating them could be religion, colour, language, customs or anything else that can engender a distinction between 'us' and 'them'.[34] In addition, however, 'ethnic groups' similar to 'races' and differently from Schmitt's political units, are also characterised by 'metaphoric or fictive kinship', that is, the belief among members that they are somehow associated by common ancestry and owe each other special duties – akin to family obligations.[35]

---

[30] Carl Schmitt, *Constitutional Theory*, translated and edited by Jeffrey Seitzer (Durham: Duke University Press, 2008 [1928]), p. 392. It has been noted many times before that the question of how peoples (friends) emerge in the first place is not dealt with in *The Concept*. It is, however, to some extent addressed in some of Schmitt's other works, for example *Constitutional Theory*. Like many others I see *Constitutional Theory*, which was published between the publication of the first and the second version of *The Concept* as the legal theoretical counterpart to it. Cf. Hofmann, *Legalität gegen Legitimität*, p. 124 and Benjamin Schupmann, *Carl Schmitt's State and Constitutional Theory: A Critical Analysis* (Oxford: Oxford University Press, 2017), p. 71.

[31] Cf. e.g. Anthony D. Smith, *The Ethnic Origins of Nations* (Oxford: Basil Blackwell, 1986), pp. 134–136, or Eric Hobsbawm, *Nations and Nationalism since 1780: Programme, Myth, Reality* (Cambridge: Cambridge University Press, 1990), pp. 18–22.

[32] Smith, *The Ethnic Origins of Nations*, pp. 154–157. See also Thomas Hylland Eriksen, *Ethnicity and Nationalism: Anthropological Perspectives* (London: Pluto, 1993), pp. 144–146.

[33] Fredrik Barth, 'Introduction', in Fredrik Barth (ed) *Ethnic Groups and Boundaries: The Social Organization of Culture Difference* (Oslo: Universitetsforlaget, 1969), pp. 9–38.

[34] Cf. e.g. Eriksen, *Ethnicity and Nationalism*, p. 16 and p. 41.

[35] Eriksen, *Ethnicity and Nationalism*, p. 17. See also Barth, 'Introduction', p. 13, and Smith, *The Ethnic Origin of Nations*, pp. 24–25. This is also congruent with the etymology of the term 'nation'. Deriving from the past principle of the verb *nasci*, meaning to be born, the Latin noun *nationem* connotes breed, origin, or race.

Reasonably, people don't come together because they mistakenly think that they are relatives, which calls for the question of how ethnic groups materialise. Noting that groups that are called 'ethnic' are a motley lot, Max Weber had insisted on the primacy of political organisation and suggested that 'it is primarily the political community, no matter how artificially organised, that inspires the belief in common ethnicity'.[36] Similarly stressing the role of political organisation, Schmitt suggested that princely absolutism had been the principal fabricator of political unity and national determination in most European states.[37] The monarchical state, he argued, 'rests on the idea that the political unity is first produced by representation through performance'.[38] It thus appears that Schmitt did not think that political friendship had to be based on kinship or be natural in any other sense[39] – political unity could be a contingent historical product generated by effective rule, through governmental technologies [Ger. *politische Sachtechnik*][40], through the dynamics of conflicts and so on.[41] Still, he insisted that a measure of homogeneity, generating a sense of shared identity, would be necessary for political friendship to persist.[42] Lars Vinx has recently suggested that in Schmitt's view, a minority would constitute an enemy and should be suppressed and eliminated for the sake of maintaining political unity.[43] Be that as it may, Vinx makes this argument with regard to political minorities who dissent from the majority position on non-trivial matters. The

---

[36] Max Weber, *Economy and Society: An Outline of Interpretive Sociology, Vol. 1*, edited by Guenther Roth and Claus Wittich (Berkeley: University of California Press, 1978), p. 389.

[37] Schmitt, *Constitutional Theory*, p. 99 and p. 101.

[38] Schmitt, *Constitutional Theory*, p. 239.

[39] This doesn't mean that Schmitt would not politically promote naturalist or mythical understandings of political community. Cf. Carl Schmitt, *The Crisis of Parliamentary Democracy*, trans. Ellen Kennedy (Cambridge: The MIT Press, 1986 [1923]), pp. 65–76.

[40] Carl Schmitt, *Dictatorship: From the Origin of the Modern Concept of Sovereignty to the Proletarian Class Struggle*, trans. Michael Hoelzl and Graham Ward (Cambridge: Polity Press, 2014), p. 9.

[41] For Schmitt's understanding of state formation see e.g. Nehal Bhuta, 'The Mystery of the State: State Concept, State Theory and State-making' in David Dyzenhaus and Thomas Poole (eds) *Law, Liberty and State: Oakeshott, Schmitt and Hayek on the Rule of Law* (Cambridge: Cambridge University Press, 2015), pp. 10–37.

[42] Schmitt, *Constitutional Theory*, pp. 239–249. Without ranking them, Schmitt argues that representation and identity are the two necessary principles of political unity. Agreeing with Bhuta ('The Mystery of the State', p. 26) it seems to me that Schmitt thinks that representation is the more significant of the two.

[43] Lars Vinx, 'Carl Schmitt's Defence of Sovereignty' in David Dyzenhaus and Thomas Poole (eds), *Law, Liberty and State: Oakeshott, Schmitt and Hayek on the Rule of Law* (Cambridge: Cambridge University Press, 2015), pp. 96–122.

minority in question is thus not necessarily an ethnoracial one.[44] And as Nehal Bhuta has highlighted, Schmitt acknowledged that 'the state has always been a unity of social multiplicity'[45] indicating that political unity for him did not exclude ethnoracial plurality.[46] It is, however, not easy to unambiguously make clear what kind or degree of homogeneity Schmitt had in mind because as Étienne Balibar has pointed out, he tends to synthesise the multiheaded people (who can never be represented as a simple homogeneity) and the state (which can be personified as one) avoiding to consider the gap between the two.[47]

As already mentioned, the key component of Schmitt's concept of the political is the *border* – not the ethnic group or the nation – and the main enemy is, logically, the denier of borders.[48] It has been noted many times before that Schmitt's purportedly strictly analytical project of defining the political is driven by the fear that its experience might disappear.[49] The main targets of *The Concept* are not any particular political enemies, but the enemies of the political, the 'fraudsters' and 'deceivers', the cosmopolitans who speak in the name of humanity.

Friendship, Enmity and the Anti-Foreigner Right of Northern and Western Europe

The French *Nouvelle Droite* (ND), a school of thought and a think-tank, was founded by a number of far right activists in the late 1960s with a view to break the cultural hegemony of the left, wage a long-term battle of ideas, and end the post-war marginalisation of the far right.[50] Inspired by the strategies

---

[44] Cf. also Lars Vinx, 'Ernst-Wolfgang Böckenförde and the Politics of Constituent Power', *Jurisprudence: An International Journal of Legal and Political Thought* 10:1 (2019), pp. 15–38, footnote 39.

[45] Carl Schmitt, 'Ethic of the State and the Pluralistic State', in Chantal Mouffe (ed), *The Challenge of Carl Schmitt*, trans. David Dyzenhaus (London: Verso, 1999), pp. 195–208, at 201.

[46] Bhuta, 'The Mystery of the State', pp. 22–23. Cf. also Schupmann, *Carl Schmitt's Constitutional and Political Theory*, p. 88.

[47] Balibar, *We, the People of Europe?*, p. 136.

[48] Raphael Gross argues that Schmitt associated the denial of the political with 'anthropological optimism', which for him was related to the denial of the Christian idea of original sin, a Jewish denial (Gross 'The "True Enemy"', p. 109). On the antisemitic undertones of Schmitt's attacks on 'anti-political thinking' more generally, see also Gross, *Carl Schmitt and the Jews*, pp. 181–183.

[49] Cf, for example Moyn 'Concepts of the Political in Twentieth-Century European Thought', p. 293 and p. 296. For a reading that tones down this aspect, see Schupmann, *Carl Schmitt's State and Constitutional Theory*, pp. 79–83.

[50] For an account of the birth and early history of the ND, see Tamir Bar-On, *Where Have All the Fascists Gone?* (Burlington: Ashgate, 2007).

and rhetoric of the New Left which they replicated, they set out to re-elaborate some of the most controversial aspects of the far right (in particular racism and the anti-democratic position) while also working to change perceptions and worldviews, so as to naturalise a politics from the right. They labelled the cultural and intellectual activities they pursued in order to win hearts and minds and conquer the mainstream, 'metapolitics'.[51]

The primary target of the thinkers affiliated with the school is liberalism and the universalism that goes with it. Echoing Schmitt, they argue that liberalism denies the specificity of politics, which 'always implies arbitrariness of decisions and plurality of goals'.[52] The universalist, and, therefore unavoidably, imperialist equality agenda of liberalism, they suggest, poses a threat to human diversity. Against the liberal menace of homogeneity, the ND champions the maintaining and cultivating of a *pluriverse*, an ostensibly non-hierarchical global society that embraces 'the plurality and variety of races, ethnic groups, languages, customs, even religions [that] has characterized the development of humanity since the very beginning'.[53] Diversity is not only presented as a value in itself, but is esteemed because it enables individuals 'to link themselves to a particular place, history, and society and thereby to possess an identity'.[54] The passion for stable and strong identities is at the centre of ND-thinking.

Thinkers of the ND stress, again echoing Schmitt, that 'one cannot be a citizen of the world, for the world is not a political category'.[55] However, contrary to Schmitt, they do not cherish the nation state, which they see as the product (or process) of centralisation and homogenisation. The nation state emerged through the suppression of the pre-existing diversity of languages, cultures and laws on given territories; its emergence dissociated people from their 'natural connections' and integrated them into the body politic as bare individuals subjected to an abstract law.[56] The nation state is

---

[51] See for example Alain de Benoist in Frank Adler, 'On the French Right – New and Old: An Interview with Alain de Benoist', *Telos* 126 (2003). The first seminar organised by the group in 1968 was titled 'What is Metapolitics?' (Bar-On, *Where Have All the Fascists Gone?*, p. 35).

[52] Alain de Benoist and Charles Champetier, *Manifesto for a European Renaissance* (London: Arktos Media, 2012 [1999]), p. 15. The ND is not a centralised and homogenous school of thought and could perhaps best be described as an ideological family. The *Manifesto* is the only attempt by key members of the school to summarise its main ideas and present their essential concepts. When not referring to this specific publication, the school will in the following be represented by its uncontested central figure, Alain de Benoist.

[53] De Benoist and Champetier, *Manifesto*, p. 42

[54] Benjamin Teitelbaum, *Lions of the North: Sounds of the New Nordic Radical Nationalism* (Oxford: Oxford University Press, 2017), p. 39.

[55] De Benoist and Champetier, *Manifesto*, p. 49.

[56] Alain de Benoist, 'The Idea of Empire', *Telos* 98–99 (1994 [1993]), pp. 81–98.

at the same time seen as an inadequate unit of political organisation in a globalised world in which 'the future belongs to large cultures and civilizations capable of organizing themselves into autonomous entities and of acquiring enough power to resist outside interference'.[57] Here, Schmitt's ideas about *Grossräume* are echoed.

The strong identities that are to be cultivated in the pluriverse are, on the one hand, local/regional, on the other hand, continental/civilisational. The pluriverse is imagined as a multipolar order in which 'great cultural groups' such as the Arab-Muslim, the North-American, the Chinese and the European 'will not supplant the ancient local, tribal, provincial or national roots, but will be constituted as the ultimate collective form with which individuals are able to identify'.[58] For Europe, this would mean a pan-European empire that, different from the EU, privileges ethnocultural concerns over economic ones and is 'bent on preserving ethnic homogeneity within the "authentic" historic regions of Europe'.[59] Unsurprisingly, there is no place for immigration in this vision for the future; the argument is that a liberal attitude to immigration implicitly and wrongly, assumes that people can easily be recontextualised.[60]

Far from Schmitt's protean take on the substance of political friendship, the ND has a clear naturalist, ethnoracial, idea about the proper basis of political community at both the local and the civilisational level: human beings have inherent identities and allegiances and are tied to specific territories, cultures and civilisations.[61] 'Authentic' communities are the ones modelled on 'the extended family'.[62] The idea of global separatism of equally valuable ethnic entities and civilisations, usually referred to as ethnopluralism[63], could be seen in the context of NDs ambition to overcome the marginalisation of the far right. Ethnopluralism and the notion of a pluriverse offers ways of severing the association of the far right with Nazism, racial hierarchies and genocide and instead attach it to the mainstream value of diversity. The 'differential antiracism' of the ND, demanding respect for 'the

---

[57] De Benoist and Champetier, *Manifesto*, p. 59.

[58] De Benoist and Champetier, *Manifesto*, p. 44.

[59] Tamir Bar-On, 'Transnationalism and the French Nouvelle Droite', *Patterns of Prejudice* 45:3 (2011), pp. 199–223, at 208. Cf. De Benoist and Champetier, *Manifesto*, pp. 52–54 and De Benoist, 'The Idea of Empire', p. 97.

[60] De Benoist and Champetier, *Manifesto*, pp. 52–54.

[61] De Benoist and Champetier, *Manifesto*, pp. 48–52. Cf. Alberto Spektorowski, 'The New Right: Ethno-Regionalism, Ethno-Pluralism and the Emergence of a Neo-Fascist "Third Way"', *Journal of Political Ideologies* 8:1 (2003), pp. 111–130, at 118.

[62] De Benoist and Champetier, *Manifesto*, p. 27.

[63] According to Teitelbaum, the term was coined in German *New Right* circles in the early 1970s. See Teitelbaum, *Lions of the North*, footnote 25 to Chapter 2.

irreducible plurality of the human species,' also entails an unconditional 'right to difference' for each and every people, suggesting for example that the authentic French people have a right to preserve their own ethnocultural identity and denying them this right would be 'racist'.[64]

Following the turn of the twenty-first century, a number of relatively small activist groups in France declared themselves to be followers of ND and used the label 'identitarian' to distinguish themselves from 'ordinary' nationalist anti-immigrant groups.[65] Although identitarian groups soon after spread across Europe, the major impact of ND has so far been indirect and through the far right political parties in Northern and Western Europe that have moved towards the mainstream and gained electoral success. Without embracing ND's wider criticism of modernity and equality or their analyses of economic systems, religions, the nation, etc., these parties have picked up, and adapted, the notion of ethnopluralism as well as some of the discursive shifts introduced by the ND, such as the inversion of egalitarian or multicultural anti-racism into a form of racism.[66]

A process of diffusion started when the French Front National in the early 1980s moved away from some the most discredited ideas of the old far right: scepticism of democracy, racial hierarchies, biological racism and antisemitism. Employing anti-political establishment rhetoric, Front National positioned itself in between the 'regular' political opposition and openly antidemocratic groups in order to bypass the charge of being against democracy.[67] To circumvent the stigma of racism, it embraced the idea of ethnopluralism, insisted on the right of the French to their difference, and accused its opponents of 'anti-French racism'.[68] The electoral breakthrough of the party in 1984 (a truly unexpected event) set in motion a process of transnational circulation whereby other anti-immigrant, white power and nationalist movements throughout Europe drew from Le Pen's repertoire in their ambition

---

[64] De Benoist and Champetier, *Manifesto*, pp. 50–52. Racism is defined by the authors of the manifesto as a 'theory which postulates that there are qualitative inequalities between the races, such that, on the whole, one can distinguish races as either "superior" or "inferior"; that an individual's value is deduced entirely from the race to which he belongs; or, that race constitutes the central determining factor in human history' (*Manifesto*, p. 50).

[65] Teitelbaum, *Lions of the North*, p. 44.

[66] Teitelbaum, *Lions of the North*, pp. 43–44; Bar-On, 'Transnationalism and the French Nouvelle Droite', p. 207.

[67] Jens Rydgren, 'Is Extreme Right-Wing Populism Contagious? Explaining the Emergence of a New Party Family', *European Journal of Political Research* 44:3 (2005), pp. 413–437, at pp. 427–428.

[68] Rydgren, 'Is Extreme Right-Wing Populism Contagious?'; Bar-On, 'Transnationalism and the French Nouvelle Droite', p. 215.

to reconcile their activism with mainstream values and gain actual political power. Highlighting this cross-national diffusion of ideas, rhetoric and strategy, Jens Rydgren has argued that the emergence of parties such as the Front National, the Belgian Vlaams Blok, the Austrian Freedom Party (FPÖ), and the Danish People's Party, and so on, should be understood in terms of a series of interdependent events.[69] The 'master frame', which connects these parties and makes them a family, has been developed by the ND and at its very centre is the notion of ethnopluralism.[70]

If the mainstream in Northern and Western Europe is committed to liberal ideals, moving in that direction in this region would logically entail that a party adapts to liberalism and makes its arguments more liberal or at least more liberal-sounding. There is, however, a tension between ethnopluralism and individual-centred liberalism, which anti-foreigner parties will have to negotiate in some way. One way of doing this is to make liberalism part of 'our' identity and to contrast it to the illiberality of the (Muslim) other. And, indeed, the far right is increasingly arguing that it only wants to exclude those who do not share 'our' liberal values such as democracy, tolerance and the rule of law.[71]

The liberalism of the anti-foreigner right is, however, not always part of a move away from a past profile and into the mainstream. A number of the anti-foreigner parties of Western and Northern Europe have, in fact, emerged from within liberal and libertarian environments. The Danish People's Party, the Swiss People's party, the Norwegian Progress Party are such examples.[72] However, the most notorious liberal anti-foreigner party is probably the short-lived Pim Fortuyn's List, which was established in early 2002 and did not for long survive its founder's, Pim Fortuyn's, murder, also in 2002. Fortuyn embodied and performed individuality, secularism, freedom of speech, and sexual liberation, his anti-Islamic civilisational rhetoric was joined with liberal positions on most issues such as gender equality, drug policy and especially gay rights. He didn't think of himself as a nativist, nationalist nor as

[69] Rydgren 'Is Extreme Right-Wing Populism Contagious?', p. 416.
[70] In the words of Jens Rydgren ethnopluralism 'is the most distinguishing ideological characteristic of the new radical right party family' (Jens Rydgren, 'Introduction: Class Politics and the Radical Right', in Jens Rydgren (ed) Class Politics and the Radical Right (Abingdon: Routledge, 2013), p. 3. See also Nigel Copsey, 'The Radical Right and Fascism', in Jens Rydgren (ed) The Oxford Handbook of Radical Right (Oxford: Oxford University Press, 2018), pp. 105–121.
[71] See the references in footnote 3 above.
[72] See for example Tor Bjørklund and J. Goul Andersen, 'Anti-Immigration Parties in Denmark and Norway: The Progress Parties and the Danish People's Party', in Patrick Hossay, Martin Schain, Aristide Zolberg et al. (eds) Shadows Over Europe: The Development and Impact of the Extreme Right in Western Europe (New York: Palgrave, 2002), pp. 107–136.

part of the far right. In his words: 'Le Pen is a petit bourgeois nationalist . . . I am a citizen of the world.'[73]

The agenda of the anti-foreigner parties originating from liberal or libertarian environments is neither driven by ethnic nationalism, nor by the urge to defend traditional identities. Instead, they are mobilised by the perceived threats against liberalism as a way of life, which they above all locate in Islam, seen as the foremost representative of religious orthodoxy, intolerance (especially against sexual minorities), patriarchy, antisemitism, in short, everything illiberal.[74] Liberal anti-foreigner parties stand for a Schmittian kind of liberalism: a liberalism preoccupied with the illiberal other and the distinction between friends and enemies; a liberalism establishing the limits of tolerance and preferring clear boundaries and decisions to compromise and negotiation. The programme of these parties comes across as a generalisation, radicalisation and a further racialisation, of the integration policy re-orientation which have taken place, to varying degrees, in most Western and Northern European states from the mid-1990s on.[75] The new orientation, pushed by political coalitions including self-described liberals and progressives, targets the sensed failure of non-Western immigrants (and their descendants) to embrace liberal-democratic norms and values.[76]

The Sweden Democratic Notion of Swedishness

The Sweden Democrats emerged from within nationalist and white supremacist skinhead environments in the late 1980s. By the early 2000s, they remade themselves to gain political influence. As they needed respectability and dissociation from their recent background as violent thugs and brutes, race warriors and Nazis, they started dressing in wholesome ways, avoided violent language and chose the blue anemone flower as a party-symbol.[77] They also adopted anti-racism as an explicit part of their party policy and launched the notion of open Swedishness according to which a person is considered

[73] Pim Fortuyn quoted in Matthew Kaminski, 'Another Face of Europe's Far Right', *The Wall Street Journal*, 3 May 2002. Available at https://www.wsj.com/articles/SB102037039985461320 (accessed 15 July 2019).

[74] Cf. Brubaker, 'Between Nationalism and Civilizationism'.

[75] On this, see for example Triadafilos Triadafilopoulos, 'Illiberal Means to Liberal Ends? Understanding Recent Immigrant Integration Policies in Europe', *Journal of Ethnic and Migration Studies* 37:6 (2011), pp. 861–880.

[76] Triadafilopoulos, 'Illiberal Means to Liberal Ends?', p. 863.

[77] On the transformation of Sweden Democrats, see for example Gabriella Elgenius and Jens Rydgren, 'The Sweden Democrats and the Ethno-Nationalist Rhetoric of Decay and Betrayal', Special Issue: What is Going on in Sweden? *Journal of the Swedish Sociological Association, Sociologisk Forskning* 54:4 (2017), pp. 353–358.

Swedish 'if defined as such by self and others'.[78] Sweden is a community, they argued, on the basis of culture, language, identity and loyalty; a community to which new members can gain entrance – if they make an effort.[79]

The Sweden Democrat who developed the idea of Open Swedishness, Mattias Karlsson, illustrated what it meant with reference to two of Sweden's most well-known football players in the early 2000s: Henrik Larsson and Zlatan Ibrahimovic.[80] Henrik Larsson whose father moved to Sweden from Cape Verde was described as an introvert with 'archetypical Swedish characteristics', while the boastful and loud Zlatan, in contrast, was not Swedish: 'His attitude does in many ways not come across as Swedish, I don't think of his body language, and language more generally, as quite Swedish'.[81] The point of contrasting Zlatan with Henrik was to show that Swedishness was not about colour: the fact that Zlatan had white skin and an all-European bloodline did not make him more Swedish than the dark-skinned Henrik.

A few years later Karlsson suggested, based on information from Zlatan's biography, that Zlatan was now in the process of becoming more Swedish thanks to his relationship and marriage with the all-Swedish blonde, Helena Seger. Zlatan's transition, Karlsson argued, shows that assimilation is possible.[82] Becoming Swedish is, however, not easy. The aspirant must be ready to lose her previous ways of being in the world, but even that might not be enough. If the culture and basic values of the community of origin of an aspirant is very different from Swedish culture and values, assimilation might not be possible at all.[83] On this basis, the party is against migration on any larger scale from countries the culture and basic values of which they judge as very different.[84]

---

[78] Sweden Democrats, 'Sverigedemokraternas principprogram: Antaget av Riksårsmötet den 4 maj 2003. Ändringar av programmet antogs vid riksårsmötet den 8 maj 2005', 8 May 2005, p. 6.

[79] See for example 'Åkesson inte rädd för nya partiet', *Sveriges radio*, 14 April 2014. Available at https://sverigesradio.se/sida/artikel.aspx?programid=83&artikel=6930909 (accessed 3 July 2019); 'Nedtonad nationalism', in *Dagen*, 13 April 2018; Sweden Democrats, 'Sverigedemokraternas principprogram 2011', 2011, p. 13.

[80] 'Zlatan är inte svensk', *Expressen*, 7 March 2007. Available at https://www.expressen.se/sport/zlatan-ar-inte-svensk/ (accessed 4 July 2019). 'SD-Karlsson kliver ut ur skuggan', *Dagens Nyheter*, 19 November 2014. Available at https://www.dn.se/nyheter/sverige/sd-karlsson-kliver-ut-ur-skuggan/ (accessed 3 July 2019).

[81] 'Zlatan är inte svensk', *Expressen*. My translation.

[82] 'SD-Karlsson kliver ut ur skuggan', *Dagens Nyheter*.

[83] Sweden Democrats, 'Sverigedemokraternas principprogram 2011', 2011, pp. 15–16 and p. 23.

[84] Sweden Democrats, 'Sverigedemokraternas principprogram 2011', 2011, pp. 15–16 and p. 23.

One group, which Sweden Democrats consider as naturally belonging to the Swedish nation, are those who have been adopted from abroad by a Swedish family at an early age.[85] Today the group consists of around 50,000 people, the majority of which have been adopted from the Global South.[86] Isolated from their social and cultural context of origin and benefitting, like Zlatan, from 'training at home', they appear as the perfect examples of assimilable individuals. Affirming the belonging of this group to the Swedish nation has the added benefit of proving that Sweden Democrats are not racists. In a video produced for the 2016 elections – Don't let yourself be silenced[87] – two non-white adoptees explain to the viewer that racism is appalling but that cherishing one's own country, culture and history is not racism, after which they are joined by the leader of the party who urges the viewer not to succumb to those who police opinions.

The political and practical implications of Open Swedishness are close enough to those of traditional ethnonationalism: the explicit favouring of the majority culture, restriction of immigration, 'encouragement' of immigrants and their children to leave the country, stricter requirements for granting citizenship, etc. The shift from a biologically to a culturally defined people, a shift Sweden Democrats have taken more seriously than most other anti-foreigner parties, has been crucial, small as it may seem, in permitting the party to mobilise against 'foreigners' while circumventing the accusation of racism. This very narrow understanding of racism – as based in biology solely – is not an invention of the party – it is close to the mainstream understanding of racism in Sweden, as well as in other Continental European countries.[88]

Sweden Democrats praise cultural homogeneity within a state, but are against 'cultural imperialism' across borders and believe all cultures should be preserved.[89] Still, they stress that all cultures are not equally good – it is

[85] Sweden Democrats, 'Sverigedemokraternas principprogram 2011', 2011, p. 15.
[86] Sweden has the highest per capita proportion of international adoptees in the world (Adoptionscentrum, 'Adoptions in Sweden', www.adoptionscentrum.se/en/Adoptions/Adoptions-in-Sweden/ (accessed 4 July 2019). On international adoptions in Sweden see for example Barbara Yngvesson, 'Migrant Bodies and the Materialization of Belonging in Sweden', *Social & Cultural Geography* 16:5 (2015), pp. 536–551.
[87] Sweden Democrats, Press release, 'SD släpper ny valfilm, "Låt er inte tystas"', 4 September 2014. Available at https://www.mynewsdesk.com/se/sverigedemokraterna/pressreleases/sd-slaepper-ny-valfilm-laat-er-inte-tystas-1050004 (accessed 4 July 2019). The video is available at https://www.youtube.com/watch?v=Uph8Mrc28dk (accessed 4 July 2019).
[88] On this see for example, Leila Brännström, 'The Terms of Ethnoracial Equality: The Swedish Courts' Reading of Ethnic Affiliation, Race and Culture', *Social and Legal Studies* 27:5 (2018), pp. 616–635.
[89] Sweden Democrats, 'Sverigedemokraternas principprogram 2011', 2011, p. 19.

'obvious that some cultures are better than others in defending basic human rights, bring about democracy, prosperity, adequate health care, high standards of education, and equality before the law'.[90] The Sweden Democratic variation on 'ethnopluralism' thus aspires to sever all attachments to biology as the basis of nationhood and collective identity, while not shying away from establishing hierarchies among cultures. It is not difficult to guess that the cultural communities to which they claim that Sweden belongs – the Nordic, North European, European and Western – are at the top of their hierarchy of cultures.[91] Even if Sweden Democrats look down on certain cultures and people originating from these cultures, they do not regard them as their political enemies. Echoing Schmitt and De Benoist, they point out the cosmopolitan, the denier of borders and the inviter of foreigners, as the real enemy.[92]

Concluding Remarks

The proper composition of the people of the land, the demographic question, is the paramount concern for anti-foreigner parties. In a constitutional order such as the Swedish, which explicitly anchors its legitimacy in the principle of popular rule, any engagement with the question of who might belong to the people will unavoidably have a constitutional dimension. As a consequence, Sweden Democrats have implicitly been involved in constitutional politics for as long as they have existed. It was, however, only in 2017 that they presented a concrete constitutional reform programme. Apart from the proposition that the Instrument of Government should begin with stories about Sweden and the Swedes, they put forth suggestions regarding non-discrimination, minority rights, the standing of international and supranational organisations, citizenship and national holidays and symbols.[93] It does not appear as a coincidence that Sweden Democrats took this initiative only a few months after Marine Le Pen launched her 'constitutional program', the first point of which was that 'the defence of the identity of our people' should be included in the constitution as a fundamental principle.[94] The

[90] Sweden Democrats, 'Sverigedemokraternas principprogram 2011', 2011, p. 20.
[91] Sweden Democrats, 'Sverigedemokraternas principprogram 2011', 2011, p. 18.
[92] See for example Aftonbladet, 'Efter fascistanklagelserna: "Jag känner mig som en operasångare"', 6 December 2016. Available at https://www.aftonbladet.se/nyheter/a/wE9mqP/sd-toppen-efter-fascistanklagelserna-kanner-mig-som-en-operasangare (accessed 20 July 2019).
[93] Motion 2017/18:878 tabled by Jonas Millard et al, 2 October 2017.
[94] Théo Fournier, 'From Rhetoric to Action, a Constitutional Analysis of Populism', *German Law Journal* 20:3 (2019), pp. 362–381.

engagement of the anti-foreigner right of Northern and Western Europe with constitutional questions has not yet been mapped and analysed systematically,[95] but the Swedish and French examples indicate that securing the identity of the proper people in constitutional texts might be one of the main items on the agenda.[96]

---

[95] There is an emergent literature on the engagement of 'populists' with constitutions and constitutionalism including Paul Blokker, 'Populist Constitutionalism', in Carlos de la Torre (ed) *The Routledge Handbook of Global Populism* (London: Routledge, 2018), pp. 113–128; Cas Mudde, *Are Populists Friends or Foes of Constitutionalism?* (The Social and Political Foundations of Constitutions Policy Brief, *The Foundation for Law, Justice and Society*, 2013), p. 4. Available at https://www.fljs.org/content/are-populists-friends-or-foes-constitutionalism (accessed 19 July 2019); and Jan Werner Müller, *What Is Populism?* (University Park, PA: University of Pennsylvania Press, 2016). Although the Western and Northern European anti-foreigner right are included in this literature as part of global populism, their constitutional engagements are not given much space. The literature deals mainly with constitutional reforms and politics in a number of Latin American and Eastern European countries. This is perhaps because the Western and Northern European anti-foreigner right has only recently engaged constitutional politics head on.

[96] Or at least part of the agenda of non-liberal anti-foreigner parties. Sweden Democrats proudly suggest that democracy and freedom of speech have deep roots in Swedish culture and history, but the influence of liberalism on their agenda is, on the whole, quite limited. The party declares itself to be socially conservative, stresses the value of cultural homogeneity, emphasises the difference between men and women, is against same-sex families having children, etc. (Sweden Democrats, 'Sverigedemokraternas principprogram 2011', 2011). In light of this, the suggestion that the far right has to adapt to liberalism to be successful in Northern and Western Europe indeed seems somewhat exaggerated.

5

Hannah Arendt and the Glimmering Paradox of Constituent Power

Hanna Lukkari

The Paradox of Constituent Power: Politics *In Medias Res*

The paradox at issue here concerns the relationship between the 'constituent power of the people' to determine the political and legal terms of its collective existence, and the constitutional framework of political and legal institutions, or the 'constituted power', that offers the medium for such freedom. 'The people's' autonomous power to determine the terms of its collective existence is mediated by institutional structures that by virtue of their very existence limit and pre-constitute such power. The paradox is that, on the one hand, in order to exercise its constituent power 'the people' needs institutional mediation – there is no 'people' capable of collective action without it – but on the other hand, all forms of such mediation are determinations of collective existence and thus are, in a constitutional democracy, held to derive their power from 'the people'.

The paradox of constituent power can also be thought of as the paradox of representation or mediation. On the one hand, 'the people' as a political collective, as a 'we' in action and not simply as an amorphous, plural multitude or population, 'does not exist independently of its representation'.[1] It needs 'shaping' and 'staging' (Claude Lefort)[2] so that it would meaningfully appear. 'The people's voice' can only be heard as mediated by someone and by some framework of speech. On the other hand, such mediation itself calls for legitimation. It calls for 'evidence' that it derives its constituted power from 'the people' as its 'true', constituent subject. Ferdinando Menga puts the paradox succinctly: '"before" the event of representation, there is no represented at all; "after" the act of representation, the represented is understood

---

[1] Lisa Disch, 'How Could Hannah Arendt Glorify the American Revolution and Revile the French? Placing *On Revolution* in the Historiography of the French and American Revolutions', *European Journal of Political Theory* 10:3 (2011), pp. 350–371, at p. 362.

[2] See Minkkinen's discussion of Lefort in this volume.

as something which must have already been presupposed to representation itself, since the original event, which enacts representation, would otherwise plunge into nothingness'.[3]

There is no 'people' nor its constituent power before an initiative that represents it as this or that. No representation simply mirrors reality. Such an initiative thus lacks authorisation by a people already in place, but as representational it claims to be authorised constituted power, to truly speak on behalf of a people already there: what is yet to come is claimed to have already taken place. Constituent power presupposes constituted power it seeks to bring about. Whether the initiative succeeds, can only be seen retroactively through the stabilisation of the articulation of 'the people' the initiative proposes.[4] Constituent power can thus be observed only indirectly, by attributing the extant order to it as that order's agent.

Because of its retroactive, indirect confirmation, a representing initiative both opens the possibility of collectivity and remains a wager, always risking to remain an empty claim. While representation empowers individuals to recognise themselves as participants in 'action in concert', as Hannah Arendt would say, it also disempowers because every representation is selective: it identifies the collective as this kind of a collective rather than as that, and offers some determination, in exclusion to others, of who participates in the action in concert and what its purpose is. The articulation of a plurality of individuals into a collective acting in concert complicates that plurality, injects limits into it: '[A] "we" can be "I plus you" or "I plus they" or even "I plus they *minus* you".'[5] The utterance spoken in 'our' name addresses a selected audience, more or less clearly defined, but there is no guarantee that the individuals interpellated as belonging to such audience recognise their political vision of the terms of collective existence in the representation that the interpellation claims to be theirs as well. There are also no guarantees that those who have not been addressed would agree to be so left out. For this reason, as Carrol Clarkson notes, 'any use of "we" raises disturbing questions about the porosity of a contingent cultural [or indeed constitutional] limit, about acts of violence perpetrated against those *excluded from* the "we" and, in some instances, against those coercively *included within* it'.[6]

---

[3] Ferdinando Menga, 'The Seduction of Radical Democracy: Deconstructing Hannah Arendt's Political Discourse', *Constellations* 21:3 (2014), pp. 313–326, at p. 321.

[4] See Hans Lindahl, 'Possibility, Actuality, Rupture: Constituent Power and the Ontology of Change', *Constellations* 22:2 (2015), pp. 163–174, at p. 168.

[5] Carrol Clarkson, 'Who are "We"? Don't Make Me Laugh', *Law and Critique* 18:3 (2007), pp. 361–374, at p. 369.

[6] Clarkson, 'Who are "We"?', p. 364. Emphasis mine.

Democratic constitutionalism is, then, an ambiguous achievement. At stake is the contingency of representational limits, their 'porosity', the possibility of their modification in response to claims that exclusion from or inclusion within are violent and alienating. The only permanent 'site' and object of politics are the limits. Politics happens *in medias res*, always against and within some pre-determination. There is something 'tragic' in constitutionalism as thinking about mediated politics/politics as a struggle with mediation: politics that challenges extant mediation itself proposes another mediation that perpetuates the paradox rather than solves it for good. The paradox suggests that democratic constitutionalism is implicated in collective disempowerment to an equal measure with collective empowerment.

I take the paradox of constituent power as real and as having important implications for democratic-constitutional theory.[7] In this chapter, I present a reading of Hannah Arendt's constitutional thinking from the perspective of the paradox and argue that it 'glimmers' in her work: it almost crystallises into an account of the tensions present in 'the act of founding', but the ambiguities are again obscured by her republican ideal of *constitutio libertatis*. I also trace an implication that, I think, comes with this obscuring of the paradox and lessens the value that Arendt's work has for a constitutional thinking of political pluralism, namely that of her 'civilisationalism'.

Participation *Versus* Representation

It is well known that Arendt's work is often difficult to interpret coherently, and this difficulty stems to a large extent from passages in her writings that seem to be incompatible with each other, if not in open contradiction.[8] It seems, for example, that she can be read as a staunch critic of representation and a proponent of direct democracy just as well as a republican elitist content with giving the status of authoritative representatives to those who are 'politically speaking' 'the best'.[9] Arendt's texts thus seem to call for a 'deconstructive' reading[10] that wants to maintain the passages in their tension – in

---

[7] See, in particular, Lindahl, 'Possibility, Actuality, Rupture'. For a critique of different versions of republican constitutionalism from the perspective of the paradox, see Emilios Christodoulidis, 'The Aporia of Sovereignty: On the Representation of the People in Constitutional Discourse', *King's Law Journal* 12:1 (2001), pp. 111–135.

[8] See e.g. Hauke Brunkhorst, 'Equality and Elitism in Arendt', in Dana Villa (ed.), *The Cambridge Companion to Hannah Arendt* (Cambridge: Cambridge University Press, 2000), pp. 178–198; Margaret Canovan, 'The Contradictions of Hannah Arendt's Political Thought', *Political Theory* 6:1 (1978), pp. 5–26.

[9] Cf. Hannah Arendt, *On Revolution* (London: Penguin Books, 1990 [1963]), pp. 277–278.

[10] See also Menga, 'The Seduction of Radical Democracy'; Rudi Visker, 'Beyond Representation and Participation: Pushing Arendt into Postmodernity', *Philosophy & Social Criticism* 35:4 (2009), pp. 411–426.

a productive paradox – rather than make choices between them. There is no strict, principled opposition and hierarchy between participation and representation in Arendt's work. In the following sections, I seek to show that representation crops up in Arendt's account of direct participation and turns participation into a form of representation.

There are, however, passages in which Arendt clearly pits 'representation versus action and participation',[11] passages that support the reading that she is hostile to representation and identifies actual participation of individuals in the sheer presence of each other as the core of genuine politics. She argues, for example, that 'the political realm rises directly out of acting together, the "sharing of words and deeds"',[12] without any pre-existing mediation. 'The space of appearance comes into being wherever men are together in the manner of speech and action, and therefore predates and precedes all formal constitution of the public realm . . . that is, the various forms in which the public realm can be organized.'[13] The constituted 'public realm' 'ultimately resides on action and speech';[14] action 'is the one activity which constitutes it'.[15] Arendt is a praxis theorist for whom politics is something that needs to appear, to be actualised, in order to exist at all, and it can be actualised only when a plurality of individuals engage in action and speech together, recognising each other as equal. Arendt insists on the importance of 'the performance itself',[16] on the importance of the actual presence of actors to each other for the emergence of (constituent) power in its collective articulation.[17]

All this seems to suggest that legitimate forms of constitutional order emerge from the direct participation in the process of their formation of all those who will be bound by the order. 'The power of making promises' is, for Arendt, the privileged way of keeping power in existence, as it ties actors together through expectations of conduct to which all have agreed, and that mitigate some of the future's and actors' own unpredictability. '[P]ower [comes] into being when and where people . . . get together and bind themselves through promises, covenants, and mutual pledges', she writes; 'only such power, which [rests] on reciprocity and mutuality, [is] real power and

[11] Arendt, *On Revolution*, p. 273.
[12] Hannah Arendt, *The Human Condition*, 2nd edn. Introduction by Margaret Canovan (Chicago: The University of Chicago Press, 1998 [1958]), p. 198.
[13] Arendt, *The Human Condition*, p. 199.
[14] Arendt, *The Human Condition*, p. 200.
[15] Arendt, *The Human Condition*, p. 198.
[16] Arendt, *The Human Condition*, p. 206.
[17] See Hannah Arendt, 'On Violence', in Hannah Arendt, *Crises of the Republic* (San Diego: Harcourt Brace & Company, 1972), pp. 103–184, at p. 143.

legitimate'.[18] It is this actual presence of the promisors to each other that is the normative source of the constituted order: all 'laws and constitutions . . . derive in the last instance from the faculty to promise and to keep promises in the face of the essential uncertainties of the future',[19] and their legitimacy is expressed by the Roman principle of *pacta sunt servanda*.[20] The practice of promising expresses the constituent power to begin something new, to found a novel order unconditioned by any extant one.

Participation As Representation

This immediacy of equals to each other, their deliberating and binding themselves to each other through the practice of promising is often taken to be what is most valuable in Arendt's work. For Andreas Kalyvas, for example, '[t]he political and constitutional order is based on the reciprocal recognition of cooperating persons who voluntarily decide to become coassociates in the institution of a new political community',[21] and Arendt leads the way in theorising constitutionalism in these terms. Representation, as it suggests making present something that is absent, seems incompatible with this emphasis on actualised reciprocity.

And yet, representation crops up. It does so in at least two ways. The first relates to the problem of non-contemporaneous participation. If the legitimacy of the public realm and laws are sourced in 'mutual promise', and this promise is to hold through time, then what about those who are not 'the founders' but come after, therefore being bound by promises they did not make? Arendt calls the 'chief perplexity' of modernity the problem whence 'to derive authority for law and power'[22] when the traditional frameworks of theological legitimation are no longer plausible, but in a way that does not destroy freedom in its quintessential modern sense of contingent newness. The constitutional order that is to be traced ultimately back to the practice of promising needs to be 'valid for all, the majorities and the minorities, the present and the future generations'.[23] Those who act now to bring forth an order seek to bring it into being for their posterity,[24] Arendt insists, that is,

---

[18] Arendt, *On Revolution*, p. 181.

[19] Hannah Arendt, 'What is Freedom?', in Hannah Arendt, *Between Past and Future. Eight Exercises in Political Thought* (New York: Penguin Books, 1993 [1961]), pp. 143–171, at p. 164.

[20] Arendt, *The Human Condition*, p. 243.

[21] Andreas Kalyvas, *Democracy and the Politics of the Extraordinary: Max Weber, Carl Schmitt, and Hannah Arendt* (Cambridge: Cambridge University Press, 2008), p. 238.

[22] Arendt, *On Revolution*, p. 161.

[23] Arendt, *On Revolution*, p. 182.

[24] Arendt, *On Revolution*, p. 229.

they include into the polity – the contours of which they determine by giving content to their mutual promise – those who are not present and cannot therefore themselves act. The speaking positions and freedom to begin of those who are not, and cannot possibly be, present are by necessity represented by those who actually speak and act.

Arendt's problem is sometimes understood to be that future generations are no longer as free as the generation of the revolutionaries, because they are forced to simply 'augment' the extant constitutional order. Freedom splits into revolutionary freedom to begin and conservative freedom to augment.[25] The freedom of subsequent generations is curtailed, in so far as their freedom is no longer the radically unconditioned freedom to begin a novel order, but only the freedom to augment and modify what already is. Therefore, revolution as the foundation of a new order seems, Arendt herself says, 'self-defeating'[26]: it locks political freedom within an established order, thus undermining the constituent agency of those who come after.

But the problem is more radical than this 'lessening' of freedom in time, this freedom-degenerating sequence from its unconditioned to conditioned actualisation. For already the very 'first' act of freedom needs to show itself as fitting into an established framework that secures its meaning and authority as a collective act, that is, as an act that can be attributed to a collective – this is what the paradox of constituent power shows. Here we come to the second way in which representation crops up in Arendt's thinking of actualised collective power as the normative source of constitutional order.

Note first what Arendt says about the seemingly self-defeating character of the revolutionary constitution of freedom. She begins by describing the American revolutionaries' 'feeling of outrage about the injustice that only [their] generation should have it in their power to "begin the world over again"'.[27] They understood political freedom exclusively in terms of 'tearing down and building up',[28] and it was this experience that, says Arendt, they wanted their posterity to have as well (lest revolutionary freedom be self-defeating). But Arendt then goes on to suggest that this self-understanding was actually 'a fallacy'[29] as a description of 'the revolutionary spirit': the founders had become blind to 'all notions of a freedom which was not preceded by liberation, which did not derive its pathos from the act of liberation'.[30] Their conceptual error

---

[25] For a reading of Arendt along these lines see Mark Wenman, *Agonistic Democracy. Constituent Power in the Era of Globalisation* (Cambridge: Cambridge University Press, 2013), p. 59.

[26] Arendt, *On Revolution*, p. 232.

[27] Arendt, *On Revolution*, p. 233.

[28] Arendt, *On Revolution*, p. 233.

[29] Arendt, *On Revolution*, p. 233.

[30] Arendt, *On Revolution*, p. 234.

was to identify the act of liberation and the act of foundation. To think that political freedom is equal to the freedom to overthrow a constitution, she says, 'sounds too fantastic'[31] to be attributed to the Founding Fathers: 'it is rather unlikely that Jefferson, of all people, should have granted the coming generations the right to establish non-republican forms of government'.[32] It is a misunderstanding of the 'revolutionary spirit' to think that it is necessarily preceded by an overthrow of an extant order. This is a mistake, because, Arendt thinks, it leads to understanding political freedom as needing no conditions at all, as necessarily acting in a void, emerging *ex nihilo*, like a divine force. To establish a republican form of government is precisely to establish *constitutio libertatis*, a lasting foundation for freedom: a republican constitution enables political freedom to actualise itself in a permanent manner that, if successful, makes revolutionary freedom as liberation inconceivable and obsolete.

There is, however, a sense in which the American Revolution truly was self-defeating in Arendt's view: its failure to constitutionalise the revolutionary spirit expressed in the organised and ordered 'elementary republics' that were the site in which the revolution itself unfolded, and the process of founding a new republic was initiated. It is thus not that an unconditioned constituent power founds a constitutional order for freedom that then denies the freedom that brought it about. There is no such sequence from the constituent to the constituted leading to a lessening of freedom. The failure in Arendt's eyes was instead that the form in which political freedom was organised in the course of the Revolution itself did not find proper recognition in the constitutional order of the republic. The revolutionary spirit was most fully actualised in those local 'revolutionary councils' of 'townhalls' that were already elementary republics in which common matters were freely debated. At no point, in her interpretation, did the American Revolution unfold in an unorderly way: 'The councils . . . were always organs of order as much as organs of action.'[33] It was, she claims, 'their aspiration to lay down the new order.'[34] for the posterity, for others to pick up as well, that remained without proper acknowledgment in constitutional terms. This was the true tragedy: not maintaining the order of freedom that the Revolution itself exemplified.

Regardless of its historical (in)accuracy or even plausibility as a historical fable,[35] Arendt's ideal of the revolutionary councils suggests a conceptual view precisely opposite to the idea that the public realm arises directly out

---

[31] Arendt, *On Revolution*, p. 234.
[32] Arendt, *On Revolution*, p. 234.
[33] Arendt, *On Revolution*, p. 263.
[34] Arendt, *On Revolution*, p. 263.
[35] See Disch, 'How Could Hannah Arendt Glorify the American Revolution and Revile the French?'.

of a plurality of individuals acting and speaking. The example of the revolutionary council rather suggests that acting and speaking always require some form of mediation in order to take place. The performances of promising take place within a framework already set in place. This seems to fit with Arendt's remark that '[t]he mutual contract by which people bind themselves together in order to form a community is based on reciprocity and presupposes equality'.[36] Equality is not, on Arendt's own account, a natural property of human beings but only emerges as they organise themselves politically – and yet all acts of explicit organisation already presuppose it.[37] Here participation is not in opposition to representation, but it is representation: it is about acting as a member of an established (even if informal) order, as empowered by a status provided by that order. One's actions can be attributed to 'the council', to a collective that distributes membership and possibilities of action in specific ways.[38]

In so far as it is Arendt's claim that promising illuminates the setting-of-the-terms-of-collective-life, her argument begs the question. No performance of promising can arise without a prior determination who the promisors are, who counts as relevant to the process of bringing about a novel polity: who belongs to 'the we' that self-founds. Arendt's normative account of the origins of 'a we' presupposes a representation of 'a we': the constituent power of promisors is necessarily constituted in some way or other. The question who are the 'cooperating persons' (Kalyvas) cannot be left wholly indeterminate, for otherwise, no deliberation occurs in the first place.[39]

Against Representative Democracy

I thus agree with Emily Zakin who argues in her contribution to this book that Arendt is, first and foremost, a republican thinker who argues against reducing the constitutional order to some amorphous, immediate 'will of the people'. I also agree with Lisa Disch, who argues that 'Arendt's "council" form is misunderstood as an exemplar of direct democracy: it is democratic

---

[36] Arendt, *On Revolution*, p. 170.

[37] See also Bonnie Honig, 'Declarations of Independence. Arendt and Derrida on the Problem of Founding a Republic', *The American Political Science Review* 85:1 (1991), pp. 97–113, at p. 103.

[38] For Arendt, also the French Revolution at one point happened through orderly republican societies, like the Paris Commune. Arendt, *On Revolution*, pp. 242–243.

[39] See also Hans Lindahl, 'The Paradox of Constituent Power: The Ambiguous Self-Constitution of the European Union', *Ratio Juris* 20:4 (2007), pp. 485–505. I think Lindahl does not fully appreciate how much Arendt's republican account presupposes representation, although her own remarks disorient the reader easily on this point.

republicanism – participatory but federated, representative and hierarchical. She presents council governance as a "new type of republican government", one that poses an "alternative for representative government" in its hegemonic form, which is the party system'.[40] Arendt is not against representation per se – indeed her core claims presuppose it – but against a specific form of representation. Arendt's critique of representative democracy of the nation state boils down to a critique of immediacy. For Arendt, representative democracy relies on the idea of representation as mirroring a 'general will' that exists prior to any institutional mediation and somehow 'automatic[ally] articulat[es]'[41] the public interest. It attributes to 'the people' 'the unanimity of the citizenry', takes it as a homogenous unit holding 'the same' 'public opinion'[42] that the spokesperson claims to know through compassion and independently of all public exchange of opinions.[43] Arendt sees representation here as fictionalising and absolutising 'the people' into a divine-like entity that serves the strategy of legitimating the centralisation of state power and marginalisation of those public fora in which citizens may gather for the purpose of opinion-formation.[44]

Arendt, in a gesture of drawing a distinction so characteristic of her writing,[45] insists on the difference between political power and legal authority[46] and is critical of the language of two, constituent and constituted, powers. She holds that law and legal authority (or constituted power) do not emerge from popular sovereignty (constituent power), understood as a unified will of the unorganised multitude, in the way that has been thought in the tradition of democratic thinking dating back to the French Revolution and its theoreticians.[47]

Her republicanism manifests in her critique of such unmediated collective agency and in her insistence on the importance of 'public things', those 'worldly' structures and institutions, legal and constitutional ones in particular, that sustain a public space capable of hosting a plurality of different-minded and non-contemporary political actors and their political debates. She finds that what is often endangered in the democratic tradition is the

---

[40] Disch, 'How Could Hannah Arendt Glorify the American Revolution and Revile the French?', p. 352; referring to Arendt, *On Revolution*, pp. 278, 267, 263.

[41] Arendt, *On Revolution*, p. 78.

[42] Arendt, *On Revolution*, p. 225.

[43] Arendt, *On Revolution*, p. 75.

[44] Arendt, *On Revolution*, p. 244.

[45] See Hannah Arendt, 'Authority in the Twentieth Century', *The Review of Politics* 18:4 (1956), pp. 403–417, at p. 413.

[46] E.g. Arendt, *On Revolution*, p. 179. See also Zakin's essay in this volume.

[47] Arendt, *On Revolution*, pp. 76–79, 155–156.

'public representation' of differing opinions.[48] Democracy looks, from the republican perspective, as the 'rule [of] public opinion' that presumes unanimity, and, for Arendt, 'no formation of opinion is ever possible where all opinions have become the same'.[49] Presuming a unified popular will means that 'the public realm has vanished' and 'government has degenerated into mere administration' of the population.[50] The 'great good fortune' of the American Revolution, in contrast to the French, was to locate the 'seat' of its power in a 'people' that was not 'a fiction and an absolute' but 'a working reality, the organised multitude whose power was exerted in accordance with laws and limited by them'.[51] If the constitutional order is thought of as a self-binding of a pre-existing collective will, order can be, Arendt thinks, only of a limited duration, for will is ever-changing.[52] It is 'the republican form of government' that 'promise[s] great durability'.[53]

Arendt's ideal is the republican constitution that offers stable (although not immutable, of course; I come back to this) institutions within which the 'public representation', or 'purification', of political opinions is a durable possibility.[54] She argues that democracies have often in the European political history been 'swayed by public opinion and mass sentiment', and thus been unstable, suggesting that their institutionalisation of representation has poorly managed the task of conflict-resolution. A republican constitution, with a federal and hierarchical structure ranging from local 'elementary republics' and state autonomy to the Senate and the Supreme Court, would, she thinks, offer better mechanisms for a genuine public display and resolution of disagreements before they turn antagonistic and end up in violence. It would prevent 'the chaos of unrepresented and unpurified opinions'[55] by offering a better medium for 'collect[ing] the voice of the people'[56] and filtering from among a plurality of opinions those that become authoritative for all members.

The Glimmering Paradox of Constituent Power

That there are passages in Arendt's writings in tension with each other, some passages insisting on constituted order emerging directly from politics, others insisting on politics being mediated by order, could be read as Arendt

---

[48] Arendt, *On Revolution*, p. 226.
[49] Arendt, *On Revolution*, p. 225.
[50] Arendt, *On Revolution*, p. 236.
[51] Arendt, *On Revolution*, pp. 165–166.
[52] Arendt, *On Revolution*, p. 163.
[53] Arendt, *On Revolution*, p. 224.
[54] Arendt, *On Revolution*, pp. 226–228.
[55] Arendt, *On Revolution*, p. 228.
[56] Arendt, *On Revolution*, p. 254.

struggling to express the paradox of constituent power. Arendt insists that novelty, or constituent power, and permanence, or constituted power, ought not to be seen as simple opposites, or contradicting each other, but proposes to see them as 'two sides of the same event': 'the act of foundation'.[57]

In several passages of her work, she also struggles to articulate the paradoxical temporality of founding. Consider first the following passage: 'every action, accomplished by a plurality of men, can be divided into two stages: the beginning which is initiated by a "leader," and the accomplishment, in which many join to see through what then becomes a common enterprise'.[58] This characterisation of action does not rest on togetherness but shows how togetherness may arise. Arendt also claims that: 'What saves the act of beginning from its own arbitrariness is that *it carries its own principle within itself,* or to be more precise, that beginning and principle, *principium* and principle, are not only related to each other, but are coeval.'[59] If 'principle' can be read here as order, something that aides a plurality to cohere in their actions, Arendt is saying that the beginning and order are contemporaneous. The beginning is a paradoxical event of representing something, an ordered collective, that the initiative, however, only seeks to bring about. In Arendt's terms, the founding of a republic presents itself as an augmentation of what already is in order to avoid arbitrariness, although before founding there is nothing to augment. To appear as authoritative, the new needs to show itself as fitting with the old, as re-presenting, presenting again and presenting in a new light, a collective already there, all the while it truly seeks to bring forth something that was not there already.

Such a paradoxical beginning offers the occasion for others to act as well: 'The way the beginner starts whatever he intends to do lays down the law of action [its principle, its order] for those who have joined him in order to partake in the enterprise and to bring about its accomplishment.'[60] The beginning is not simply the first step in a temporal sequence, but presupposes, represents, its end, that what it seeks to bring about – and requires the recognition by others who join it in order to receive evidence as non-arbitrary and authoritative, to count as an act that can be attributed to the collective and thus expressive of political, collective freedom and 'our' constituent power. Only retroactively may a 'beginner' be seen as such; 'either they were founders and, consequently, would become ancestors, or they

[57] Arendt, *On Revolution*, pp. 223–224.
[58] Hannah Arendt, 'Personal Responsibility under Dictatorship', in Jerome Kohn (ed.), *Responsibility and Judgment* (New York: Schocken Books, 2003), pp. 17–48, at p. 47. See also Arendt, *The Human Condition*, pp. 177, 189.
[59] Arendt, *On Revolution*, p. 212.
[60] Arendt, *On Revolution*, pp. 212–213.

had failed'.[61] Perhaps Arendt's revolutionary 'elementary republics' can also be seen as exemplifying this paradoxical temporality: already representing in their functioning the order that they sought to bring about. And the tragedy was that their initiative was not picked up and constitutionally recognised and confirmed as authoritative, and in this sense the revolutionaries did not become 'ancestors' and constituent power, and the American Constitution adopted in Arendt's eyes a less republican form of representation.[62]

Paradoxically then, at the moment of founding, constituent power presents itself as a constituted one, and only within a constituted order may that event be confirmed to have been constituent. Emily Zakin[63] also interprets (what I call) the temporal paradox of constituent power as the recursive temporality of the future anterior of the American founding event. She notes how, for Arendt, this event was an appeal to future generations to sustain a temporal loop that would confer the status of founders on the framers by holding past and future together. Arendt sees the legal order as guaranteeing a common political space for a plurality of non-contemporaneous, equal individuals, as forming an 'in-between' that is, in Zakin's words, 'sturdy enough' to sustain conflicting interpretations, heterogenous points of view, dissent and disagreement. Acting now on the political possibilities offered by the constitutional order effectively is an act of recognition of oneself as an heir and of the framers of the constitution as one's authoritative ancestors, thus binding non-contemporaneous individuals into the same political-constitutional tradition and collective.

Thus it is not that political action and legal authority simply have 'different lineages' as Zakin suggests, following Arendt, but as Zakin's own analysis of the temporal loop suggests, the lineages paradoxically bend over each other. The 'transtemporal' political collective is already presupposed by the acts of setting the legal order that thus claim to simply re-set, augment, what already is, although bringing forth a novel order, and by acting on the possibilities opened up by this initiative/order, political actors recognise it as 'theirs' as well and therefore as authoritative, non-arbitrary law.

But can politics be neatly located within the constitutional frame, as both Arendt and Zakin seem to suggest? Is not the retroactive recognition of the framers as ancestors and oneself as an heir a contingent one, implying the possibility of non-recognition? If the framers require heirs to become founders, it is certainly also possible that not all whom the legal order claims to include as members recognise themselves as such and, by the same token, the

[61] Arendt, *On Revolution*, p. 203.
[62] See Arendt, *On Revolution*, p. 251.
[63] See Zakin's contribution in this volume.

framers as authoritative founders. What about those who *dis*identify from the status of 'heirs' of the founders that the constitution seeks to impose on them?

Arendt never goes as far as to explicitly assume the paradox as her position, nor to explore its difficult implications,[64] which would have complicated her republican ideal of representation as the promise of an unambiguously authoritative *constitutio libertatis*. In this sense, the paradox of constituent power only 'glimmers' in her work, almost surfaces in its full tension only to find this tension obscured by the insistence on the ideal of containing political freedom and constituent power within republican institutions and their augmentation.

Blind Spots of Republican *Constitutio Libertatis*

For Arendt, there is a form of mediation, a form of constituted order, that allows for political freedom as a durable possibility. However, all mediation is necessarily an ambiguous achievement: a republican order offers a certain frame for the actualisation of political freedom while marginalising other possibilities. It empowers and disempowers. As Arendt herself suggests, it excludes political possibilities that are seen by the judging authorities (who hold the task of 'purification' of opinions, as she puts it)[65] as anti-republican. Republican politics is limited politics.

Arendt thinks of the contingency and modification of the frame in terms of amendment and augmentation, and federation. A constitutional order does have a contingency of its own as it may be debated upon and amended in response to new political claims. Its authority rests on people's consent, and dissent, or 'civil disobedience', is a signal of a crisis of authority that calls for a legal and even constitutional response through legal innovations. Arendt herself proposes, notably, two constitutional amendments: legal recognition of civil disobedience as a political right, and of the political and legal equality of the African American population. The first of these amendments would, she thinks, recognise that the polity and its authority rest on people's consent by allowing for the expression of its lack, thereby helping to prevent political conflicts from escalating into civil strife and revolution.[66] The constitutional recognition of dissent is important precisely because participation is representation: '[w]hoever participates in public life at all . . . is implicated in one way

---

[64] See also Menga, 'The Seduction of Radical Democracy', p. 326, footnote 82.

[65] See Arendt, *On Revolution*, p. 227.

[66] Hannah Arendt, 'Civil Disobedience', in Hannah Arendt, *Crises of the Republic* (San Diego: Harcourt Brace & Company, 1972), pp. 49–102, esp. at pp. 82–83. See also Arendt, 'On Violence', p. 140.

or another in the deeds of the regime as a whole',[67] and so not dissenting counts as consenting. The constitutional right to dissent would include dissensual acts within the scope of those acts that express in their very performance the recognition of the authority of the extant constitutional order, by allowing at least some disagreements concerning this order to fall within its purview, rather than presenting fundamental challenges to it. The second of Arendt's amendments would both function as a corrective to the historical wrong of slavery and respond to contemporary debates concerning the status of African Americans, by including them as full-fledged members.[68]

Another form of combining newness and durability, constituent power and constitutional stability, is, for Arendt, through a federal unification of separate powers. Federation is the principle of bringing together, within a shared larger framework, loci of political power without effacing their differences and their 'original power to constitute': 'the federal principle', Arendt holds, 'the principle of league and alliance among separate units, arises out of the elementary conditions of action itself'.[69] Indeed, she sees the initiative of elementary councils as pointing to other power centres at different levels (local, state, national, international) joining in to an augmenting alliance that secures both plurality and unity.

In Arendt's republican-federal vision, then, limited 'spaces of appearances' or 'oases in a desert'[70] have porous limits that can include always new beginnings, individuals and political collectives, within an ever-growing shared world of freedom. The blind spot of this vision is the ambiguity of such porosity: the renewal is precisely *republic-preserving* renewal, which means that not all kinds of novelty can register. It is too optimistic to hold, as one reader of Arendt's republican constitutionalism does, that '[l]aw, for Arendt, must be understood both as an ordering and stabilising force in politics, and also as a *radically open* and revisable ongoing practice, which is open to intervention and interruption through political contestation'.[71] For clearly republican constitution cannot be 'radically open' to political contestation: it ultimately only hears political claims that authorities can come to see as *constitutional*, as a modification, and re-entrenchment, of the extant order. A *constitutio libertatis* is 'a framework of stability [that] provide[s] the wherein for the flux of change'.[72] Arendt's republican constitution of freedom excludes

---

[67] Arendt, 'Personal Responsibility under Dictatorship', p. 33.

[68] Arendt, 'Civil Disobedience', p. 91.

[69] Arendt, *On Revolution*, p. 267.

[70] E.g. Arendt, *On Revolution*, p. 275.

[71] James Muldoon, 'Arendt's Revolutionary Constitutionalism: Between Constituent Power and Constitutional Form', *Constellations* 23:4 (2016), pp. 596–607, at p. 596. Emphasis mine.

[72] Arendt, 'Civil Disobedience', p. 79.

every political disagreement that is deemed, by the relevant authorities (ultimately the judges of the Supreme Court), to propose non-republican and non-constitutional terms of collective life.

Arendt's blindspot is the ambiguity of the initiative. While others may join in and recognise the initiative as a legitimate beginning of their joint action, it never fully overcomes its arbitrariness. It remains *a claim to* representativeness and authority. Others may also *not recognise* themselves as 'the heirs' of the constitutional tradition into which they see themselves as forcibly included. Arendt does not entertain the possibility that some individuals and groups (in her paradigmatic case of the US, the First Nations and groups promoting black nationalism), who were included in 'a people' by a successful foundation and distribution of membership might come to hold their inclusion as an injustice that cannot be repaired by an inclusion in new terms. Or, more precisely, she does not view such anti-republican claims as genuine political disagreements and is prone to view them as irrational and leading to violence.[73]

Furthermore, for Arendt the possibility of political action within a shared world, and the renewal of this world through politics, is what counts as *the most human*. The space of freedom is 'the space where I appear to others as others appear to me' and 'where men exist not merely like other living or inanimate things but make their appearance explicitly',[74] that is, as 'men'. Not to appear on such a stage

> means above all to be deprived of things essential to a truly human life: to be deprived of the reality that comes from being seen and heard by others, to be deprived of an "objective" relationship with them that comes from being related to and separated from them through the intermediary of a common world of things, to be deprived of the possibility of achieving something more permanent than life itself.[75]

In brief, as Rudi Visker puts it, '[t]o be deprived of such a space is . . . to lack that without which one cannot be human'.[76]

Such 'civilisationalism'[77] means then that political change can only be understood as the inclusion into a constituted order of republican freedom: inclusion into such an order counts as inclusion into fully human humanity. It is this identification with the *constitutio libertatis* and the humanness of

---

[73] Arendt, 'On Violence', pp. 122–123.
[74] Arendt, *The Human Condition*, pp. 198–199.
[75] Arendt, *The Human Condition*, p. 58.
[76] Visker, 'Beyond Representation and Participation', p. 413.
[77] See A. Dirk Moses, '*Das römische Gespräch* in a New Key: Hannah Arendt, Genocide, and the Defense of Republican Civilization', *The Journal of Modern History* 85:4 (2013), pp. 867–913.

humanity that shows itself in key moments of Arendt's narrative, like in the notorious passing over in silence the violence that the British settlers exercised toward the First Nations that Arendt describes as 'worldless', as 'isolated tribes ... vegetating their lives away when first discovered on new continents by European explorers, tribes that the Europeans then either *drew into the human world* or eradicated without ever being aware that they too were human beings'.[78] The violence the colonialists exercised does not appear as an act of injustice, in so far as Arendt sees the inclusion of the First Nations as a civilisational upgrade, as a movement from a state of not-being-fully-human into a *constitutio libertatis* of full humanity.[79]

A porous *constitutio libertatis* is about augmenting the sphere and the scope of what is truly human: it thus is structurally blind to the possibility of inclusion as a political problem, as unjust domination and political alienation.[80] Exclusion from the constituted order does not make sense as a political possibility. All claims to exclusion by individuals and groups who find themselves included without their consent can only be heard as violent, non-political claims. This is indeed how Arendt treats claims of black nationalists in her essays on civil disobedience and violence. She refuses to see that racism in the US is perhaps not merely an internal affair and an injustice that can simply be rectified with full inclusion of the African American population as equals. She refuses to see that it also has a transnational colonial dimension. Arendt reviles black student movements of the 1960s as violent and non-political (because they were anti-republican), but they saw themselves as taking part in transnational anti-colonial political struggles and thus against inclusion as an unambiguously only normative answer to the history of slavery.[81] Because they saw the extant constitutional order as colonial, and hence did not see themselves as its 'heirs', inclusion (even if in modified terms) was not the answer *but the problem*.

---

[78] Hannah Arendt, *The Promise of Politics* (New York: Schocken, 2005), p. 176. Emphasis mine.

[79] See also Turpeinen's essay in this volume for an account of the complex contemporary situation in which the Native Americans both assert their claim over the land both as exclusively theirs – a claim presented against the inclusivism of the colonialist state – and as inclusively public – a claim made in defence of the state and its 'public things' against neoliberal privatisation.

[80] My account is indebted to Hans Lindahl, 'Recognition as Domination: Constitutionalism, Reciprocity and the Problem of Singularity', in Neil Walker and Jo Shaw (eds), *Europe's Constitutional Mosaic* (Oxford: Hart Publishing, 2011), pp. 205–229.

[81] See Patricia Owens, 'Racism in the Theory Canon: Hannah Arendt and "the One Great Crime in which America Was Never Involved"', *Millenium: Journal of International Studies* 45:3 (2017), pp. 403–424.

A federation in Arendt's narrative understands difference only as plurality within a common frame and conceives of radical strangeness that lies beyond its limits only as the non-human, non-political and violent. What Arendt does not see as a possible question of justice, is the federation's response to claims that legal inclusion dominates rather than liberates, misrecognises the political identity of a people rather than opens a stable order for its political freedom.

For Arendt, the 'elementary republics' exemplified a constituted order where '"the voice of the whole people would be fairly, fully, and peaceably expressed, discussed, and decided by the common reason" of all citizens',[82] and the federation expresses this same 'revolutionary spirit' on a larger scale.[83] This 'republican optimism'[84] prevents her from seeing that no amount of participation and augmentation will authentically express 'the voice of the whole people', since 'the people' as a unity is not reducible to any number, big or small, of gathering individuals, nor to any augmentation of that number. This is not to deny the normative importance of securing equal access to participatory institutions – Arendt's famous 'right to have rights'[85] – but only to remind that 'the whole people' is not a sum of its members. It is a represented unity that does not correspond to any actual reality and thus is irreducibly conflictual in a way that no constitutional framework can fully contain. Political claims may also be made for the right *not* to have the rights[86] that a legal order endows, for the right not to be included within an order that is 'not ours' and that 'we' see as making 'our' political freedom impossible. Arendt does not see that sometimes, at least, politics is not, in Rancière's words, 'based on right but wrong'.[87]

The paradox of constituent power challenges the idea that political freedom and power can find a locus in the 'common world' *in the singular*. It manifests as the difficulty of voicing political claims in institutional settings that do offer the framework of audibility and visibility for claim-making, but simultaneously curtail what novelty can be heard. Politics cannot, therefore, be thought as unambiguously actualising itself within a *constitutio libertatis*. The radical, incommensurable and 'non-federable' plurality of possible political collectives offers the point of departure for constitutional thinking of plurality that goes beyond civilisational hierarchies.

---

[82] Arendt, *On Revolution*, p. 250, Arendt cites Jefferson.

[83] See Arendt, *On Revolution*, p. 266.

[84] Cf. Emilios Christodoulidis, 'Constitutional Irresolution: Law and the Framing of Civil Society', *European Law Journal* 9:4 (2003), pp. 401–432, at p. 403.

[85] Arendt, *The Origins of Totalitarianism* (Orlando: A Harvest Book, Harcourt Inc., 2017 [1951]), p. 296.

[86] I owe this expression to Nanda Oudejans, 'The Right Not to Have Rights: A New Perspective on Irregular Immigration', *Political Theory* 47:4 (2019), pp. 447–474.

[87] Jacques Rancière, *Disagreement*, trans. Julie Rose (Minneapolis: University of Minnesota Press, 1999), p. 78.

6

Constituent Power from Cultural Practice: Implications from the Malheur Wildlife Refuge Occupation

Juho Turpeinen

Introduction

I present here a defence of the people as the subject of constituent power, a case against ardently utopian thinking.[1] The conjunctures in which bounded political entities are constituted are messy and problematic, but not hopeless or dystopian. This is to say, oppressive power relations are not always only oppressive, but should be viewed in context. The armed occupation of the Malheur National Wildlife Refuge, which took place in Oregon in 2016, makes for an illustrative case study of political identity formation, the foundation of a political regime rooted in popular rule.[2] How are such identities, the discursively constructed subject positions of democracy, possible in the first place? What allows them to be called democratic? What role does land play in this process?

Adopting the cultural studies ethos of studying not only meaning but how meaning is produced, I approach the question of the people as the subject of constituent power by arguing for an interpretation of sovereignty as cultural practices of meaning-making, as discursive struggles over cultural meaning that challenge and are challenged by relations of power. Sovereignty as cultural

---

[1] For an example of what I consider 'utopian', see the discussion on Jean-Luc Nancy and Jacques Rancière in Ari Hirvonen and Susanna Lindroos-Hovinheimo's chapter in this collection.

[2] As Wendy Brown puts it, 'Democracy detached from a bounded sovereign jurisdiction (whether virtual or literal) is politically meaningless: for the people to rule themselves, there must be an identifiable collective entity within which their power sharing is organized and upon which it is exercised'. Wendy Brown, 'We Are All Democrats Now. . .', in Giorgio Agamben, Alain Badiou, Daniel Bensaïd, Wendy Brown, Jean-Luc Nancy, Jacques Rancière, Kristin Ross, and Slavoj Žižek, *Democracy in What State?*, trans. William McCuaig (New York: Columbia University Press, 2011), p. 49. Compare with the argument for the necessity of 'the people' for democracy in Gill-Pedro's chapter in this collection.

practice gives us a framework for understanding these processes of identity formation on three related and synchronous levels of politics. This approach should not be confused with 'cultural sovereignty', whether defined as a kind of bundle of intellectual property rights protective of indigenous cultures,[3] or as a normative political project that posits the right to define 'sovereignty' from within indigenous cultures, and in which tradition is to form the foundation of group identity and political action.[4] I do, however, share with this latter conceptualisation an effort to reconsider the relationships between law, politics and culture. Indeed, to understand the workings of sovereignty in the abstract as well as in a specific temporal and spatial context, I employ the interdisciplinary approach of cultural studies, seeking the fecund interplay of theories from different traditions, and ultimately, the understanding a synthesis from therein may yield. As such, I aim to show that the conceptual frameworks of this collection relate to tangible political struggles.

I begin by grounding sovereignty, a contested and controversial concept,[5] in politics as a struggle over cultural meaning, as practices of meaning-making constitutive of a people. As these struggles bound meaning, they bound cultural entities, which constitute antagonistic groups that battle over cultural hegemony. This boundedness is not rigid, and especially in the case of the democratic subject, appears to be endangered, even fragile. I then consider sovereignty's relationship with land – juxtaposing it with neoliberalism and anti-statism, which threaten to undo the people as a subject of constituent power, and thus popular rule. I complicate this reading by placing it in the context of post-colonial America. I conclude that sovereignty not only remains a powerful counterforce to neoliberal, anti-democratic projects but that alliances with the state to construct the people as the subject of constituent power can serve this purpose. At the same time, the post-colonial context undermines these alliances as an emancipatory force.

Sovereignty as Constitutive Meaning-Making

I ground sovereignty as cultural practice in the relationships between politics and culture. Politics constructs culture, just as politics, as a cultural product,

---

[3] Jason Zenor, 'Tribal (De)Termination: Commercial Speech, Native American Imagery and Cultural Sovereignty', *Southwestern Law Review* 48:1 (2019), pp. 81–104, at p. 83, note 13.

[4] Wallace Coffey and Rebecca Tsosie, 'Rethinking the Tribal Sovereignty Doctrine: Cultural Sovereignty and the Collective Future of Indian Nations', *Stanford Law & Policy Review* 12:2 (Spring 2001), pp. 191–222.

[5] Costas Douzinas, 'Athens Revolting: Three Meditations on Sovereignty and One on Its (Possible) Dismantlement', *Law & Critique* 21:3 (2010), pp. 261–275, at p. 262. For an extended critique of the concept of sovereignty, see Michael Hardt and Antonio Negri, *Assembly* (New York: Oxford University Press, 2017).

is shaped by the culture in which it is produced. William Henry Sewell Jr. argues that the word 'culture' can be understood as two distinct concepts. Firstly, there is the analytical category of culture that is 'abstracted out from the complex reality of human existence' and designated as a field, sub-field or a method of study.[6] 'Culture', in this sense, 'is neither a particular kind of practice nor practice that takes place in a particular social location. It is, rather, the semiotic dimension of human social practice in general'.[7] In the second meaning, 'culture' is understood to refer to one of many 'bounded world[s] of beliefs and practices',[8] or simply as 'a way of life'.[9] I refer to 'culture' in both of these meanings, depending on the context: in the former sense, when I attempt to theorise how politics functions as a mechanism of constructing cultural meanings and vice versa; in the latter sense, when I focus on specific, bounded cultural meanings in the temporal and spatial context of the Malheur occupation. It is true, however, that in this latter meaning of the word as well, cultures are best conceptualised as 'partially coherent landscapes of meaning' whose 'boundedness is only relative and constantly shifting'.[10] 'Culture' is, thus, inseparable from 'politics'; politics are the various struggles to, among other things, imbue social life with a degree of coherent if unstable and contested meaning.

Sewell points out that when dominant actors attempt to affect culture, they cannot do so merely by ordering cultural homogeneity, but more often resort to organising difference.[11] Such a conception of culture is commensurate with an understanding of politics as a struggle over hegemony.[12] Because this struggle relies on dominant (or hegemonic) practices that aim to produce meanings, and on the reactions to those practices from oppositional or marginalised groups, the struggle forms a 'dialectical dance' which 'far from demonstrating that cultures lack coherence, may paradoxically have the effect of simplifying and clarifying the cultural field'.[13] This

---

[6] William H. Sewell, Jr., 'The Concept(s) of Culture', in Victoria E. Bonnell and Lynn Hunt (eds.), *Beyond the Cultural Turn: New Directions in the Study of Society and Culture* (Berkeley: University of California Press, 1999), pp. 35–61, at p. 39.

[7] Sewell, Jr., 'The Concept(s) of Culture', p. 48.

[8] Sewell, Jr., 'The Concept(s) of Culture', p. 39.

[9] Neil Campbell and Alasdair Kean, *American Cultural Studies: An Introduction to American Culture,* 3rd edn. (New York: Routledge, 2012), p. 6.

[10] Sewell, Jr., 'The Concept(s) of Culture', p. 58.

[11] Sewell, Jr., 'The Concept(s) of Culture', p. 56.

[12] Indeed, Sewell is ambivalent about whether 'culture' in the second meaning is called 'culture' or 'hegemony'. Sewell, Jr., 'The Concept(s) of Culture', p. 58. For a post-Gramscian understanding of hegemony in political theory, see Ernesto Laclau and Chantal Mouffe, *Hegemony and Socialist Strategy: Towards a Radical Democratic Politics,* 2nd edn. (London: Verso, 2014).

[13] Sewell, Jr., 'The Concept(s) of Culture', pp. 56–57.

process, in which meaning is articulated and re-articulated, is the political struggle over culture.[14]

Crucially, understanding culture as 'a way of life', as one of many, implies a focus on the particular and the local. Even Sewell, who argues that we can no longer think of societies as separate from one another, with 'corresponding and well-integrated "culture[s]"',[15] admits that 'much cultural practice is concentrated in and around powerful institutional nodes including . . . most spectacularly, states'.[16] Although there are powerful dimensions of cultural practices that are global, giving reason to suspect whether Sewell's analysis is still relevant, much of social life can still be made intelligible through the concept of the nation state.[17] This is particularly true in the United States, where national identity remains a notable issue of interest, even as the coherence of any such concept has come under considerable criticism as both homogenising and inward-looking.[18] More broadly, the recent surge in popularity of ethnonationalist movements in Europe and the United States serves as a testament to the enduring power of national identity. Furthermore, as Davina Cooper argues, 'recognizing the state-shaped character of social life makes it possible to explore the complex ways state and other (including grass-roots) governance logics and processes combine rather than assuming they meet as discrete independent forces'.[19]

To interpret the logics of this bounding of cultural identity and its relationship with democracy, I draw on Panu Minkkinen's division of theories of sovereignty into three categories: autocephalous, or sovereignty defined in legal terms as the power of the people or the authority of the state; heterocephalous, or political power that resists a single point in which sovereignty can be identified, marking a constellation of power relations; and acephalous, or sovereign self-knowledge that predates legal constitution.[20] As this distinction makes clear, 'theories of sovereignty have been characterised by so many contortions and impasses that one could be justified in thinking that they are dealing with different phenomena'.[21] Instead, I use

---

[14] In other words, the 'transformational act of resignification – which is irreducibly discursive – is the generative source from which political rupture and social change is born'. Kobena Mercer, 'Introduction', in Stuart Hall, *The Fateful Triangle: Race, Ethnicity, Nation*, ed. Kobena Mercer (Cambridge: Harvard University Press, 2017), pp. 1–30, at p. 18.

[15] Sewell, Jr., 'The Concept(s) of Culture', p. 57.

[16] Sewell, Jr., 'The Concept(s) of Culture', pp. 55–56.

[17] Campbell and Kean, *American Cultural Studies*, p. 2.

[18] Campbell and Kean, *American Cultural Studies*, pp. 2–5.

[19] Davina Cooper, 'Transformative State Publics', *New Political Science* 38:3 (2016), pp. 315–334, at p. 318.

[20] Panu Minkkinen, *Sovereignty, Knowledge, Law* (New York: Routledge, 2009), pp. 8–9.

[21] Douzinas, 'Athens Revolting', p. 262.

these different 'heads' to refer to different levels of sovereignty that exist synchronously rather than as related groupings of theoretical approaches. Moreover, I understand autocephalous sovereignty to refer not only to constituent power in the juridical sense but to entities of bounded cultural meaning. For Minkkinen:

> the theory that posits a constitutionally ordered state already presupposes a subject that has reached full self-knowledge and that is also capable of 'knowing' the world that surrounds it. In that sense, the 'containing' that a constitutional framework provides is introduced by a sovereign subject, that is, the subject of knowledge and science.[22]

Building on this concept, I refer to acephalous knowledge not only in the context of producing the framework for a legal constitution but in subjectivising a group of people as a political entity, a subject of constituent power, a player that can then act on the heterocephalous stage of politics. While cultural studies has recently approached law and legitimacy from the perspective of culture,[23] my approach here is to look at how the concept of sovereignty, derived from legal theory, can be used to understand the processes of cultural identity formation that found the subjects of constituent power at the heart of democratic politics.[24] In other words, I transpose the legal onto the cultural plane.

Public Lands, Neoliberalism and Anti-Statism

I now turn to the case of the armed occupation of the Malheur National Wildlife Refuge to show how a cultural conceptualisation of sovereignty can help us understand the construction of bounded political entities that constitute popular rule. The occupation, which lasted forty-one days in early 2016, saw Western ranchers, entrepreneurs, and other malcontents – predominantly white and male – journey to southeastern Oregon, and take over the remote wildlife refuge, owned by the federal government and managed by the United States Fish and Wildlife Service. The occupation had seemingly splintered off from a peaceful protest in the closest city, Burns, a small town of fewer

---

[22] Minkkinen, *Sovereignty, Knowledge, Law*, p. 8.

[23] Jaafar Aksikas and Sean Johnson Andrews (eds.), *Cultural Studies and the 'Juridical Turn': Culture, Law and Legitimacy in the Era of Neoliberal Capitalism* (New York: Routledge, 2017).

[24] This can be juxtaposed with institutional mediation-oriented (see Lukkari's chapter in this collection) and human rights-oriented (see Gill-Pedro's chapter in this collection) approaches to the question of constituent power.

than 3,000 people, against the impending federal imprisonment of two local ranchers, held thirty miles away.[25] In the media, the occupiers' claims were largely communicated through brothers Ammon and Ryan Bundy, the apparent leaders of the occupation.[26] The occupiers claimed that the federal government had no right to the land and that their attempt to seize the land was for the economic well-being of ranchers and private citizens.[27] The occupation was widely condemned by legal experts, politicians and commentators in mainstream and social media.[28] It ended with all occupiers arrested, save for one who was shot to death by Oregon State Patrol. While the majority of the accused pleaded guilty, many of the key figures of the occupation, including Ammon and Ryan Bundy, were later acquitted of conspiracy charges.[29]

While scholars from different fields have taken an interest in the values that the occupiers represent, values that may resonate with a much broader

[25] Carissa Wolf, Peter Holley, and Wesley Lowery, 'Armed men, led by Bundy brothers, take over federal building in rural Oregon', *The Washington Post*, 3 January 2016. Available at https://www.washingtonpost.com/news/post-nation/wp/2016/01/03/armed-militia-bundy-brothers-take-over-federal-building-in-rural-oregon/ (accessed 26 July 2019).

[26] See e.g. Ralph Ellis, Holly Yan, and Sara Sidner, 'Oregon protest leader: "There is a time to go home", *CNN*, 7 January 2016. Available at https://edition.cnn.com/2016/01/06/us/oregon-wildlife-refuge-armed-protest/ (accessed 29 July 2019); John Sepulvado, Oregon Public Broadcasting, 'Ryan Bundy: We'll leave if community want us to', *Public Broadcasting Service*, 5 January 2016. Available at https://www.pbs.org/newshour/nation/ryan-bundy-well-leave-if-community-wants-us-to (accessed 29 July 2019).

[27] Les Zaitz 'Oregon militant leader Ammon Bundy exudes calm as he presides over occupation', *The Oregonian*, 3 January 2016. Available at https://www.oregonlive.com/pacific-northwest-news/2016/01/ammon_bundy_exudes_calm_as_he.html (accessed 29 July 2019).

[28] See e.g. Erwin Chemerinsky, 'Private: No Legal Issue in Oregon', American Constitution Society (blog), 7 January 2016. Available at https://www.acslaw.org/expertforum/no-legal-issue-in-oregon/ (accessed 29 July 2019); Dana Ford, 'Oregon governor tells armed protesters to leave', *CNN*, 8 January 2016. Available at https://edition.cnn.com/2016/01/07/us/oregon-wildlife-refuge-armed-protest/ (accessed 29 July 2019); Josh Zeitz, 'Sorry, Ranchers, You're Actually Big-Time Government Moochers. What Ammon Bundy doesn't get about U.S. history', *Politico*, 7 January 2016. Available at https://www.politico.com/magazine/story/2016/01/bundhy-protest-ranchers-actually-government-moochers-213510 (accessed 29 July 2019); Wilfred Chan, 'Oregon Standoff? Call it a "Y'all Qaeda" attack, say Internet users', *CNN*, 4 January 2016. Available at https://edition.cnn.com/2016/01/04/us/oregon-standoff-social-media-reaction/ (accessed 29 July 2019).

[29] Courtney Sherwood and Kirk Johnson, 'Bundy Brothers Acquitted in Takeover of Oregon Wildlife Refuge', *The New York Times*, 27 October 2016. Available at https://www.nytimes.com/2016/10/28/us/bundy-brothers-acquitted-in-takeover-of-oregon-wildlife-refuge.html (accessed 29 July 2019).

audience,[30] the media at the time focused on the sensational character of the militia-esque occupiers, giving them the opportunity to articulate their anti-statist rhetoric. Although their messaging was at times ambiguous,[31] their anti-statism is what links the armed occupation to neoliberalism. As Carolyn Gallaher puts it, 'the occupier's stated goal – to seize public land and "give it back" to ranchers – is inconsistent with neoliberal goals but ultimately dovetails with its solutions'.[32] After all, in the United States, neoliberalism manifests in the context of 'long-established antistatism and new managerialism'.[33] Greg Walden, the US Representative for Oregon's second congressional district, reiterated the relevance of anti-statism to contemporary Republican politics by agreeing with the aims albeit not the means of the armed occupiers.[34]

The anti-statist occupiers construct a rhetorical group identity that closely resembles the 'sovereign citizen' movement, which holds the federal government to be largely illegitimate.[35] In this heterodox interpretation, the federal government has extremely narrow powers that can almost never be expanded upon; actions usually considered to be well within the legal powers of the federal government are seen by militia groups as illegitimate if they encroach on 'the freedoms of particular – usually white and male – citizens'.[36] Such an interpretation relies on historically derived notions of racial hierarchy and

---

[30] See for example Carolyn Gallaher, 'Placing the Militia Occupation of the Malheur National Wildlife Refuge in Harney County, Oregon', *ACME: An International E-Journal for Critical Geographies* 15:2 (2016), pp. 293–308. Available at https://www.acme-journal.org/index.php/acme/article/view/1312/1173 (accessed 24 July 2019); Michael C. Blumm and Olivier Jamin, 'The Property Clause and Its Discontents: Lessons from the Malheur Occupation', *Ecology Law Quarterly* 43:4 (2016), pp. 781–826. From the perspective of sovereignty, Courtney Irons has discussed patriarchy and masculinity in the occupiers' rhetoric. Courtney Irons, 'The Patriarch and the Sovereign: The Malheur Occupations and the Hyper-Masculine Drive for Control', *Columbia Journal of Law and Social Problems* 51:3 (2018), pp. 479–522.

[31] See for example Ashley Fantz, Joe Sutton and Holly Yan, 'Armed group's leader in federal building: "We will be here as long as it takes"', *CNN*, 4 January 2016. Available at https://edition.cnn.com/2016/01/03/us/oregon-wildlife-refuge-protest/index.html (accessed 29 July 2019).

[32] Gallaher, 'Placing the Militia Occupation', p. 298.

[33] Wendy Brown, *Undoing the Demos* (New York: Zone Books, 2015), p. 20.

[34] Mike DeBonis, 'Oregon congressman: Those occupiers kind of have a point', *The Washington Post*, 6 January 2016. Available at https://www.washingtonpost.com/news/powerpost/wp/2016/01/06/oregon-congressman-those-occupiers-kind-of-have-a-point/?noredirect=on&utm_term=.18660ecdcb11 (accessed 29 July 2019).

[35] Lane Crothers, *Rage on the Right: The American Militia Movement from Ruby Ridge to Homeland Security* (Lanham: Rowman & Littlefield, 2003), pp. 58–61.

[36] Crothers, *Rage on the Right*, p. 58, pp. 58–61.

antagonism towards the federal government.[37] In a 'sovereign citizen' interpretation, any autocephalous justification of the federal government's power is severely questioned. The government is largely viewed as an oppressive political power in the heterocephalous realm. Ammon and Ryan Bundy's father, Cliven Bundy, had previously tried to use such a failed defence in court in relation to his land dispute in Nevada.[38] Following in his father's footsteps, '[Ammon] Bundy used the occupation to repeatedly declare federal land ownership unconstitutional, and BLM [Bureau of Land Management] powerless to manage federal lands'.[39]

The occupiers' anti-statism can also be read in the context of the Sagebrush Rebellion, a movement that right-wing politicians tapped into in the 1970s and 1980s.[40] Although some states are exceptions, the current trend for the federal government is, and has been for decades, to diminish rather than increase the amount of federal lands. This has been the case in the eleven contiguous western states as well. However, the Sagebrush rebels' call to simply transfer federal lands to the states has been unsuccessful.[41] Critics have long held that the argument that federal lands should be transferred to the states is not much more than a ruse under which public lands would be privatised.[42]

Seemingly at the intersection of these traditions, the militant, armed occupiers that took control of the facilities at the refuge, claimed they were doing so to help the people and the community.[43] The 'economics' that the occupiers talked about could supposedly only be achieved through local or private means.[44] According to a County Commissioner, however, Harney County would not be able to afford to manage what are currently federal lands.[45]

---

[37] Crothers, *Rage on the Right*, p. 60. Although, as Crothers notes, militias do not necessarily see themselves as racist, but defend their views as constitutional. Crothers, *Rage on the Right*, p. 73.

[38] Blumm and Jamin, 'The Property Clause', pp. 788–789.

[39] Blumm and Jamin, 'The Property Clause', p. 793.

[40] Richard White, *'It's Your Misfortune and None of My Own': A New History of the American West* (Norman: University of Oklahoma Press, 1991), pp. 567–568.

[41] Carol Hardy Vincent, Laura A. Hanson, and Carla N. Argueta, 'Federal Land Ownership: Overview and Data', US Congressional Research Service, R42346, 3 March 2017. Accessed at Federation of American Scientists, available at https://fas.org/sgp/crs/misc/R42346.pdf (accessed 29 July 2019), pp. 15–20.

[42] White, *It's Your Misfortune*, pp. 567–568.

[43] The Oregonian, 'Militant leader explains intentions on Oregon refuge takeover', YouTube, 3 January 2016. Available at https://www.youtube.com/watch?v=eb8Oq83Uzb0 (accessed 29 July 2019); Sepulvado, 'Ryan Bundy'.

[44] Zaitz, 'Oregon militant leader'; Oregonian, 'Militant leader explains intentions'.

[45] Samantha White, 'County Court Continues Conversation Concerning Refuge Occupation', *Burns Times-Herald*, 27 January 2016. Available at http://btimesherald.com/2016/01/27/county-court-continues-conversation-concerning-refuge-occupation/ (accessed 29 July 2019).

For Bonnie Honig, such privatisation of public things would lead to an undoing of popular rule through erosion of the foundations of a democratically oriented people.[46] Honig connects sovereignty to public things, comparing public things to a blanket or toy, through the use of which an infant learns to think of 'itself as a unit as well', but transposes this object-relations concept from personality in developmental psychology to collectivity in political theory.[47] In the political realm, this could mean that transitional objects help individuals move towards thinking about the world beyond themselves, towards a democratic imagination.[48] For Honig, such objects are public. While private things may have a 'magic' of their own, they lack the political magic of public things. Honig concedes that we cannot know whether private things can or cannot serve this function, but that the fetishist obsession with the same privately owned things (such as iPhones) appears to be 'more like the ruin' that reminds us of our need for public things in neoliberal times.[49]

Although Honig argues for 'a democratic politics based not on identity and inclusion',[50] public things bound cultural meaning through acephalous knowledge. They 'press us into relations with others',[51] and have the potential to 'constitute citizens equally as citizens'.[52] Public things equalise privilege inherent to wealth and various social intersections, such as gender, race and ethnicity, while private things cannot equalise privilege – after all, they are not available to all. It follows that, if public things are a necessary condition of democracy, then all efforts to wrest land from public control are inherently anti-democratic. Privatisation of public lands, either directly or because the county or state could not afford to manage the lands,[53] threatens the democratically subjectivising knowledge of public lands. What is at stake is not just the loss of the political power of the people in the heterocephalous sense, but the people in which autocephalous sovereignty is grounded, due to a loss of acephalous sovereign knowledge, undoing constituent power. As Jason Frank puts it, what Honig 'diagnoses is the disappearance of the political itself . . .

---

[46] Bonnie Honig, *Public Things: Democracy in Disrepair* (New York: Fordham University Press, 2017).

[47] Honig, *Public Things*, pp. 16–17.

[48] Honig, *Public Things*, p. 17.

[49] Honig, *Public Things*, pp. 30–31.

[50] Felicity Collins, 'Disturbing the Peace: The Ghost in Bedevil and The Darkside', *Critical Arts* 31:5 (2017), pp. 107–114, at p. 110.

[51] Honig, *Public Things*, p. 6.

[52] Honig, *Public Things*, p. 11. Public things also 'provide a basis around which to . . . reimagine various modes of collective being together in a democracy'. Honig, *Public Things*, p. 24

[53] Gallaher, 'Placing the Militia Occupation', p. 304.

the capacity of ordinary people to respond collectively to challenges they commonly face'.[54]

The 2016 occupation was not, of course, the first time Euro-Americans laid claim to the ancestral lands of the Northern Paiutes. Seemingly reflecting on this past, Ryan Bundy reportedly claimed that the occupiers 'recognize that the Native Americans had the claim to the land, but they lost that claim . . . There are things to learn from cultures of the past, but the current culture is the most important'.[55] Despite the occupiers' later rhetoric that they welcomed the Burns Paiute Tribe to discuss the federal treatment of Paiute artefacts with them (an invitation the tribe refused),[56] any attempt at allegiance was undermined by the general implications of an armed, exclusive occupation that aimed at the privatisation of a public thing. Instead of building alliances, the white male occupiers' 'assembly' radically excluded others. Due to the armed nature of the occupation, the Malheur protesters were attacking the right to public land, the right of the Burns Paiute Tribe to have the federal government manage the land, and the right of locals – who, subsequently, assembled at other public sites[57] – to protest against the occupiers' presence.

In cases where students have seized university buildings, Judith Butler argues, they have claimed them for public education, to wrest them from neoliberalism.[58] The Malheur occupiers, on the other hand, claimed public land for privatisation. Yet, does this act not signify the precarity of the occupiers, and demand that that precarity be redressed, even if it cannot be

[54] Jason Frank, 'Collective Actors, Common Desires', *Political Research Quarterly*, 68:3 (2015), pp. 637–641, at p. 637. In Honig's words: 'Without public things, we have nothing or not much to deliberate about, constellate around, or agonistically contest'. Honig, *Public Things,* p. 5.

[55] Rebecca Boone, Associated Press, '4,000 artifacts stored at Oregon refuge held by armed group', *Business Insider*, 15 January 2016. Available at https://www.businessinsider.com/ap-4000-artifacts-stored-at-oregon-refuge-held-by-armed-group-2016-1?r=US&IR=T&IR=T (accessed 29 July 2019).

[56] Sam Levin, 'Fresh outrage after militia seen rifling through tribal artifacts at Oregon refuge', *The Guardian*, 21 January 2016. Available at https://www.theguardian.com/us-news/2016/jan/21/oregon-militia-standoff-malheur-wildlife-refuge-native-american-artifacts-paiute-tribe (accessed 29 July 2019); LaVoy Finicum 'Jan 20 Native American Artifacts', YouTube, 21 January 2016. Available at https://www.youtube.com/watch?v=EzFhWAcu3i0 (accessed 29 July 2019).

[57] Conrad Wilson and Ryan Haas, Oregon Public Broadcasting, 'Oregon residents in packed town hall want armed militia to leave', *Public Broadcasting Service*, 7 January 2016. Available at https://www.pbs.org/newshour/nation/oregon-residents-in-packed-town-hall-want-armed-militia-to-leave (accessed 29 July 2019).

[58] Judith Butler, *Notes Toward a Performative Theory of Assembly* (Cambridge: Harvard University Press, 2015), pp. 94–95.

redressed by the means they propose? Is it not liveable life that the Malheur occupiers demand? Is their precarity not, thus, related to protests against the very neoliberal ideals they implicitly support?[59]

Claiming Sovereignty in the Post-Colonial Context

Conversely, the Burns Paiute Tribe, the ancestors of whom were the original habitants of the area, articulated a different kind of relationship with land, sovereignty and the federal government. Charlotte Rodrique, the Burns Paiute Tribal Chair at the time, made an attempt to retain a distinction between cooperation with the government and a ceded heterocephalous sovereignty, to maintain a political and not just cultural distinction in relation to the United States. The Burns Paiute Tribe was adamant when talking to the press that it had not in fact given away its land; by signing the treaties in 1868, the Paiutes only entrusted the federal government to be the land's guardian.[60] In *The Oregonian*, Rodrique is quoted saying that the tribe has a 'good working relationship' with the federally owned and managed refuge, and hold the federal government to be 'a protector of [their] cultural rights in that area'.[61] At the same time, Rodrique maintains that 'we as a tribe view that this is still our land no matter who's living on it'.[62] This claim should be considered in the context of the juridical status of Native Americans in the United States. Although rulings of the Supreme Court have been interpreted to afford Native American tribes varying degrees of sovereignty,[63] Congress retains plenary powers over Indian affairs, and whether and to what degree Native American treaties and rights are upheld. Courts tend to defer to this power 'when it is to the detriment of tribes, while asserting judicial review over congressional acts that benefit tribes'.[64]

In practical terms, then, it makes sense for the Burns Paiute Tribe to maintain a relationship with the federal government. Working towards heterocephalous power and autocephalous sovereignty without antagonising the

---

[59] Cf. Butler, *Notes*, pp. 126–127.

[60] E.g. Ian K. Kullgren, 'Burns Paiute Tribe: Militants need to get off "our land"', *The Oregonian*, 6 January 2016. Available at https://www.oregonlive.com/pacific-northwest-news/2016/01/burns_piaute_tribe_militants_s.html (accessed 26 July 2019).

[61] Kullgren, 'Burns Paiute Tribe'.

[62] Kullgren, 'Burns Paiute Tribe'.

[63] Federico Lenzerini, 'Sovereignty Revisited: International Law and Parallel Sovereignty of Indigenous Peoples', *Texas International Law Journal* 42:1 (2006), pp. 155–189, at pp. 165–169.

[64] Michalyn Steele, 'Plenary Powers, Political Questions, and Sovereignty in Indian Affairs', *UCLA Law Review* 63:3 (2016), pp. 666–710, at p. 671. See also pp. 669–671.

federal government would seem to require a deft hand. Parallels can be drawn between the events of 2016 and the character of Sarah Winnemucca, a controversial nineteenth-century figure.[65] Like Rodrique in 2016, Winnemucca appeared 'to imagine a form of incorporation that does not require dissolution of Northern Paiute sovereignty, a form the United States is reluctant to acknowledge'.[66]

After federal war efforts against the Paiutes brutally concluded, a treaty between the parties created the Malheur Indian Reservation in 1872, on the Paiutes' ancestral lands.[67] Experiences and interpretations vary on what the Malheur Indian Reservation actually was. Winnemucca described the (by then abolished) reservation as the 'Paiutes' home'.[68] Conversely, historian Nancy Langston argues that the reservation was 'intended to free up land for ranching' and soon 'became a site of constraint and anger for the Paiute' when ranchers and Indian agents tried to force the Paiutes out of their nomadic ways and into farming.[69] Regardless, ranchers and settlers soon began to take over the lands of the reservation, leading to a Paiute uprising that was quickly crushed.[70] In 1879, the Malheur Paiutes were forcibly moved to another reservation in 'a 350-mile journey that took a number of lives'.[71] Ranchers then fully took over the Malheur Indian Reservation, which was finally abolished in 1889, returning the land to the public domain.[72] During the early twentieth century, the environmental devastation wrought by agricultural developments, not just in Malheur but across the United States, sparked interest in conservation efforts. President Theodore Roosevelt established the Malheur Lake Bird Reservation in 1908,[73] and in 1934, when the cattle empire was in ruins, the rest of the area was obtained by the federal wildlife refuge system.[74]

Winnemucca struggled to restore the Malheur Reservation to the Paiutes, but the area remained largely public land and eventually became the wildlife refuge. Cari M. Carpenter argues that regardless of their ostensible failure,

---

[65] Cari M. Carpenter, 'Sarah Winnemucca Goes to Washington: Rhetoric and Resistance in the Capital City', *American Indian Quarterly* 40:2 (Spring 2016), pp. 87–108, at pp. 97–98.

[66] Carpenter, 'Sarah Winnemucca', p. 96.

[67] Nancy Langston, *Where Land and Water Meet: A Western Landscape Transformed* (Seattle: University of Washington Press, 2003), p. 32.

[68] Carpenter, 'Sarah Winnemucca', p. 94.

[69] Langston, *Land and Water*, p. 32.

[70] Langston, *Land and Water*, pp. 32–34.

[71] Carpenter, 'Sarah Winnemucca', p. 87.

[72] Langston, *Land and Water*, pp. 33–34.

[73] Langston, *Land and Water*, p. 67.

[74] Langston, *Land and Water*, p. 63.

Winnemucca's attempts represent resistance. They represent a performance of heterocephalous power in a time when federal policy was shifting away from treating Native American tribes as external nations and towards 'inward surveillance and manipulation'.[75] The tension between struggles for political distinction and for cultural distinction within political assimilation continues to this day.[76] The latter, what Carpenter refers to as 'multiculturalism', is a way of conceptualising Native Americans as culturally different rather than politically sovereign.[77] Carpenter, drawing on Maureen Konkle,[78] seems to suggest that 'multiculturalism' is a euphemism that undermines or undercuts indigenous heterocephalous sovereignty.[79] Carpenter argues that multiculturalism 'functions in part as a colonial effort to forcibly incorporate and thus dissolve "difference"'.[80] Native Americans must resist this rationality and fight for 'the rights of US citizenship without ceding the independence promised to Natives' in a 'complex dance' for heterocephalous sovereignty.[81]

Winnemucca remains, especially among the Northern Paiutes, a contentious figure, implicated in the white colonial agenda, and the assertion of the Paiutes during the Malheur occupation performs a similar function; it continues the 'complex dance'. It may well be, as it appears here, that 'the disruptive and challenging assertions made by the excluded in equality's name [are] always entangled with the "police" order rather than separate from it'.[82] Furthermore, as Cooper points out, '[r]eading such action as resistance, necessarily located outside centers of power, can obscure and attenuate the power that subordinate forces can and do make use of through their state location'.[83]

At the same time, it may be this colonial heritage at the heart of the federal government that allows the government to recognise, cooperate with, and defend Native Americans, when it happens to reinforce its own legitimacy, such as by condemning the white conservative militia types that came to Malheur to oppose and question that legitimacy. When the Paiutes maintain that they have good relations with the federal government, they too seem to maintain the colonial hegemony of the federal government in which the Indigenous are subaltern and assimilated to the 'American' narrative.

---

[75] Carpenter, 'Sarah Winnemucca', pp. 90–91.
[76] Carpenter, 'Sarah Winnemucca', pp. 97–98.
[77] Carpenter, 'Sarah Winnemucca', p. 90.
[78] Maureen Konkle, *Writing Indian Nations: Native Intellectuals and the Politics of Historiography, 1827-1863* (Chapel Hill: The University of North Carolina Press, 2004), p. 35.
[79] Carpenter, 'Sarah Winnemucca', p. 90.
[80] Carpenter, 'Sarah Winnemucca', p. 104.
[81] Carpenter, 'Sarah Winnemucca', p. 104.
[82] Cooper, 'Transformative State Publics', p. 318.
[83] Cooper, 'Transformative State Publics', p. 318.

If public lands as public things have an important, even formative relationship with democracy, they cannot by their colonial nature directly grant the Burns Paiute Tribe their heterocephalous sovereignty. Understood against the backdrop of the legal and political status of Native Americans in the United States, the struggle for political recognition has troubling implications for the 'democratic' dimension of public lands and perhaps even the pre-neoliberal liberal democracy that birthed them. Considering the colonial legacy of liberal democracy in the United States, one whose problems are not merely a historical backdrop, but an actively oppressing force in contemporary times, can such democracy be defensible?[84]

In other words, if public lands have a political magic that private ones do not, it is one tempered by a lack of democratic mapping.[85] Public lands, as conceived of through the nation state, are delimited in terms of democracy by the framework of the nation state; even if public land is mapped democratically, which is certainly not always the case, it is only democratic to the degree that the nation state itself is. Honig recognises the issue, arguing that the creation and maintenance of public things, including public lands, cannot be limited to the means of the state. Honig argues that while 'criticisms of public things as falsely universal, falsely inclusive, colonial, appropriative, and statist have been tremendously important and apt',[86] we should not see this as:

> a reason to oppose public things, as such, or to be reluctant to claim and mobilize their powers now, or to shrink from building new ones. Nor is it a reason to conflate public things with state sovereignty, which these days is just one of the mechanisms of their reproduction and can be one of the mechanisms of their betrayal.[87]

In addition to the state, there is potential for the support of public things in other political powers, including agency in relation to the state as well as 'alternative sovereignties' constructed by 'with-drawalists' – powers that are not always compatible with each other.[88] At this level, Honig's theorising can be read as a web of heterocephalous political power. Yet, the idea that 'the

---

[84] Compare with the discussion on Hannah Arendt's writings on African Americans and the indigenous peoples of North America in Lukkari's chapter in this collection.

[85] See Bonnie Honig, 'What Kind of Thing Is Land? Hannah Arendt's Object Relations, or: The Jewish Unconscious of Arendt's Most "Greek" Text', *Political Theory* 44:3 (2016), pp. 307–336, at p. 318.

[86] Honig, *Public Things*, p. 91.

[87] Honig, *Public Things*, p. 92.

[88] Honig, *Public Things*, pp. 92–93.

state itself is a public thing and worth fighting for' remains explicitly at the core of Honig's theorising.[89]

The complicated discursive performance by the Burns Paiute Tribe brings these threads together. It resists the notion of Native Americans as merely culturally different, and it rejects the notion that the federal government is the rightful owner of the land while maintaining the possibility of a heterogeneous alliance to keep the land public.[90] To contain democratically vital elements, such an effort need not be done to promote democracy; even when ostensibly aimed at discursively claiming heterocephalous sovereignty and producing conditions for survival, the performance produces not only a discursive alliance in the face of anti-democratic tendencies but also affirms public lands. Indeed, '[f]ollowing the Paiutes' lead', locals of Harney County assembled to protest the armed occupation.[91] To draw on Butler, 'through their action, they [brought] the space of appearance into being'.[92]

For democratic society to exist, the subject capable of democratic knowledge must be constituted in such terms. This is possible through the magic of public things, including public lands, which are, in fact, a prime example of what can be read as the acephalous sovereign even during times of neoliberal assault:

> [P]ublic things stand out as a point worth insisting upon, something that must not be allowed to become part of the morass of despair. Their thingness still enchants, even as their publicness is under pressure. Anyone who has visited a national park can attest to this.[93]

In this sense, the nation state, regardless of its factually limited heterocephalous sovereignty, continues to shape the democratic imagination. One can be critical of the nation state, the ways in which it produces domination and is limited in its politically emancipatory potential, and yet one can recognise how the nation state produces democratic imaginaries in the very moment we live in.

---

[89] Honig, *Public Things*, p. 92. Honig still clearly has an affinity for the nation state that informs the 'publicness' of 'public things'. This is obvious from the examples used in the book.

[90] E.g. Kullgren, 'Burns Paiute Tribe'.

[91] Mariya Strauss, 'Keeping Public Lands Public: How Oregon's Rural Communities Rescued the Malheur Wildlife Refuge', *New Labor Forum* 26:3 (2017), pp. 83–87, at pp. 84–85.

[92] Butler, *Notes*, pp. 88–89.

[93] Honig, *Public Things*, p. 32.

Conclusions

In the above, I have tried to show the need for a cultural interpretation of sovereignty, one that allows us to understand constituent power in democratic politics. By connecting politics to struggles over cultural meaning, we can use sovereignty as a tool for locating the formation of political subject positions. Mirroring what Minkkinen calls the acephalous, autocephalous and heterocephalous heads of sovereignty – that is, knowledge, law and politics – cultural struggles draw on (acephalous) subjectivising knowledge, and perform (autocephalous) social constitution and (heterocephalous) political struggle through discursive performances. These practices challenge and are challenged by relations of power, and the boundedness they delineate is not rigid, but always open to discursive renegotiation.

The subject positions we can analyse through the concept of sovereignty as cultural practice are not necessarily constructed on the concept of democracy itself; it is not always the need for democracy that creates democratic conditions, but our social actions that demand liveable life in the face of precarity. As Giunia Gatta puts it, it is not:

> that suffering is constitutive of *all* political action, but rather that debates around the meaning and the best way to contain our suffering and the suffering of fellow human beings are at the core of contemporary politics, and they constitute often an impetus to engage in political enterprises.[94]

The immediate needs and desires of people, for land and sovereignty, are not necessarily thought of in terms of 'democracy', but they can be foundational in producing democratic conditions by constructing democratically subjectivising knowledge out of political alliances and things held in common. They may even do this as they clash with power relations in ways that undermine emancipatory potential.

Social action by itself can be directed in many ways. It can ally a statist conception of public things with Native American sovereignty, or it can be directed towards anti-statist, neoliberal, even discriminatory desires. The armed occupiers' claims were exclusionary, ostensibly an attempt at fighting a perceived or experienced precarity but poised to deepen precarity and anti-democratic politics. The acephalous notion of the sovereign citizen

---

[94] Giunia Gatta, 'Suffering and the Making of Politics: Perspectives from Jaspers and Camus', *Contemporary Political Theory* 14:4 (2015), pp. 335–354, at p. 351. Here, like Gatta, I argue for a disruption of 'the binary proposed by Honig between lamentational politics and agonistic humanism'. Gatta, 'Suffering and the Making of Politics', p. 336.

is the root of autocephalous group identity, juxtaposed with the federal government, which is viewed as a hostile competitor on the heterocephalous stage of politics. The historically developed marriage of this type of anti-statism with neoliberalism threatens the acephalous, democratically subjectivising knowledge of public lands.

While the Burns Paiute Tribe at once reject the exclusionary attempts of the occupiers and reaffirm public lands as the lands managed by the federal government, they also assert their claim over the land both as exclusively theirs and as inclusively public. Performatively, the articulation allies a statist conception of democracy with democratic action that does not presuppose a state, and public land as common to both. At the same time, the complexities of context confound any easy answers, exemplified by the colonial history of public lands. This land is the acephalous knowledge that subjectivises a people that is sovereign in the autocephalous sense and struggling for political recognition in the heterocephalous realm.

We can understand the implications of this conjuncture – and the construction of political identity in general – through the concept of sovereignty as cultural practice.

For Eduardo Gill-Pedro, the act of claiming human rights is a political one; to make the claim, we need to see ourselves as potential members of a democratic collectivity. As such, the central task is to bring the process of democracy into being.[95] This process – or discursive struggle over cultural hegemony – is, I argue, rooted in rhetorically constructed subject-positions, which in turn are founded on sovereign knowledge. Here that knowledge is, in the first place, precarity, propelling the inaugural act, and in the second, political alliances that constellate around things held in common. The potential for collective self-recognition as a part of a democratic collectivity appears to already be present in the acknowledging of shared precarity, but as that precarity entails a desire for land and sovereignty, it seems to be derived from (the spectre of) the subjectivising knowledge of public things.

If public lands, like public things in Honig's argument, subjectivise democratic thought, it is the struggle, from precarity, to performatively produce land as public that can challenge the neoliberal threat to democracy. However, because state power produces the subaltern in relation to itself, any effort to ally with the state comes from a compromised starting point and is easily taken as an implicit agreement of how the state operates in regard to

[95] See Gill-Pedro's chapter in this collection.

land. The democratically subjectivising knowledge of the precariat may be lost. Yet, in the process, it may help create a democratically oriented auto-cephalous sovereign that can then exercise its democratic principles on the heterocephalous stage. The acephalous sovereign is at once decapitated and capable of producing democratic conditions.

7

Claiming Human Rights: The Reflexive Identity of the People

Eduardo Gill-Pedro

Introduction

In this chapter, I try to discern the shape of a phantom.[1] The phantom is the people in a democracy. The first argument which will be put forward is that democracy cannot exist without such a phantom. But this phantasmagorical presence of the people in society can threaten the very democracy which it makes possible in two ways. First, the phantom can prove to be no more than that – a mere figment of the imagination, a fantasy without any substance. If that were the case, then any claim that law could be legitimated as popular rule would be a fraud. Second, the phantom could acquire a concrete existence in society. As any reader of ghost stories will know, where a ghost becomes flesh, becomes incarnated in the land of the living, things do not turn out well for those affected.

There is another fate possible for this phantom. Drawing on the theory of Claude Lefort, I will set out how the people can remain in the transcendental realm, and act as a symbol, a symbol to which all can refer, but no one can possess. It is only when the people is so understood that democracy is possible. The second argument which will be put forward in this chapter is that the conditions which allow this phantom to stay in this state, and neither dissolve into a mirage nor be incarnated into society, are human rights.

The role of human rights in precluding the incarnation of the people, and at protecting individuals from being crushed by the incarnation of the people in society is widely accepted. Human rights are traditionally seen as entitlements which individuals have against popular rule, against power exercised in the name of the collective subject, and which protect individuals from being

---

[1] This chapter builds on and develops research which I conducted for my doctoral thesis, subsequently published as Eduardo Gill-Pedro, *EU Law, Fundamental Rights and National Democracy* (Abingdon: Routledge, 2019).

sacrificed for what is claimed to be the greater good. But in this chapter, I will focus on another aspect of the role of human rights – the role they play in preventing the phantom of the people from dissolving into mirage, in making possible the symbolic existence of the people as constituent power.

These arguments draw primarily on three political theorists. Claude Lefort, whose image of the empty place of power is essential if we are to understand how democracy can exist in a pluralist society, Hans Lindahl, whose understanding of the reflexive identity of the people allows us to develop an ontology of the people which comes into being through the mode of questioning, and Jacques Rancière, whose understanding of the rights of man allows us to see them as symbolically inscribed in the political community, and not in the individuals who bear them.

Democracy and the Empty Place of Power

The starting point for the first argument is that law claims legitimacy as democratic law, and such a claim has some possibility of being valid. Such a claim presupposes the existence of 'the People', because the nature of the claim is that law in some way emanates from the people, or represents the will of the people, or is in some other way under the control of the people. For the claim of legitimacy to make sense, it must refer to the people as a unity. This is because such a claim must refer to a legal order[2] within which the validity of any particular norm can be determined.

However, as Lefort observed, with the advent of modernity there is no longer any pole within which the sphere of law, the sphere of power and the sphere of knowledge can be condensed.[3] Power, previously to the advent of

---

[2] The presupposition that law constitutes an order is a fundamental element of both positivistic and non-positivistic theories of law. Kelsen's pure theory of law sees the legal system as a self-contained system, in that the validity of any particular norm can only be assessed by reference to another norm of the same legal system. See generally Hans Kelsen, *Introduction to the Problems of Legal Theory*, trans. Bonnie and Stanley Paulson (Oxford: Clarendon, 1992), pp 10–14. Tuori also sees law not only as a social practice, but as a normative order. Kaarlo Tuori, *Critical Legal Positivism* (Farnham: Ashgate, 2002), pp 121–127. Hart conceives of law as union of primary and secondary rules – the application of secondary rules, in particular the rule of recognition – allows for the conclusive identification of primary rules of obligation. H.L.A. Hart. *The Concept of Law* (Oxford: Oxford University Press, 1961), p. 95. Non-positivists such as Dworkin also presuppose law as a unity – famously as a unity characterised by its integrity, which requires legal officials to approach it as if it was created by a single author. See Ronald Dworkin, *Law's Empire* (Cambridge, MA: Harvard University Press, 1986), pp. 225–232.

[3] Claude Lefort, 'The Question of Democracy', in Claude Lefort, *Democracy and Political Theory*, trans. David Macey (Cambridge: Polity, 1988), pp. 9–20, at p. 17.

modernity, was embodied in the person of the King,[4] whose very body was the symbol for the unity of the kingdom. The advent of modernity brought about the dissolution of the markers of certainty and with it the disentanglement of power from knowledge and from right. With the King, who constituted the symbol of the unity of the kingdom, gone, there is no pole through which society can orient itself.

But while the body of the King is taken away, the place that is thus vacated remains, but it remains as an empty place. This empty place forms the stage in which conflicts and divisions in society can be acted out, and resolutions proposed. These conflicts and divisions, and their enactment in the political stage are the necessary and irreducible element of democracy.[5]

Democracy is presented as a form of society where it is no longer possible to assert the legitimacy of law by reference to any person or institution. Democracy instead:

> invites us to replace the notion of a legitimate law with the notion of a debate about what is legitimate and what is illegitimate, a debate which is necessarily without any guarantor and without any end.[6]

The Necessity of the People for Democracy

Where does 'the People' come into this picture, though? Andrew Arato claims that Lefort elides the people as any kind of presence in his understanding of democracy. The 'empty place of power' on this reading, is the space within which 'symbolic meta-norms that transcend the real can be located within a political model of legitimacy'.[7] Lefort is thus understood as proposing a notion of democracy that 'puts in doubt the notion of popular sovereignty' and which puts in place 'a scheme of plural legitimating possibilities rather than the monistic scheme of populism based on popular sovereignty and identification'. In fact, on Arato's reading 'all attempts to identify the people, and all claims of identity or unity of the people are, and can only be, usurpations of democracy'.[8]

This does not seem a very credible reading of Lefort. According to Lefort, democracy requires an understanding of the people as a unity, and it is not possible to separate democracy from popular rule, nor can democracy be

---

[4] Lefort relies extensively on the image of the King's two bodies. See in particular Claude Lefort, 'On the Permanence of the Theologico-Political', in Claude Lefort, *Democracy and Political Theory*, trans. David Macey (Cambridge: Polity, 1988), pp. 213–255.

[5] Lefort 'On the Permanence of the Theologico-Political', p. 227.

[6] Lefort 'The Question of Democracy', at p. 39.

[7] Andrew Arato, *Post Sovereign Constitution Making: Learning and Legitimacy* (Oxford: Oxford University Press, 2016), p. 277.

[8] Arato, *Post Sovereign Constitution Making*, p. 290.

concretised without the presence of 'the people' as the constituent power.[9] In his words:

> The people do indeed constitute a pole of identity which is sufficiently defined to indicate that it has the status of a subject. The people possess sovereignty, they are assumed to express its will, power is exercised in their name.[10]

I argue, contra Arato, that the people, as a unity capable of having a will, remains an ineluctable part of democracy as Lefort understands it. Such a people cannot exist as a collective subject, acting in society.[11] Nonetheless, it must exist as the symbol through which society can relate to itself. Indeed, as Lefort puts it, if the distinction between power as symbolic agency and power as real organ disappears then 'the authority of those who make public decisions vanishes, leaving only the spectacle of individuals or clans, whose one concern is to satisfy their lust for power'.[12] A society in which there is no people as a symbolic locus of power, where those who exercise power cannot claim to do so in the name of the people, but instead are 'exposed to the threat of appearing as individuals or groups concerned solely to satisfy their own desires',[13] such a society cannot claim to be democratic.

The Totalitarian Danger

In his exploration of democracy as a political form of society, Lefort contrasts democracy with another political form, which he termed 'totalitarianism'. This methodological choice allows Lefort to bring into starker relief what he considers to be the key feature of democracy.[14] From the point of view of this chapter, the most relevant such feature concerns the identity of

---

[9] Cf. von Bogdandy, who argues that '[t]he principle of democracy must be concretised independently from the concept of people. Armin von Bogdandy, 'Founding Principles', in Armin von Bogdandy and Jürgen Bast (eds), *Principles of European Constitutional Law*, 2nd edn. (Oxford: Hart, 2010), pp. 11–54, at p. 48.

[10] Lefort, 'On the Permanence of the Theologico-Political', p. 232

[11] See James Ingram, 'The Politics of Claude Lefort's Political: Between Liberalism and Radical Democracy', *Thesis Eleven* 87:1 (2006), pp. 33–50, at p 44.

[12] Lefort, 'On the Permanence of the Theologico-Political', p. 233. As Minkkinen points out in this volume, Lefort conceives of totalitarianism and democracy as political forms that 'share a kinship, but operate in diametrically opposite ways'. It is by highlighting these differences that Lefort is able to illuminate the way in which democracy operates.

[13] Claude Lefort. 'The Image of the Body and Totalitarianism', in Claude Lefort, *The Political Forms of Modern Society: Bureaucracy, Democracy, Totalitarianism,* trans. Alan Sheridan (Cambridge, MA: MIT Press, 1986), pp. 292–306, at p. 305.

[14] As Geenens puts it, reliance on this contrast allows Lefort to uncover the key characteristics of democracy '*ex negative.*' Raf Geenens 'Modernity Gone Awry: Lefort on Totalitarian and Democratic Self-representation', *Critical Horizons* 13:1 (2012), pp 74–93, at p. 76.

the people. In a totalitarian political form of society, 'the people' is wholly immanent in society. The locus of power is the image of the People-as-One[15] – there is a symbolic orientation of society towards the image of the people, and this people is imagined as identical with the state. Totalitarian thinking conceives of the people as being wholly immanent in society. Although Lefort does not explicitly engage with Carl Schmitt, one can see striking parallels between Lefort's presentation of the totalitarian form of political society and Schmitt's understanding of democracy. Because for Schmitt 'all democratic thinking rests on the idea of immanence and every departure from immanence would destroy the identity of the people'.[16] So for Schmitt, 'the people' as the constitution making power, is, and must be, always conceived as immanent within society. But not only is the people identical with the state, but the state is identical to the people – the state coincides with the people, and the people with the state which, according to Lefort, results in 'an impossible swallowing up of the body in the head [and] an impossible swallowing up of the head in the body'.[17] In other words, in a totalitarian political society, the constituent power of the people is identical with the constituted power of those who act in its name.

By contrast, in a democratic form of society, the identity of the people can never be immanent within society, but must always be latent.[18] The people exists, not as a concrete order present in society, but as the symbolic orientation through which society can relate to itself. This orientation is not towards something in society, embodied in a particular group, person or party, but as something that transcends that society. What we have in a democratic form of society is thus not a people who is present in that society, but conflicting claims to represent the people, claims which can never be definitely confirmed. Because if they are so confirmed, if any group, person or party is able to authoritatively claim to represent the people and to prevent anyone else from challenging that claim, democracy will end. As Chantal Mouffe emphasises, 'the democratic character of a society can only be based on the fact that no limited social actor can attribute to herself the representation of the totality and claim to have mastery of the foundation.'[19]

---

15 Claude Lefort. 'The Logic of Totalitarianism', in Claude Lefort, *The Political Forms of Modern Society: Bureaucracy, Democracy, Totalitarianism,* trans. Alan Sheridan (Cambridge, MA: MIT Press, 1986), pp. 283–291, at p. 287.

16 Carl Schmitt, *Constitutional Theory,* trans. Jeffrey Seitzer (Durham, NC: Duke University Press, 2008), p. 266.

17 Lefort, 'The Image of the Body and Totalitarianism', p. 302.

18 Lefort, 'On the Permanence of the Theologico-Political', p. 230.

19 Chantal Mouffe, *The Democratic Paradox* (London: Verso, 2000), p. 100.

So in this first part, I argued, with Lefort, that democracy requires the presence of a people, as the symbolic pole which orientates the democratic debate. However, this people cannot be conceived as immanent within society. In Bonnie Honig's memorable phrase 'the people are always unde-cidably present and absent from the scene of democracy'[20], present in that every claim to exercise legitimate power must claim it as emanating from the people, but absent in that no one person or social actor can claim to appropriate it.

Operationalising 'the people'

The methodological approach chosen by Lefort, which seeks to discern the characteristics of democracy by contrasting it with totalitarianism, results in a rather one-sided understanding of democracy as a political form of society. We are told what democracy is *not,* and great emphasis is placed on demonstrating the danger which totalitarianism entails for democracy, and how democracy can degenerate into totalitarianism.[21] The defining charac-teristic of democracy is, as discussed above, that the locus of power becomes an empty place. But what constitutes that empty place is not looked at in detail. As Lefort himself states, 'there is no need to dwell on the details of the institutional apparatus'[22], and nowhere in his work does Lefort set out in detail the implications of his theory of the empty place of power from an institutional point of view.[23]

This one-sidedness, and the focus on what democracy is not, has the effect of emphasising the danger that 'the people', when conceived in the image of the People-as-One, poses for democracy. So Lefort goes into some detail in showing how the image of the people can be a threat to democracy when it acquires totalising force, but does not spell out how the people, as the symbol of the unity of society, is an ineluctable part of democracy. What we are told is that the actual empirical society is riven with divisions, and the reference to an empty place 'implies a reference to a society without

---

20 Bonnie Honig, 'Between Decision and Deliberation: Political Paradox in Democratic Theory', *American Political Sciences Review* 101:1 (2007), pp 1–17, at p. 5.

21 The term which Lefort uses is 'mutation': 'modern totalitarianism arises from a political mutation, from a mutation of the symbolic order' Lefort 'The Question of Democracy', p. 12. Nonetheless, it is beyond doubt that he views this mutation in a negative light – Lefort is clearly 'on the side of democracy'. For a discussion of the normative commitments in Lefort's political philosophy, see Raf Geenens, 'Democracy, Human Rights and History: Reading Lefort', *European Journal of Political Theory* 7:3 (2008), pp. 268–286.

22 Lefort, 'The Question of Democracy', p. 17.

23 Geenens, 'Modernity Gone Awry', p. 88.

any positive determination, which cannot be represented by the figure of a community'.[24]

Therefore Lefort's theory of democracy requires that the people can function as a symbol in reference to which claims of legitimacy can be made, but such a people can never be conceived as having an actual existence in society, nor can such a people be represented in society by the figure of a community. This leaves open the question of how democracy functionalises that unity.[25] In the next section, I will set out how Lindahl proposes to address that question by an exploration of the reflexive identity of the people.

The Ontology of 'the people'

Lindahl begins his exploration by highlighting the distinction, which was first proposed by Heidegger, between the identity of a *thing*, which can only be established in terms of what it *is*, and the identity of a human being, which not only is, but is also reflexive, 'in that this being relates to itself as the one who acts and who ultimately is at stake in such acts.'[26] Lindahl then expands this understanding of the reflexive identity of a human being to be applicable also to the identity of collective beings. The identity of a collective being such as 'the People' is not like the identity of a thing, which *is,* but is more akin to the identity of a human being. The people is a being who relates to itself as the one who acts (collectively), and whose (collective) identity is at stake in such acts. Having set out the particular ontological nature of the collective person, Lindahl links it to Kelsen's basic norm. According to Lindahl:

> The basic norm offers the key to an ontology of collective selfhood: the collective self 'exists' in the form of self-attributive acts by individuals.[27]

These self-attributive acts are individual acts, which necessarily have to presuppose the existence of a collective. When individuals act in this way,

---

[24] Lefort, 'On the Permanence of the Theologico-Political', p. 226.

[25] Hans Lindahl, 'Democracy and the Symbolic Constitution of Society', *Ratio Juris* 17:1 (1998), pp 12–37, at p. 15. Lindahl seeks to address that question by taking, as his point of departure, the political and legal theory of Hans Kelsen. See in particular Hans Lindahl, 'Constituent Power and Reflexive Identity: Towards an Ontology of Collective Selfhood', in Martin Loughlin and Neil Walker (eds), *The Paradox of Constitutionalism* (Oxford: Oxford University Press, 2008), pp 10–22, at p. 12.

[26] Lindahl, 'Democracy and the Symbolic Constitution of Society', p. 15.

[27] Lindahl, 'Democracy and the Symbolic Constitution of Society', p. 19.

they do not attribute those acts to themselves as individuals, but to themselves as a collective: 'a "We" the existence of which is not simply a summation of a manifold of individual acts of attribution'.[28]

Lindahl goes on to analyse these acts of (collective) self-attribution in order to locate precisely where the ontology of the collective is made apparent. He identifies three elements which are crucial for there to be such self-attribution. The first element is the claim to act in the name of the collective. There must be an act by which someone 'seizes the initiative to determine what interests are shared by the collective and who belongs to it'.[29] But this claim, by itself, cannot bring into being the collective, because such a claim must already be presented as an act of representation. By claiming to act in the name of the collective, and to determine what interests are shared by it, the individual must necessarily refer to something which precedes that act. The initial claim must, therefore, be considered as an exercise of constituted power, rather than constituent power, because it entails an invocation of a people who would constitute the authority whom the person claims to represent.[30] The invocation of the people in the original act can only originate such a people by claiming to represent it.[31] Representation thus constitutes what it represents.[32]

This understanding of the ontology of the people appears to 'reveal a fundamental passivity at the heart of the political unity: instead of initiating, the collective is initiated by the act of constituent power'.[33] Indeed, if the person claiming to represent the people is able, by merely making the claim, to bring that people into existence, then any understanding of democracy as the power of the people would be a fraud – the people, in this understanding, would be a mere prop – a passive symbol to be used by those who claim to

---

[28] Lindahl, 'Constituent Power and Reflexive Identity', p. 20.

[29] Lindahl, 'Constituent Power and Reflexive Identity', p. 22.

[30] That is not to say that the claim to represent the people is an act which is *intended* to bring about the existence of the people. The claim of representation must presuppose the existence of the people, and therefore is an essential step in bringing about the existence of such a people. But those who exercise constituted power do not necessarily 'seek to bring about constituent power'. Cf. Lukkari's chapter in this volume.

[31] We can thus see that on this understanding, 'the people' cannot be seen as a concrete entity which, through its action, creates the constitutional order. The people is therefore not the cause, but rather 'the effect of the attempt to exercise joint control over what men and women perceive to be the situation of their life.' Alexander Somek, 'The Constituent Power in a National and Transnational Context', *Transnational Legal Theory* 3:1 (2012), pp 31–60, at p. 31.

[32] Matthias Lievens, 'From Government to Governance: A Symbolic Mutation and Its Repercussions for Democracy', *Political Studies* 63:1 suppl. (2015), pp. 2–16, at p. 3.

[33] Lindahl, 'Constituent Power and Reflexive Identity', p. 18.

act in its name. Lindahl rescues the people from its passivity by pointing out that this claim to initiate a collective only succeeds if the addressees of that claim 'retroactively identify themselves as member of a polity in constituent action'.[34] The claim to act on behalf of the political community 'always comes too soon', because such a claim can never 'reveal a people immediately present to itself as a collective subject'.[35] Instead, this claim opens up the possibility for the political community to reveal itself retroactively.

Lindahl's ontology of the people provides us with two important ingredients. First, it conceives of the people as a unity capable of action, which is not merely the action of several individuals, but is the action of one community, a community which has the capacity of being the author of the legal order. This ontology of the people provides us, therefore, with an understanding of constituent power which can never be reduced to pure decision that emanates from nothingness. Second, it provides us with an ontology of the people that does not rely on that community as a unified, monolithic, concrete order, immanent within the social space, but instead allows for the fact that sociologically, there is great plurality, diversity and disagreement between the members of the actual community of persons that are claimed to be 'the people'. Indeed, the very act of representation establishes a gap between 'the people' as the transcendental, symbolic locus of constituent power, and the society which is given meaning by it. This gap prevents any one person, group or party to claim authoritatively and unilaterally that they represent the people. Any such claim depends on the putative people, in whose name the constituent power was exercised, to 'retroactively identify themselves' as a community with the capacity and the will to act.[36]

Reflexive Identity not as Recognition but as Questioning

The exploration of the ontology of the people set out above showed that in order for the people to come into being there must be a claim to represent the people and the retroactive identification of a people as being represented in that claim. This would seem to imply that the key to the ontology of the people is the recognition, by the addressees of the claim to represent, that they are being represented by the one making the claim. By recognising the claim

---

[34] Lindahl, 'Constituent Power and Reflexive Identity', p. 19.

[35] Lindahl, 'Constituent Power and Reflexive Identity', p. 18.

[36] As Lindahl puts it, in the context of the European Union: 'Europe is not simply at the disposition of the constituent powers that claim to represent it in the process of attributing legislation to the European Union.' So the claim to represent cannot entail a reproduction, or copy, of the original. Hans Lindahl, 'The Paradox of Constituent Power: The Ambiguous Self-Constitution of the EU', *Ratio Juris* 20:4 (2017), pp. 485–505, at p. 496.

to act on their behalf as binding on them, the people as subjects of law identify themselves as part of the people who is the author of the law. Lindahl himself seems to suggest this, in the context of the EU, where he states that:

> By invoking direct effect, individuals do not attribute the Treaty to a collective from a third person perspective; they attribute it to themselves in the first person plural, understanding their acts as part and parcel of the ongoing process whereby a "We" gives shape to a common market.[37]

There is something problematic about an understanding of 'the people' which bases the identification of the people on recognition, by the addressees of the claim of representation, that they are being represented by the one making the claim. Such an understanding would bring the constituent power of the people into the social space. The people would no longer be a symbolic pole which transcended society but would be an identifiable entity, immanent within the social space, who would, by their acceptance of the claim to represent them, have the power to authoritatively determine who the people is and what the people wants. Lefort's understanding of the symbolical nature of the political rejects an understanding of politics which reduces it to a 'particular set of facts circumscribed within a particular social sphere'.[38]

Furthermore, the mere acceptance by an individual of what is given by the person making the claim is not enough to show that reflexive identification has taken place. So to use Lindahl's EU example of the invocation of direct effect, it may well be that an individual may take advantage of the opportunities that are provided by the EU Treaties and claim directly effective rights granted by those Treaties, without necessarily seeing herself as someone who is part of some putative 'European people'. Similarly, mere compliance with the strictures imposed by the EU Treaties does not entail a recognition of the EU as constituting a community of which one is a part.[39] There are many reasons why people may view a particular law as binding on them which do not entail the acceptance that they constitute a political community.

So rather than reducing reflexive identity to the act of recognition, I propose to explore a point made by Lindahl: 'individuals retroactively identify themselves as a member of a polity in constituent action by exercising the powers granted to them by the constitution.'[40] In this reading, reflexive

---

[37] Lindahl, 'The Paradox of Constituent Power', p. 498.

[38] Lievens, 'From Government to Governance', p. 4.

[39] There are particular difficulties in applying this understanding of reflexive identity in the context of the EU, in particular the fact that the EU, as a multi-level polity, claims authority over the member states, rather than the citizens. For an overview of this difficulty, see Gill-Pedro, *EU Law, Fundamental Rights and National Democracy*.

[40] Lindahl, 'Constituent Power and Reflexive Identity', p. 19.

identity is not an act of acceptance, or of recognition – of taking what one is given – but is instead an exercise of power. This raises the question of what form that exercise of power takes, and how such an exercise of power may allow individuals to reflexively identify themselves as members of the polity. Lindahl does not provide us with an answer to this question, but he makes a suggestion that may be helpful when he states that 'the collective self exists in the modes of *questionability* and, by way of its acts, of *responsiveness.*'[41]

This indicates that the powers which allow individuals to identify themselves as members of the collective self are powers to respond to and to question the claim to represent that collective self. I argue that the key is not acceptance, nor recognition, but questioning. It is when the addressees of a claim to act on behalf of a collective self exercise their powers to respond, to question and to challenge that claim, that they reflexively identify themselves as members of that collective self. In the next, final section, I argue that such a questioning always entails a claim to human rights.

Human Rights and the Identity of the People

Lefort insists that human rights are 'indissociable from the birth of the democratic debate.'[42] They sustain and make possible that democratic debate, and whenever they are threatened, democracy is threatened.[43] However, Lefort does not specify how human rights are connected to the birth of the democratic debate, neither does he elaborate on the nature of the connection between the subject of the rights and the political community.[44] The argument I make here is that this connection is to be found in the act of claiming human rights – it is this act that makes possible the reflexive identity of the people.

As set out above, Lindahl observed that it is when individuals exercise the 'powers granted to them by the constitution'[45] that they are able to retroactively identify themselves as members of the political community. The act of claiming human rights is such 'an exercise of powers granted to individuals by the constitution'. Note that it is an exercise of power, not an enjoyment of a right, which is the key. As I set out above, mere acceptance does not entail identification, and human rights are not 'legal goods' which are 'rationed

[41] Lindahl, 'Constituent Power and Reflexive Identity', p. 21
[42] Lefort, 'The Question of Democracy', p. 18.
[43] Lefort, 'The Question of Democracy', p. 18.
[44] Mark Blackwell, 'Lefort and the Problem of Democratic Citizenship', *Thesis Eleven* 87:1 (2006), pp. 51–62.
[45] Lindahl. 'Constituent Power and Reflexive Identity', p. 19.

and allocated to the subject as the state sees fit'.[46] Merely demanding the allocation of a particular good by a power who claims to act in the name of the people does not necessarily acknowledge that such a people exist. The act of claiming human rights, on the other hand, is an intrinsically political act and necessarily presupposes the existence of a political community. This is because of the particular nature of human rights as legal norms.

As Lefort emphasised, human rights are inextricably connected to the political. Lefort rejects an understanding of human rights which sees them as protecting private interests against the state.[47] Lefort explicitly addressed Marx's criticism of the rights of man as 'the rights of egoistic man, of man separated from other men and from the community'[48] by insisting that human rights, in their symbolic dimension, are 'a constitutive element of political society'.[49] In order to explore how human rights may operate in their symbolic dimension, I rely on the thought of Jacques Rancière, who states that the rights of man:

> are inscriptions of the community as free and equal . . . Even though actual situations of rightlessness may give them the lie, they are not only an abstract ideal, situated far from the givens of a situation. They are also part of the configuration of the given. What is given is not only a situation of inequality, it is also an inscription, a form of visibility of equality.[50]

---

[46] Ingeborg Maus, 'On Liberties and Popular Sovereignty: Jürgen Habermas' Reconstruction of a System of Rights', *Cardozo Law Review* 17:1 (1996), pp. 825–882, at p. 852–853. This point is echoed by Lefort, who emphasises that 'human rights would no longer count for anything if the authority of the state were measured solely on its ability to enable . . . and if its citizens' demands were reducible to a demand for well-being'. Claude Lefort, 'Human Rights and the Welfare State', in Claude Lefort, *Democracy and Political Theory*, trans. David Macey (London: Polity, 1998), pp. 21–44, at p. 23.

[47] Claude Lefort, 'Politics and Human Rights', in Claude Lefort, *The Political Forms of Modern Society: Bureaucracy, Democracy, Totalitarianism*, trans. Alan Sheridan, (Cambridge, MA: MIT Press, 1986), pp. 239–272, at p. 245.

[48] Karl Marx, 'On the Jewish Question' [1843], in Robert Tucker (ed.), *The Marx-Engels Reader*, 2nd edn. (New York: Norton & Company, 1978), pp. 26–52, at p. 43.

[49] Lefort, 'Politics and Human Rights', p. 259. Not everyone found Lefort's rebuttal of Marx persuasive. Shortly after the publication of 'Politics and Human Rights', Marcel Gauchet and Pierre Manent, two French thinkers and Lefort's contemporaries, both launched critiques of Lefort's understanding of rights, which they see as underestimating the capacity of rights to atomise society and deprive the political of its vital force. For a discussion of these critiques, see Justine Lacroix, 'A Democracy Without a People? The 'Rights of Man' in French Contemporary Political Thought', *Political Studies* 61:3 (2013), pp. 676–690. For a very recent reaffirmation of Marx's critique of the role of rights in reinforcing forms of domination, see Christian Boonen, 'Limits to the Politics of Subjective Rights: Reading Marx After Lefort', *Law and Critique* 30:2 (2019), pp 179–199.

[50] Jacques Rancière, 'Who Is the Subject of the Rights of Man?', *The South Atlantic Quarterly* 103:2 (2004), pp. 297–310, at p. 303.

This allows us to see human rights as a symbolic inscription that is part of the 'configuration of the given' whenever a claim of authority is made. To return to the investigation into the nature of reflexive identification sketched out above, we know that reflexive identification requires a claim to represent the people. More precisely, a claim of authority is made which bases its purported legitimacy on the people. But we know that the mere making of such a claim, while necessary, is not sufficient. The truth of such a claim cannot be verified by reference to any particular social fact, such as the fact that it was made by a particular person, party, or group, or that it is supported by any particular section in society. In a democracy, the people cannot be seen as immanent within society, so the claimed legitimacy cannot be grounded on the immanent authority of the person or institution who makes it. Neither it is sufficient that those over whom the claim is made accept that claim.

It is instead, as Lefort insists:

> the very fact that every single individual over whom that authority is claimed has the right to reject that claim, and denounce it as hollow and wrong, which gives any claim of authority democratic legitimacy.[51]

The possibility to claim democratic legitimacy, that is to say, to claim authority in the name of the people, rests on the possibility of those over whom that authority is claimed, to challenge it.[52]

The argument which is put forward in this chapter is that this act of challenging a claim of authority, when done as a claim to human rights, is the act which constitutes the people as the symbolic reference on which the democratic legitimacy of the legal order can be claimed. This argument needs to be broken down somewhat. First, the argument implies a political conception of human rights, which sees them as norms which 'protect those interests tied to equal political membership'[53] of that collective. As Rancière points out, human rights are 'inscriptions of the community', so they are not something which the individual carries with them, but they are something which is (potentially) already inscribed in the social space in which the individual claims them, as a symbolic representation of a 'people' which transcends that social space. Second, and closely related, the act of claiming human rights is not a complaint that one has not been given what one is entitled to as an individual, or as member of a particular group or class. Rather, the act

---

[51] Lefort, 'Human Rights and the Welfare State', at p. 41.

[52] As Lukkari points out in her chapter in this volume, for 'the people' as a collective entity to have meaning and to be able to act politically, it needs 'staging'.

[53] Samantha Besson, 'Human Rights and Democracy in a Global Context: Decoupling and Recoupling', *Ethics & Global Politics* 4:1 (2011), pp. 19–50, at p. 23.

of claiming human rights entails a claim that one has not been treated as an equal member of the political community. Claiming human rights is a political act because it requires us to see ourselves as (potential) members of a community of free and equals, and rejecting a claim of authority that fails to acknowledge us as such.

This challenge is the act which inaugurates the debate which constitutes democracy. Lefort observed that 'democracy invites us to replace the notion of a legitimate law with a debate about what is and what is not legitimate'.[54] The act of challenging the claim to represent the community,[55] on the grounds that the act was not a true representation of the will of that community, or that if failed to take into account the interests of all those who should count as members of the community, initiates that debate, and therefore makes it necessary for those who participate in that debate to reflexively identify with the community whose identity and interests are the subject of contestation.[56]

Such a community can never be grasped as a unity by any one person or institution. The symbolic location of political power means that the political subjects 'are not definite collectives' but are 'names that set out a question or dispute about who is included in their count'[57] and:

> Freedom and equality are not predicates belonging to definite subjects. They open up a dispute about what they exactly entail and whom they concern in which cases.[58]

But on the other hand, the dispute which is opened up is about the identity of the people – whatever freedom and equality entail, and whomever they may concern, they relate to freedom and equality as a member of a community, not as a merely private individual. The disputes that are opened up, and the divisions that they reflect, refer to one community. We can only understand the concept of social divisions if we see them as divisions within one and the same society.[59]

---

[54] Lefort, 'Human Rights and the Welfare State', p. 39.

[55] And this again reminds us of the need for conceiving of the legal order as a unity – the addressee of the law can only challenge the claim of authority which the law makes by reference to the unity which that claim seeks to represent.

[56] The initial seizure of the initiative can never initiate a debate, because a debate requires more than one party: it is only when that initial claim is challenged that there is possibility of a debate. The etymology of the very word 'debate', from the Old French *debatre*, implies a fight or contestation.

[57] Rancière, 'Who Is the Subject of the Rights of Man?', p. 303.

[58] Rancière, 'Who Is the Subject of the Rights of Man?', p. 303.

[59] Lindahl, 'Democracy and the Symbolic Constitution of Society', p. 15.

The Act of Claiming Human Rights and Constituent Power

We can now return to the phantom simile. The argument is that the people is a phantom which is brought into being, as a transcendental entity, by the act of claiming human rights. It is those who claim that they are not recognised as equal members of the community who have the power to bring into being that community, as a democratic community. Popular rule is, to appropriate Rancière, 'not the power of the population or of the majority, but the power of anyone at all, the equality of capabilities to occupy the positions of governors and of the governed.'[60]

This is the 'scandal of democracy'. That the constituent power that may give meaning to any claim of popular rule resides with those who have no titles or qualifications to exercise it, those whose very status as an equal of the ones claiming authority is denied.[61] Because human rights, as Rancière again points out, are 'the rights of those who have not the rights that they have and have the rights that they have not'.[62] The power to claim human rights can only be exercised by those who are denied the rights that they have.[63]

And the power to claim human rights is constituent power, in that it constitutes the people as a transcendental entity, which is simultaneously capable of symbolising the unity of society and providing a locus through which society can identify with itself while preventing that unity from manifesting itself with totalising force.

To clarify, the argument which is advanced in this chapter is not that those whose rights are denied are the 'true people'. To repeat the point made by Honig, the people must be undecidably present *and* absent from the scene of democracy.[64] What the act of claiming human rights allows is for the addressees of claims of authority to reflexively identify themselves with the 'absent presence'[65] of a people who would be able to ground such a claim of authority. The possibility for those who claim the authority to do so on the basis of democratic legitimacy depends on those whose rights they deny.

[60] Jacques Rancière, *Hatred of Democracy*, trans. Steve Corcoran (London: Verso, 2006), p. 49.
[61] Rancière describes popular sovereignty as 'a way of including democratic excess . . . the government of those who are not entitled to govern'. Rancière, *Hatred of Democracy*, p. 76.
[62] Rancière, 'Who Is the Subject of the Rights of Man?', p. 302.
[63] As Minkkinen points out in his chapter to this volume, Lefort's understanding of rights emphasises their 'contestability'. Any demand for a right will only be successful if such a demand can be seen as conforming with existing rights, and such a matter will inevitably be contested and must therefore be a subject for the democratic debate.
[64] Honig, 'Between Decision and Deliberation', p. 5.
[65] In the felicitous phrase which Blackwell, echoing Honig, employs. Blackwell, 'Lefort and the Problem of Democratic Citizenship', p. 57.

Such an act requires a certain attitude on the part of those who carry it out. As already noted, Lindahl insists that 'the collective self exists in the modes of *questionability* and, by way of its acts, of *responsiveness*.'[66] I interpret this as implying that the act of claiming human rights must be undertaken as a response to the claim to represent the people, and must question the truth of that claim. But it must respond in a specific way, which carries with it an acceptance of the possibility that there is a 'people' who could be represented. Remember that the act of claiming human rights is the demand to be recognised as an equal member of the political community. If the addressee of the claim of authority does not respond to the claim as made, but instead denies that there is a political community that could legitimise such a claim, or who responds merely in terms of her or his personal interests, then the act is not one of claiming human rights.

Such an understanding of human rights and of democracy places a great responsibility on the addressees of claims of authority.[67] They must first question claims of authority, which deny their equal status as members of the putative people in whose name such authority is claimed. If they fail to do so, and if they unquestionably accept the truth of claims to represent the people, then the locus of power will no longer be an empty place – the phantom of the 'people' will become incarnate in society, and democracy will be no more.

But on the other hand, if those addressees do not respond to the claim of authority by reference to the people, but seek merely to protect their own private interests, then the phantom of the people will remain mere illusion, a mere will-o'-the-wisp which those with power can use to mislead the populace, and any understanding of 'popular rule' or of 'the people' as constituent power will remain impossible.

---

[66] Lindahl, 'Constituent Power and Reflexive Identity', p. 43 (emphasis in the original).

[67] And this argument chimes perhaps with Honig's point that, ultimately, it is the decision to accept or reject the legitimacy of the lawgiver that the people determine who they are and form themselves into the particular people they are and are to be. Honig, 'Between Decision and Deliberation', p. 6.

Part 3

Democracy and Populism

8

Katechontic Democracy? Carl Schmitt and the Restraining Mediation of Popular Power

Hjalmar Falk

Introduction: the Crisis of Democratic Capitalism

The observation that democracy is under stress is in itself not new. We have been hearing about the 'hollowing' of Western democracy for years,[1] and it has long been suggested that we have moved into a state of 'post-democracy'.[2] The condition, however, is clearly worsening. In the words of Wolfgang Streeck, we have entered into a 'delayed crisis of democratic capitalism'.[3] The diverging paths of economic and social forces are tearing at the post-war political compact that up until a decade ago was promising a post-historical steady state. These strains, increasingly violent, seem to be threatening the compromise that came to rule Western states following World War II. While this has led Streeck himself to raise questions regarding an impending end of capitalism, an astute critic has asked if what Streeck is describing is not rather the end of *democratic* capitalism.[4]

The populist explosion of 2016 and the unceasing waves following it seem to confirm fears that liberal democracy is coming apart at the seams and that we are facing a clash of illiberal democracy and undemocratic liberalism.[5] In the words of William Davies, 'politics is being reenchanted' in reaction to

[1] Peter Mair, *Ruling the Void. The Hollowing of Western Democracy* (London: Verso, 2013).

[2] Colin Crouch, *Post-Democracy* (Cambridge: Polity, 2004).

[3] Wolfgang Streeck, *Buying Time. The Delayed Crisis of Democratic Capitalism* (London: Verso, 2017).

[4] Jerome Roos, 'From the Demise of Social Democracy to the "End of Capitalism": The Intellectual Trajectory of Wolfgang Streeck', *Historical Materialism*, 27:2 (2019), pp. 248–288.

[5] Yascha Mounk, *The People vs. Democracy: Why Our Freedom is in Danger and How to Save It* (Cambridge, MA: Harvard University Press, 2018). For further examples of this line of argument, see Patrick J. Deneen, *Why Liberalism Failed* (New Haven, CT: Yale University Press, 2018) and Roger Eatwell and Matthew Goodwin, *National Populism. The Revolt Against Liberal Democracy* (London: Penguin, 2018).

neoliberalism's 'disenchantment of politics by economics' and the 'intoxication of popular power and of demagoguery is being experienced in visceral ways for the first time since 1968, or possibly longer'.[6] This reenchantment of politics has given rise not only to fears but also to hopes of a possibility for deeper democratisation, following the crisis of neoliberal hegemony. However, as the number of newly published books dedicated to discussion of an 'end' or the 'death' of democracy indicates,[7] the crisis has undoubtedly also given rise to a widespread political apocalypticism. The dissolution of the knot holding liberal democracy together is often envisaged as leaving us with the stark choice between neoliberal technocracy and demotic populism, both inherently non-democratic. In this chapter, I will argue that the current crisis and ongoing transformation of democracy concerns something more fundamental than the perceived conflict between technocracy and populism as forms of rule, namely the mediation of popular power within existing political systems.

This will be illustrated through a discussion of the theory of democracy developed by Carl Schmitt, together with aspects of his political theology. Schmitt has of late become an important point of reference in the discussion on populism and technocracy. My concern here is not the theoretical or political rehabilitation of Schmitt as a theorist or democrat, but rather the ominous implications of his thought for our contemporary predicament. At the centre of the discussion will be a politico-theological motif, the *katechon*. The *katechon* is a Biblical figure, often translated and viewed as 'the restrainer' holding back the advent of the Antichrist and, thereby, the end of days. Its implications for an understanding of contemporary democracy and the problem of mediation of political power may not be self-evident, but that is the overarching objective of this chapter to show. What is at stake here is therefore not the normative conception of terms like democracy or populism and their potential interrelation.[8] Rather, I want to make the case for using the concept of a *katechontic* democracy, in a Schmittian vein, to understand current developments concerning democracy as a state form.

[6] William Davies, *The Limits of Neoliberalism. Authority, Sovereignty and the Logic of Competition*, rev. edn. (London: Sage, 2016), p. xx.

[7] For recent prominent examples, see Steven Levitsky and Daniel Ziblatt, *How Democracies Die* (New York: Broadway Books, 2018) and David Runciman, *How Democracy Ends* (London: Profile Books, 2018). See also the overview of an emerging field in Tom Gerald Daly, 'Democratic Decay: Conceptualising an Emerging Research Field', *Hague Journal on the Rule of Law* 11:1 (2019), pp. 9–36.

[8] For an enlightening discussion of dominant tendencies in current populism research, see Vergara's chapter in this volume.

In what follows, I will continue by examining two seemingly contradict-ing appeals to Schmitt's relevance for understanding the state of democracy in our so-called 'populist moment'.[9] Then, I go on to outline what Schmitt's *katechontism* consists in. After that, I turn to Schmitt's theory of modern democracy and its *katechontic* framing of the mediation of popular power. Finally, I discuss the resonance of Schmitt's thought with the contempo-rary problems concerning the mediation of popular power in contemporary European politics.

Carl Schmitt and the Populist Moment

Schmitt's resonance with contemporary challenges to liberal democracy can be illustrated with the help of two recent influential interpretations of his thought. These are particularly interesting since they, at first sight, seem to contradict each other by both, in turn, placing him on opposite sides of the perceived divide between authoritarian populism and neoliberal technocracy. Yet, both highlight important aspects of Schmitt's theory of democracy and place him firmly in the midst of the populist moment.

The first of these two examples of Schmitt being used as a tool for grasp-ing contemporary political challenges can be found in Jan-Werner Müller's *What is Populism?*. To Müller, populism represents an anti-elitist and anti-pluralist moralistic imagination of politics.[10] It formulates a sort of identity politics based on the idea of a unified, moral, 'ultimately fictional' people.[11] Populism is growing today, Müller suggests, by feeding on the discontent with the depoliticised, delegitimised technocratic rule of elites that has come to characterise Western democracies during the last few decades.[12] Against this order, populists claim to speak the public's mind and to represent the true will of the people.

Populists may invoke the popular will, but in their version the people is always vague and 'out there', uninstitutionalised, and in Müller's words a 'purely symbolic unity'.[13] And it is here we can see where Schmitt comes into the picture: 'This notion of the people was influentially theorised by the right-wing legal theorist Carl Schmitt during the interwar period'.[14] It then

---

[9] This term is borrowed from Chantal Mouffe, *For a Left Populism* (London: Verso, 2018), as a suitable description of our current predicament.

[10] Jan-Werner Müller, *What is Populism?* (Philadelphia: University of Pennsylvania Press, 2016), p. 19.

[11] Müller, *What is Populism?*, p. 20.

[12] Müller, *What is Populism?*, p. 96.

[13] Müller, *What is Populism?*, p. 27.

[14] Müller, *What is Populism?*, p. 27.

served as a 'conceptual bridge from democracy to nondemocracy', laying the basis for an identitarian claim that 'fascism could more faithfully realise and instantiate democratic ideals than democracy itself'.[15] The populist claim to represent is, therefore '[m]ore *Volksgeist*, if you like, than *volonté générale*'.[16] Müller claims that this is true for Schmitt as well. His emphasis on the shared identity between ruler and ruled as a cornerstone of democracy is an example of this, not least since Schmitt claims that this identity is primary and more decisive than any actual outcomes of elections or opinion surveys in determining the people's will.[17] To Müller, then, Schmitt can be seen as a spiritual forebear or an intellectual expression of the same logic as contemporary populist movements, who grow out of their confrontation with the technocratic rule of the current global neoliberal regime.

A sharply contrasting perspective can be found in the work of Wolfgang Streeck, already mentioned above. In an essay bearing the title 'Heller, Schmitt and the Euro', Streeck describes an essentially neoliberal state structure on the European level, institutionalised in the Eurozone, as reminiscent of the 'authoritarian state' theorised by Schmitt – understood as building on an 'authoritarian liberalism', in terms borrowed from Schmitt's contemporary and critic Hermann Heller – during the last crisis-ridden phase of the Weimar Republic.[18] According to Schmitt's analysis, Weimar democracy had weakened the state and its pluralism had opened up the state institutions for infiltration by particular social interests – primarily, Streeck points out, the worker's movement.[19] In effect, Weimar democracy had become a 'total state' that intervened in all social sectors, but it was 'totalitarian out of weakness', since it was guided by organised particular special interest groups. The point of Schmitt's authoritarian state was to acquire the strength with which it could suppress social intervention in for instance the economy, thereby protecting private property from claims for redistribution, and not least guarantee its own basic integrity. The leading principle was, as the title of one of Schmitt's lectures from the time reads, 'strong state and sound economy'.[20]

The common ground between Schmitt's ideas and the fundaments of our contemporary neoliberal order consists in 'the insulation of a politically

---

[15] Müller, *What is Populism?*, p. 28.

[16] Müller, *What is Populism?*, p. 29.

[17] Müller, *What is Populism?*, pp. 52–53.

[18] Wolfgang Streeck, 'Heller, Schmitt and the Euro', in Wolfgang Streeck, *How Will Capitalism End?* (London: Verson: 2016), pp. 151–163.

[19] Streeck, 'Heller, Schmitt and the Euro', p. 151.

[20] Carl Schmitt, 'Strong State and Sound Economy: An Address to Business Leaders', in Renato Cristi, *Carl Schmitt and Authoritarian Liberalism: Strong State, Free Economy* (Cardiff: University of Wales Press, 1998), pp. 212–230.

instituted market economy from democratic politics'.[21] The authoritarian language favoured by Schmitt may have fallen 'out of fashion in today's Europe' to be replaced by technocratic claims of 'superior expertise', but the effect and intent is similar.[22] The juridical structure of the EU and the Eurozone functions as a shield against popular appeals for social justice and economic control, but the loss of the latter was in part a conscious handing over of power to 'an institutional context which was designed to not be suitable for democratisation'.[23] In the very structure of transnational experts and economic forces that make up the European technocratic elite, the prime target of Müller's Schmittian populists, Streeck, therefore, sees the realisation of the Schmittian model for the modern state – or 'the strong total state'.

Perhaps quite surprisingly, both Müller and Streeck are correct in identifying central elements of Schmitt's theory of the modern state. In fact, it is rather in the meeting of these two descriptions that the proper character of the Schmittian democratic state becomes visible. Müller is on to something when he notes that the two supposed 'arch rivals' of technocracy and populism 'mirror each other' in their common tendency towards depoliticisation.[24] In neither case, conflict and antagonism within the political unit is accepted, nor do they show any understanding for internal dissensus.[25] This is, of course, Schmitt's basic position: conflict must be externalised; enmity must not appear within the political unit. Still, this only explains a very general feature of Schmittian thought regarding political order, not how both Müller's and Streeck's partial descriptions are brought together within Schmitt's seemingly contradictory theory of democracy through its *katechontic* structure.

The *Katechon* and the Politics of Avertive Apocalypticism

The *katechon*, generally translated as 'the restrainer' or 'that which restrains', is a figure first mentioned by St Paul in the Second Letter to the Thessalonians. There, the *katechon* is described first as an impersonal force and then as a masculine person, as a force or person restraining 'lawlessness' and 'the

---

[21] Streeck, 'Heller, Schmitt and the Euro', p. 155. Schmitt's relationship with the intellectual sources of contemporary neoliberalism is complicated. For an enlightening discussion, see Quinn Slobodian, *Globalists. The End of Empire and the Birth of Neoliberalism* (Cambridge, MA: Harvard University Press, 2018), pp. 10, 115, and 206.

[22] Streeck, 'Heller, Schmitt and the Euro', p. 156.

[23] Streeck, 'Heller, Schmitt and the Euro', p. 156.

[24] Müller, *What is Populism?*, p. 97.

[25] Müller, *What is Populism?*, p. 97.

lawless one' respectively (2 Thess. 2: 6–7). St Augustine concluded that the figure of the *katechon* was obscure and that Paul's intention with this passage had been lost. It has nevertheless made a politico-theological mark as an artefact of Christian tradition. The standard interpretation identifies 'the lawless one' with the Antichrist, and several among the church fathers came to interpret the restraining force as the Roman Empire, an interpretation strengthened by the Edict of Milan and the Christianisation of the empire and one that can be found among some of the Church Fathers, particularly Tertullian.[26]

According to this interpretation, the *katechon* holds back the coming of the Antichrist, but this act of restraining also holds back the events that will lead on to the end times and thereby the Second Coming. It thus becomes a figure invested with great eschatological importance, though its way of relating to the Last Judgement is non-Messianic. The figure of the restrainer represents a very different type of apocalyptical figure than the Millenarian 'hastener' of the end times. During the Reformation, the identification between empire and the *katechon* was challenged, not least by Calvin, after which it disappeared from learned discussions. Schmitt has been described as the most important modern representative of a 'stateaffirming' understanding of this piece of political theology, in contrast to another, less influential 'statecritical' tradition.[27]

A series of critical writings have emphasised the importance of the *katechon* for understanding Schmitt's authoritarian conception of order and its implications for his antisemitism, decisionism, imperialism and the gnostic tendencies of his theology.[28] These features of Schmitt's thought are thus, in this reading, connected to the apocalyptic tone of his writings, and apocalypticism is

[26] For a discussion of the traditional reading of the *katechon* and Schmitt's use of it, see Felix Grossheutschi, *Carl Schmitt und die Lehre vom Katechon* (Berlin: Duncker & Humblot, 1996). See also Marc de Wilde, 'Politics Between Times: Theologico-Political Interpretations of the Restraining Force (*katechon*) in Paul's Second Letter to the Thessalonians', in Ward Blanton and Hent de Vries (eds.), *Paul and the Philosophers* (New York: Fordham University Press, 2013), pp. 105–126.

[27] de Wilde, 'Politics Between Times', p. 106.

[28] For a discussion of Schmitt's concept of the *katechon* that summarises this line of reception and reads it through the lens of German imperialism, see Julia Hell, 'Katechon: Carl Schmitt's Imperial Theology and the Ruins of the Future', *The Germanic Review*, 84:4 (2009), pp. 283–326. For a sharply contrasting perspective, see Michele Nicoletti, 'Religion and Empire: Carl Schmitt's *Katechon* between International Relations and the Philosophy of History', in Martti Koskenniemi, Mónica Gárcia-Salmones Rovira, and Paolo Amoroso (eds.), *International Law and Religion: Historical and Contemporary Perspectives* (Oxford: Oxford University Press, 2017), pp. 363–379.

traditionally often understood as inherently associated with radical and extrem-ist politics, and with the intent of 'hastening' the end.[29]

However, as some contemporary scholars of apocalyptic imagery and movements have noted, 'avertive apocalypticism' is a powerful strain in West-ern eschatological traditions.[30] Schmittian *katechontism* can be viewed as a specific political expression of this strain. In a recent discussion of Schmitt's view of history, Matthias Lievens emphasises the paradoxical theologically driven defence of a profane and non-Messianic philosophy of history that forms the basis of his *katechontism*. Lievens suggests that what is fundamen-tally at stake in Schmitt's political eschatology is the risk of an end to the political, which would mean the triumph of a depoliticised and absolute con-ception of enmity.[31] This example clearly highlights the avertive character of Schmitt's apocalypticism, as his emphasis on the antagonistic aspect of the political ultimately is supposed to shield politics from absolute brutalisation.

The *katechon* appeared as a theological fascination late in Schmitt's work. His more consistent use of the figure or concept is particularly vis-ible around 1950. After a more ambiguous view of it in the early 1940s, Schmitt came to develop a positive interpretation of the figure later in the decade, only to stop using it all together sometime during the late 1950s. The concept itself could thus be seen as a rather marginal feature of Schmitt's writings, but it has been described by Jacob Taubes as naming a major theme in it, since Schmitt's thought can be described as animated by a 'catechontic [sic] impulse'.[32] According to Taubes, Schmitt 'thinks apocalyptically, but from above, from the powers that be', and central to

---

[29] A central point of reference in this discourse is Norman Cohn, *The Pursuit of the Mil-lennium. Revolutionary Millenarians and Mystical Anarchists in the Middle Ages*, rev. and expanded edn. (London: Paladin, 1970 [1957]). For a contemporary application of this line of thinking in the analysis of totalitarianism as a form of apocalyptic religiosity, see Emilio Gentile, *Politics as Religion* (Princeton: Princeton University Press, 2006).

[30] Daniel Wojcik, 'Avertive Apocalypticism', in Catherine Wessinger (ed.) *The Oxford Handbook of Millennialism*, (Oxford: Oxford University Press, 2011), pp. 66–88. See also Bernard McGinn, *Visions of the End. Apocalyptic Traditions in the Middle Ages* (New York: Columbia University Press, 1998), p. 32.

[31] Matthias Lievens, 'Carl Schmitt's Concept of History', in Jens Meierheinrich and Oliver Simmos (eds.) *The Oxford Handbook of Carl Schmitt* (Oxford: Oxford University Press, 2017), pp. 401–421. Compare Schmitt's distinction between 'real' and 'absolute' enmity in Carl Schmitt, *The Theory of the Partisan. A Commentary/Remark on the Concept of the Politi-cal*, trans. A.C. Goodson (East Lansing: Michigan State University Press, 2004), pp. 64–68. For related discussions of Schmitt's concern with the end of the political as a potentially catastrophic threat, see both Brännström's and Wittrock's chapters in this volume.

[32] Jacob Taubes, *The Political Theology of Paul* (Stanford: Stanford University Press, 2004), p. 69.

this line of thinking is an 'experience of time and history as a delimited respite, a term or even a last respite'.[33] 'Schmitt's interest,' Taubes observes, 'was in only one thing: . . . that the chaos not raise to the top, that the state remain'.[34]

Taubes' description of Schmitt's *katechontism* is important because it helps us to identify the implications of Schmitt's political eschatology in a more precise way. Throughout his diaries from the time, Schmitt seemingly toys with a diverse set of characters that may have acted as *katechon* during different times, but he simultaneously appears dead serious about the *katechon*'s inherent relation to Christian faith.[35] This seriousness can also be seen in the discussion of the office of Holy Roman Emperor as *katechon* – a secular agent imbued with sacred *auctoritas* – in *The Nomos of the Earth* from 1950,[36] as well as in the short and pithy essay 'Three Possibilities for a Christian Conception of History',[37] published the same year.

In the latter, Schmitt discusses the *katechon* as one of three possible figures out of which to reconstruct a Christian philosophy of history, out of and against the devastation wrought by what he views as the secularised eschatology of modern political faiths, particularly Marxism.[38] In Schmitt's view, politico-ethical problems, like the use of the new weapons of mass destruction, can no longer be answered through any other resources than that of a philosophy of history. Hence, the need for counter-images and counter-myths with which to confront the eschatological faiths that are used to mobilise the modern masses. Through the figure of the *katechon*, 'which defers the end and suppresses the evil one',[39] the Christian can find a mythological model through which to act historically and politically, an answer to the challenge of both enchanted mass politics and disenchanted technocracy (and their conflict). The Holy Roman Emperor in Schmitt's reading illustrates this *katechontic* function well, in his mission of staving

---

[33] Jacob Taubes, 'Carl Schmitt: Apocalyptic Prophet of the Counterrevolution', in Jacob Taubes, *To Carl Schmitt. Letters and Reflections*, trans. Keith Tribe (New York: Columbia University Press, 2013), pp. 1–18, at p. 13.

[34] Taubes, *The Political Theology of Paul*, p. 103.

[35] See Carl Schmitt, *Glossarium. Aufzeichnungen aus den Jahren 1947 bis 1958. Erweiterte, berichtigte und kommentierte Neuausgabe* (Berlin: Duncker & Humblot, 2015 [1991]), pp. 47, 52, 60, 85, 94, 116, 124, 192, 206, and 207.

[36] Carl Schmitt, *The Nomos of the Earth in the Jus Publicum Europaeum*, trans. G.L. Ulmen (New York: Telos Press Publishing, 2006), pp. 59–66.

[37] Carl Schmitt, 'Three Possibilities of a Christian Conception of History', trans. Mario Wenning, *Telos* 147 (2009), pp. 167–170.

[38] Schmitt, 'Three Possibilities', p. 167.

[39] Schmitt, 'Three Possibilities', p. 169.

off evil and lawlessness, thereby restraining the Antichrist's coming and with it the end of days.

The essay on the Christian conception of history effectively elucidates Schmitt's eschatology of modern politics. In its attention to the dynamics of political myth, Schmitt's essay connects to themes prominent in his earlier work on the crisis of parliamentarism, to which I will turn shortly. The consistency is as will be shown obvious, down to the fact that Schmitt's proposed solution appears to be reliance on some sort of politico-theologically framed 'counter-myth'. Granted, in content Schmitt's post-war outspokenly Christian mythology is different from his reliance on a nationalist political mythology in the 1920s and 1930s. However, the function and form of these respective mythologies are the same, as they are both supposed to help restrain the destructive tendencies of modern political myth in the name of order and unity.

Thus, it is possible to discern the basic elements of *katechontic* politics. *Katechontism* is a specific form of avertive apocalypticism oriented towards worldly politics, but without the idea of directing its eschatological convictions toward transcendence and salvation. On the contrary, the *katechontic* worldview regards the introduction of salvation and Messianic hope into politics as profoundly dangerous. It is also important to note the secular nature of the *katechon* itself. Even if it is endowed with an eschatological mission, and thereby becomes sacralised, it remains a fundamentally secular agent, its field of operations being strictly those of worldly politics. The aim of *katechontic* politics is to avert the end and foreclose fundamental changes to the reigning order. It is a mythology of stability and restraint.

Schmitt's *Katechontic* Democracy and the Mediation of Popular Power

Schmitt found liberal parliamentarianism's turbulent crisis during the interwar years to be an inevitable consequence of democracy's development following the extension of the franchise and the emergence of 'the masses' as a political phenomenon. Schmitt wrote relatively little about mass society as such, but the fear of the masses, a strong feature of bourgeois thought throughout the nineteenth and early twentieth century (and possibly experiencing a resurgence in the guise of contemporary anti-populism), definitely made an imprint on his social thought. But for all his expressed fears of impending anarchist violence and social upheaval, Schmitt saw popular enthusiasm and activity as not only an inevitable feature of modern political life but also as something inherently useful for sustaining political order. Without the direction of popular enthusiasm into a system of political representation, the state would lose its grandeur and potential to inspire awe. Following, though not uncritically appropriating, the theories of Georges Sorel, Schmitt approaches this problem through the term political myth.[40]

According to Schmitt, the success of political myth in the twentieth century shows the extent to which rationalism and liberal appeals to rational deliberation have lost their explanatory value for political decision-making. Following the advent of proper mass politics, society is ruled through command and enticement in the public sphere, through 'symbols' and slogans.[41] But this state of affairs cannot be either ignored or simply mourned. Instead, it needs reckoning and a proper model of political rationality, something that Schmitt finds in his conception of 'the political form' in Roman Catholicism. Against a rationalist vision of reason oriented towards exposing and eradicating irrationality, Schmitt suggests the symbolic rationality of Catholicism, which instead intends to give direction and purpose to the 'irrational darkness of the human soul'.[42] He also suggests that the sovereign political order can be saved from internal devolution into civil conflict between special interests through the myth of the nation.[43]

It is important to note that Schmitt in proposing this was not an ideological German nationalist per se, but rather something of a fanatic for order. Schmitt recognised that democracy was the dominant modern form of rule and therefore the only way to order modern states.[44] Democracy, 'properly' instituted, could become a way to uphold state sovereignty and, through it, established political order. Popular mass activity and the energies it produced should be redirected, the people repurposed as a restraining force rather than be left to devolve into a chaotic hastener of law destroying revolutions. Nationalism is simply very suitable for this ulterior motive since it appears as a 'stronger myth' than class struggle.[45]

Behind this reasoning was the insight that democracy as a form of state built on the status of the people as constituent power. The very foundation

---

[40] See the extensive discussion of Sorel's theory of political myth in the final chapter of Carl Schmitt, *The Crisis of Parliamentary Democracy*, trans. Ellen Kennedy (Cambridge, MA: MIT Press, 2000), pp. 65–76.

[41] Schmitt, *The Crisis of Parliamentary Democracy*, p. 6.

[42] Schmitt, *Roman Catholicism and Political Form*, trans. G.L. Ulmen (Westport, CT: Greenwood Press, 1996), p. 14. Translation modified, see the German original, Carl Schmitt, *Römischer Katholizismus und politische Form* (Stuttgart: Klett-Cotta, 2008 [1923]), p. 24.

[43] Schmitt, *The Crisis of Parliamentary Democracy*, p. 76.

[44] Schmitt, *The Crisis of Parliamentary Democracy*, pp. 22–25. See also the discussion of the passing of monarchical legitimacy in Carl Schmitt, *Political Theology. Four Chapters on the Concept of Sovereignty*, trans. George Schwab (Chicago: The University of Chicago Press, 2005), p. 56.

[45] Schmitt, *The Crisis of Parliamentary Democracy*, p. 76.

of legitimacy in the democratic state, that is, the people, is at the same time constantly an uncontrollable opening towards a complete reordering of constitutional foundations.[46] Just as legal positivism cannot accommodate the sovereign decision over the exception,[47] liberalism cannot accommodate the democratic people's ultimate control over the basic principles of legality. The same sort of paradoxical 'ungrounding' of established legal order in the name of the principle of order thus appears here as in the more famous discussion of the sovereign decision in *Political Theology*.[48]

As Carlo Galli has noted, for Schmitt 'a political order cannot be founded on stability (or staticity) but only on an openness to disorder'.[49] In the case of the democratic state, it is therefore simply not enough to have strong, constitutionally-guaranteed institutions. Schmitt's conception of a functional modern state instead builds on stable juridified institutions combined with 'the power of the presence of the people', as 'Schmitt understood state institutions to be permanently crossed and disquieted by constituent power, by the originary presence of the people'.[50] According to Galli, this is one of Schmitt's fundamental insights into the fate of modern political life. This 'tragic', unresolvable unity of popular presence and political representation must be understood as an 'always active disequilibrium between constituent power and State powers'.[51] However, it is a disequilibrium that energises and revitalises the state and political order.

In Schmitt's view, the ideal of rational mediation via parliamentary politics was thus just one of many possible ways of organising democratic life, and one not very well suited for the challenges of mass society. Schmitt distrusted the attempts to mediate particular interests and social conflict through parliamentary parties and the organs of party democracy, believing these to be institutionally weak. Their open acknowledgement of social conflict also risked sowing discord within the polity. Still, he could not give up on some sort of principle of political mediation, which becomes apparent in his theory of representation. This is perhaps best understood through his 1923 essay *Roman Catholicism and Political Form*. Schmitt's ecclesiological institutionalism contains a politico-juridical theory of an authority that

---

[46] For Schmitt's conception of constituent power (translated as 'constitution-making power'), see Carl Schmitt, *Constitutional Theory*, trans. Jeffrey Seitzer (Durham: Duke University Press, 2008), pp. 125–135.

[47] A central tenet of Schmitt, *Political Theology*.

[48] Schmitt, *Political Theology*, pp. 12–15.

[49] Carlo Galli, *Janus's Gaze. Essays on Carl Schmitt* (Durham: Duke University Press, 2015), p. 6.

[50] Galli, *Janus's Gaze*, p. 16.

[51] Galli, *Janus's Gaze*, p. 17.

manages to incorporate and bind the element of popular activity to itself. It needs a form akin to the church's conception of the office, verified and answered by the active acclamation of the congregation.[52]

The Roman Catholic conception of the office, Schmitt argues, treats it as a 'concrete, personal representation of concrete personality'.[53] The concrete personality represented by the church official is, of course, Christ,[54] but Schmitt's formal way of reasoning shows the relevance of his idea of Roman Catholicism for his constitutional theory. The political person of the state that represents the democratic polity must work in a similar way, as a public body uniting 'ruler and ruled' in a sort of congregation.[55] In this way, the ecclesiological form presented in *Roman Catholicism and Political Form* as eminently political is generalisable to the institutions of political organisation and understood as one that could give life to the idea that spiritual energy can breathe life into the structure of offices.

Thus, Schmitt emphasises the way in which the *complexio oppositorum*, the 'complex of opposites', of the Catholic Church escapes and mediates the dualities presented as given in modernity,[56] for instance between formal bureaucratic legality and the popular enthusiasm of the congregation. Schmitt's politics, therefore, build on neither mediation, nor immediacy, but rather, in Carlo Galli's words, 'the tragic coexistence of mediation and immediacy, that does not admit any dialectical resolution'.[57] His model of 'tragic coexistence' between state officials and the power of an 'energetic' people is imagined without the interference of organised private interests, like parliamentary parties or social movements.[58] What is left is a peculiar form of 'charismatic bureaucracy', a 'plebiscitarian-technico-authoritarian'[59] model that brings together what appears as contradicting forces in our current 'populist moment', that is: popular power and technocratic legality. Overcoming their division, to Schmitt always visible in parliamentary party machinations

---

[52] Schmitt, *Constitutional Theory*, pp. 275, 304. Compare Carl Schmitt, *Volksentscheid und Volksbegehren* (Berlin: Duncker & Humblot, 2014 [1927]), p. 52, where Schmitt is more candid about the politico-theological, ecclesiological origins of his concept of the acclamation (complete with a reference to Erik Peterson).

[53] Schmitt, *Roman Catholicism*, p. 14.

[54] Schmitt, *Roman Catholicism*, p. 14.

[55] Schmitt, *Constitutional Theory*, p. 264.

[56] Schmitt, *Roman Catholicism*, pp. 7–9.

[57] Galli, *Janus's Gaze*, p. 11.

[58] Besides Schmitt, 'Strong State and Sound Economy', see also Schmitt's specific and detailed description of the 'faults' of Weimar pluralist party democracy in Carl Schmitt, *Der Hüter der Verfassung* (Berlin: Duncker & Humblot, 1996 [931]), pp. 62–63.

[59] Galli, *Janus's Gaze*, p. 22.

and ultimately threatening social cohesion and political stability, was the aim of his democratic theory and, hence, at the heart of his *katechontism*.

Conclusion: *Katechontic* Democracy and the Populist Moment

Obviously, Schmitt's predictions did not come to pass, since post-war order was dominated by party democracy, but they have acquired a new sense of relevance in the populist moment. This development has not come about by accident. As Wendy Brown has put it, 'undoing the demos' and its popular sovereignty has been the goal of 'neoliberalism's stealth revolution',[60] along lines akin to those described by Streeck in his analysis of the Eurozone's authoritarian liberal economic constitution. Undermining the diverse institutions mediating conflict in its reconfiguration of society in the image of its economistic models, neoliberalism has left us without a democratic *demos*. Instead, social conflict now assumes the form of a contestation between legalistic technocracy and the unmediated will of the people as the source of 'pure' popular legitimacy. The diverse attempts to remedy this situation now come to mirror Schmitt's *katechontic* model of democracy.

Some observers note the deeper social connections between the two ideological tendencies, relating them both to deeper ongoing structural shifts within Western democracies. What is effectively foreclosed in both technocratic and populist forms of politics is the mediation via political parties and movements that was so fundamentally important to the post-war political compact of 'party democracy'.[61] The latter can in this context be defined as 'the mediation of social conflict through the institution of the political party understood as a means for the articulation of particular interests into comprehensive – although competing – conceptions of the common good'.[62] Besides a particular form of institutional mediation, it also represents a procedural conception of political legitimacy,[63] to which could be added an open acknowledgement of social conflict as in itself inescapable. I would argue that the latter aspect is particularly unacceptable to Schmitt, and that his need for other forms of democratic mediation and legitimacy stems from this foreclosure of social conflict within established political order.

---

[60] Wendy Brown, *Undoing the Demos. Neoliberalism's Stealth Revolution* (New York: Zone Books, 2015).

[61] See for example Christopher Bickerton and Carlo Invernizzi Accetti, 'Populism and technocracy: opposites of complements?', *Critical Review of International Social and Political Philosophy* 20:2 (2017), pp. 186–206, and Danielle Caramani, 'Will vs. Reason: The Populist and Technocratic Forms of Political Representation and Their Critique to Party Government', *American Political Science Review* 111:1 (2017), pp. 54–67.

[62] Bickerton and Invernizzi Accetti, 'Populism and technocracy', p. 189.

[63] Bickerton and Invernizzi Accetti, 'Populism and technocracy', p. 189.

Schmitt's *katechontic* interpretation of the democratic constitution clearly resonates with the observations on the passing of party democracy. His theory of democracy would thus seem the ideal form for a convergence of disparate forces in the post-democratic, populist moment we have entered. In this way, Müller's populist Schmitt and Streeck's technocrat-elitist Schmitt can be brought together through a deeper understanding of the *katechontic* Schmitt, a figure that provides a theory for the state structure emerging in Western politics after the decline of party democracy. This theory strives to bring together populist and elitist tendencies within the overarching frame of a restraining political order that manages to depoliticise the people and mobilise its apocalyptic potential as tamed constitutive power. By directing the myth-driven 'enthusiasm' of the self-subordinating people directly towards and into the apparatus of the state, social peace is reached through majoritarian consent to an affirmed authority. In such a way, the people itself becomes a restraining force, limiting its own potential for disruption. Thus, democracy is ordered – or pacified.

The current problems of the capitalist-democratic state model are often framed as limited to the rise of authoritarian populism in conflict with different types of more or less international elites, economic, liberal, and/or cultural. However, the turn toward more repression and increasing inequality also implicates the political centre as colluding with or gradually assuming the worldview of so-called 'illiberal' forces in attempts to restrain the breaking down of the established democratic-capitalist order.

In fact, one may even claim that the centrist-populist conflictual axis in itself presents us with the political logic of a *katechontic* democracy, since it reduces politics to the two depoliticising forces described by Müller and Streeck respectively. It should be added that no success of the authoritarian-populist movements has led to any substantial break with the logic of technocratically imposed economic austerity, and the number of centrist political actors who have no problem implementing the authoritarian aspects of populist programmes illustrates the objective conditions under which these forces operate. The *katechontic* democracy envisioned by Schmitt actually looks a lot like their ideal point of convergence, walling borders and containing all demands for increased economic redistribution. It seems that we are not just dealing with a 'political-economic ideology having turned into a religion',[64] as Wolfgang Streeck puts it, but rather with a politico-eschatological regime aimed at restraining the end-crisis of 'democratic capitalism' as a state form.

---

[64] Streeck, *Buying Time*, p. 174.

Katechontism represents the endpoint of a long decline of faith in democratic social reform. What remains is the holding on to the static forms of an ageing and increasingly less substantial democracy. Under the strains of austerity and inequality, and the declining influence of organised social interests in party form, what hope is there beyond that in popular restraint and the direction of apocalyptic energies into a fear of the end? The real question would then appear not to be the by now well-known 'Orbán or Macron?', but rather to what extent the logic of that much-attested conflict risks boiling down to a kind of narcissism of small differences. After the decline of party democracy, are there any alternatives for the mediation of popular power left, besides some form of democratic *katechontism*?

9

The Power of the People

Ari Hirvonen and Susanna Lindroos-Hovinheimo

Introduction

> 1) What is the Third Estate? *Everything*. 2) What has it been until now in the political order? *Nothing*. 3) What does it want to be? *Something*.
>
> – *Emmanuel-Joseph Sieyès[1]*

Emmanuel-Joseph Sieyès' definition seems to make no sense. It includes an aporia between being nothing and being everything, an impossible paradox that is not only political but also ontological. For us, this aporia encapsulates the idea of the people as constituent power. The power of the people, as Alain Badiou says, is sovereignty as 'a relation of totality to totality, of the people to itself'.[2] This definition of the people is our premise, but how to understand this cryptic nothing, which is simultaneously not merely everything but also a drive to become something?

In *Qu'est-ce que le Tiers-État?* ('What is the Third Estate?'), a pamphlet published in the first days of January 1789, Sieyès explains his definition of the Third Estate. Following the spirit of the revolutionary times, Sieyès condemns the privileged classes and the inequalities that divide the French nation. The privileged are 'the actual enemies of the common interest' and the 'simple citizens'.[3] Freedom does not derive from privileges but from the equal rights of the citizens. These rights belong to all. Sieyès goes further by affirming that the common people constitutes the entire French nation. The pamphlet shows us that this 'something' that the people desires to be is the constituent power. The people – being everything but oppressed to the point of nothingness – wants to be a voluntary and

---

[1] Emmanuel-Joseph Sieyès, 'What is the Third Estate?', trans. M. Blondel, in Emmanuel-Joseph Sieyès, *The Essential Political Writings*, ed. Oliver W. Lembcke and Florian Weber (Leiden: Brill, 2014), pp. 43–117, at p. 43.

[2] Alain Badiou, *Metapolitics*, trans. Jason Barker (London & New York: Verso, 2005), p. 91.

[3] Sieyès, 'What is the Third Estate?', p. 116.

free act of will. Simultaneously, the people wants to be the constituent power that creates the constitution; this very power rests with the people, that is, with 'everything'.

Becoming something is to be everything. This is what Robespierre claimed in April 1791 when he opposed the distinction between active citizens, who were eligible to vote and run for election because they were able to make a financial contribution, and passive citizens who were excluded from electoral participation. This kind of exclusion from the formation of the law is 'anti-constitutional and anti-social'.[4]

Based on Sieyès' definition, our thesis is that the people counted as nothing has an inalienable will to become something through political action and solidarity, that is, to be everything. To elaborate our thesis, we have to take a step backwards. Sieyès introduced popular sovereignty, constituent power and human rights into the revolutionary political discourse in a brand-new way. However, his theoretical and political thinking would not have been possible without Jean-Jacques Rousseau's theory of social contract, even though in his writings Sieyès mentions Rousseau only once. For Jean-Luc Nancy, Rousseau 'is the first to understand that "society" is merely an association of interests without any higher interest (or disinterest)'.[5] He 'surveys everything with a straightforward air, in a way that few before or after him have done'.[6]

For us, the revolutionary concepts of constituent power and popular sovereignty are still relevant as possible conditions of radical emancipatory and egalitarian politics. We 'are still in the sequence opened up by the French Revolution'.[7] Perhaps, we may understand sovereignty as 'the revolt of the people'.[8] To open a dialogue with the revolutionary past and the contemporary non-revolutionary situation, we bring Jean-Luc Nancy and Jacques Rancière into a discussion with Rousseau. We invite Jean-Jacques to discuss with Jean-Luc and Jacques, since the political and philosophical thinking of these three is never very far from Sieyès' conception of the people as nothing, something and everything.

---

4   Maximilien Robespierre, 'On the Silver Mark', in Maximilien Robespierre, *Virtue and Terror*, trans. John Howe (London: Verso, 2007), pp. 5–19, at p. 6.
5   Jean-Luc Nancy, 'Politics and Beyond, An Interview with Jean-Luc Nancy', trans. P. Armstrong and J. E. Smith, *Diacritics* 43:4 (2015), pp. 90–108, at p. 92.
6   Nancy, 'Politics and Beyond', p. 92.
7   Alain Badiou, *Philosophy and the Event*, trans. L. Burchill (Cambridge & Malden, MA, 2013), p. 23.
8   Jean-Luc Nancy, *The Creation of the World or Globalization*, trans. F. Raffoul and D. Pettigrew (Albany, NY: State University of New York Press, 2007), p. 109.

General Will

'The principle of political life is', Rousseau points out in *On the Social Contract*, 'in the sovereign authority.'[9] The executive power is the brain, but since the body may go on living in a vegetative stage, the legislative power is central to the life and heart of the body politic. Rousseau situates the legislative power as follows: 'the laws are only authentic acts of the general will', and thus the sovereign merely acts when 'the populace is assembled'.[10] The law is the expression of the general will and 'the first rule of the public *economy* is that the administration should be in conformity with the laws'.[11]

Numbers do not generalise a will: only a common interest unites a will. However, Rousseau admits that there are those who oppose the laws and that the general will is 'the vote of the majority [that] always obligates all the others'.[12] Even the will of an association that is a general will for its members is a mere particular will for the whole society. Rousseau specifies that 'the most general will is always the must [most] just also, and that the voice of the people is in fact the voice of God'.[13] The criterion of the general will is that it '*always* tends towards the conservation and well-being of the whole and of each part' and is '*always* for the common good'.[14] Rousseau does not hesitate to conclude that this will is '*always* right'.[15] That is, the general will as constituent power is not merely the source of the laws. It also constitutes the normative criteria about what is just and unjust.

The general will is the singular will of the common political body, a commonly shared or generative view that is to be separated from particular wills. For Rousseau, nothing is more dangerous than 'the corruption of the legislator, which is the inevitable outcome of particular perspectives'.[16]

Is Rousseau's general will a conversion of a multitude into a single person? The general will that has absolute sovereignty seems to be based on unanimous

[9] Jean-Jacques Rousseau, *On the Social Contract*, in Jean-Jacques Rousseau, *The Basic Political Writings*, trans. D. A. Cross, (Indianapolis, IN & Cambridge: Hackett Publishing, 1987), pp. 141–227, at p. 194.
[10] Rousseau, *On the Social Contract*, p. 195.
[11] Jean-Jacques Rousseau, *Discourse on Political Economy*, in Jean-Jacques Rousseau, *The Basic Political Writings*, trans. D. A. Cross (Indianapolis, IN & Cambridge: Hackett Publishing, 1987), pp. 111–138, at p. 118.
[12] Rousseau, *On the Social Contract*, p. 206.
[13] Rousseau, *Discourse on Political Economy*, p. 115.
[14] Rousseau, *Discourse on Political Economy*, pp. 114–115, emphasis added.
[15] Rousseau, *On the Social Contract*, p. 155, emphasis added.
[16] Rousseau, *On the Social Contract*, p. 179.

consent rather than a multiplicity of opinions.[17] We see this as democratic politics because the general will is the becoming of politics. The general will is a form of fidelity to the emergence of the political and to egalitarian aims.[18] As a part of the general will and the constituent power of everyone, even those who have no authority whatsoever are capable of becoming something and sharing being everything.

For Rancière, the general will includes emancipatory potential. The presupposition of equality may give rise to 'the right of the individual as non-right of the state, the entitlement of anyone at all to question the state or to serve as proof of its infidelity to its own principle'.[19] The general will 'must presuppose the equality of the one who commands and the one who is commanded'.[20] However, for Rancière, for whom the presupposition for democratic politics is equality, there is a risk that the social contract theory breaks down the people into autonomous and isolated individuals. This exorcises politics and turns it into a war of all against all.[21] Rousseau recognises this threat, but for him the cause of the possible dissolution does not lie in particular individuals but in social interest groups.

If for Rousseau, the existence of the general interest 'has as its sole content *the declaration of its existence*', this requires a political event. Moreover, even if the general will is subjected to particular wills and interests, a possibility which Rancière recognises, it is still an existing will. What it requires is to be declared in, through and as a collective political event. Perhaps Rancière's conception of the political comes closer to this than he would admit. The political event is a manifestation of the general interest, the content of which is simply the manifestation of its existence. Hence, for Rancière, the general will would always be situational and, as such, related to a general interest and/or a general wrong. The general will is here understood as related to a political event, where declaration takes place as the voice of the people. Such an event is simultaneously a confrontation between politics and police.

---

[17] Hannah Arendt, *On Revolution* (London: Penguin, 1990), p. 77. See also Peg Birmingham, *Hannah Arendt and Human Rights: The Predicament of Common Responsibility* (Bloomington & Indianapolis, IN: Indiana University Press, 2006), p. 43.

[18] Alain Badiou, *Being and Event*, trans. Oliver Feltham (London: Continuum, 2005), pp. 344–354. See also Nina Power, 'Towards an Anthropology of Infinitude: Badiou and the Political Subject', *Cosmos and History: The Journal of Natural and Social Philosophy* 2:1–2 (2006), pp. 186–209, at p. 194.

[19] Jacques Rancière, *Disagreement: Politics and Philosophy*, trans. Julie Rose (Minneapolis, MI: University of Minnesota Press, 1999), p. 79.

[20] Jacques Rancière, *Hatred of Democracy*, trans. S. Corcoran (London & New York: Verso, 2006), p. 48.

[21] Rancière, *Disagreement*, p. 78.

The general interest is formed by different particular interests which are in opposition to each other.[22] The general will does not pre-exist as a given truth but is formed in, through and as a political event of the constituent power, which is not just an abstract concept but a concrete revolutionary or periodic institutional assembly.

The general will is a central part of civil liberty in a society, which differs from the concept of natural freedom: 'To choose freely is to choose in accordance with the general will, which means that one chooses for all.'[23] This 'consists in obedience to a law that I give myself'.[24] The law is hence consistent with the autonomy of the subject. Since the citizens make their own laws, instead of being in slavery they obey only themselves. This is what positive freedom is. Freedom and equality are not contradictory concepts. The expression of individual freedom is included in collective autonomy, and equality is the expression of that freedom. Rousseau moves from the concept of authority to the concept of power. Citizens who have been subjects to law become political actors who may overturn or transform the law.[25] Rousseau presents a 'topology that does not presuppose' any position of mastery.[26] The general will is not the authority invested in an office or a constitution that would require unquestioning recognition of the authority by those compelled to obey.

The general will presents – not *re*presents – an infallible and inviolable will that is in itself correct. Its justification is immanent to it insofar that motivation, will, decision and justification are simultaneously present in the general will. On the other hand, there is no time span between deliberation and declaration, no spatial difference between interiority and exteriority. The body politic itself is 'a moral being which possesses a will', that is, a general will.[27] The objective (general) and subjective (moral being) wills are blended. The absolutely immanent will is the true voice of the people and the truth of the people's voice. The only spatial-temporal differences are between the

---

[22] Rousseau, *On the Social Contract*, p. 156.

[23] Simon Critchley, 'The Catechism of the Citizen: Politics, Law and Religion in, after, with and against Rousseau', in Ari Hirvonen and Janne Porttikivi (eds.), *Law and Evil: Philosophy, Politics, Psychoanalysis* (London & New York: Routledge, 2010), pp. 169–196, at p. 176.

[24] Critchley, 'The Catechism of the Citizen', p. 175.

[25] Peg Birmingham, 'On Violence, Politics, and the Law', *The Journal of Speculative Philosophy* 24:1 (2010), pp. 1–20, at p. 8; see also Hannah Arendt, *On Violence* (New York: Harcourt, Brace & Co., 1969), p. 45.

[26] Jacques Rancière, *The Politics of Aesthetics*, trans. Gabriel Rockhill (London: Continuum, 2006), p. 49.

[27] Rousseau, *Discourse on Political Economy*, p. 114.

legislative body, which makes legal propositions, and the general will, which makes the correct decision. The general will is the political will and the constituent power of the autonomous people prior to any representative institution or government.

Nancy would argue that the general will is a sharing among political subjects, 'the disposition of community . . . the destination of its sharing', which affirms that 'the political is not dissolved in the sociotechnical elements and forces and needs'. Thus, the general will inscribes 'the sharing of community . . . [and] the experience of its sharing'.[28] In Nancy's terms, the general will is about exposition, which is not the substance of the general will (or the supposed general will) but the finite existence of particular wills in their exposition to each other and to the general will. Thus, the power of the people is what is exposed.[29] Then again, for Nancy, the concept of democracy – government by the people – refers to the process of identification, which is not identification with an essence.[30] This is exactly how we understand the concept of the general will as the democratic power of the people. The general will does not exist. It takes place and happens. Hence, it is to be understood as a political concept that simultaneously unbinds the given transcendental or immanent whole and re-establishes a non-essential whole. It is neither a given nor a complete will corresponding to some pre-given meaning. It is, as Nancy says, an incompletable question of 'not merely "what do we want?" but first "who we are" and "do we want/will ourselves?"'[31]

Social Contract

Rancière appreciates Rousseau's attack on social inequalities in the *Discourse on the Origins of Inequality*, which he considers as a declaration of wrong. As Rancière says, 'politics is not based on right but wrong'.[32] Then again, the general will is always right. However, Rousseau's social contract theory should not be thought to be without relationship to the inequalities and wrongs of the society. Being a presentation of right and justice, the general will is what brings forth the wrong, since it is based on the equality of the people in their solidarity. Equality is the presupposition of the people, even though the prevailing state may be based on inequality.

---

[28] Jean-Luc Nancy, *The Inoperative Community*, trans. Peter Connor, Lisa Garbus, Michael Holland, and Simona Sawhney (Minneapolis, MN: University of Minnesota Press, 1991), p. 40.

[29] Nancy, *The Inoperative Community*, p. xxxix.

[30] Jean-Luc Nancy, 'Un peuple ou des multitudes?', *L'Humanité*, 26 December 2003.

[31] Nancy, 'Politics and Beyond', pp. 94, 96.

[32] Rancière, *Disagreement*, p. 78.

For Rousseau, equality is the aim of every system of legislation. Another fundamental object of the law is liberty: 'Liberty, because all particular dependence is that much force taken from the body of the state; equality, because liberty cannot subsist without it.'[33] Rousseau considers a form of political community that balances the claims of freedom and equality. It demands equal loyalty and obedience from every member of the society. The duty of a citizen takes precedence over the various particular duties that people have. For a virtuous citizen, his particular will conforms to the general will. And the body politics itself is a moral being possessed of a will, that is, the general one. How, then, is the general will combined with freedom and equality?

The social contract, 'the most voluntary act', provides the solution for what Rousseau calls 'the fundamental problem', that is, how freedom and equality can exist together in a non-conflictual way in a society.[34] The true foundation of society is this covenant through which a people becomes a people and which 'defends and protects with all common forces the person and goods of each associate'.[35]

Equality is a necessary element of the social contract. Through the social contract, the forced alienation of the state of war is turned into a conscious, free and voluntary total alienation: 'All men are equal in alienation, since it is total for each of them.'[36] Everyone gives all he is and has. The second moment consists of an advantageous exchange, which includes individual interests. An individual wants and gets back what he has given away. Simultaneously, he has to want to give the same to others because of the formal equality produced by the alienation. I wish the happiness of each one because I am myself 'each'. This is the basis of general equality. Particular interests, thus 'forced into the generality of equality',[37] are paradoxically the foundation of and an obstacle to the general interest. An individual gets back even more than he gives because he gives himself to himself, to his own liberty. Once again, equality and liberty form an intimate couple.

Rousseau argues for the same reality of equality that Rancière considers not as a goal to be attained but a presupposition and actuality. The people is made of equal subjects who are interchangeable in their equality even though they 'construct a situation in time out of their

---

[33] Rousseau, *On the Social Contract*, p. 170.

[34] Rousseau, *On the Social Contract*, pp. 205, 148.

[35] Rousseau, *On the Social Contract*, p. 148.

[36] Louis Althusser, *Montesquieu, Rousseau, Marx: Politics and History*, trans. Ben Brewster (London: Verso, 1982), p. 142.

[37] Althusser, *Montesquieu, Rousseau, Marx*, p. 143.

own lives and experiences'.[38] For Rancière, as for Rousseau, politics means the exercise of a capacity that everybody has. What Rancière wants is a democracy where anyone can act as a political subject, stage her otherness, take different roles and make visible the fluid boundaries between the same and the other. Hence, for Rancière, democracy has a built-in logic of heterogeneity.[39] But 'democracy' is understood neither as a form of government nor a form of social life. Democracy *is* politics. It is the principle that says that the power to rule is founded on nothing. The basis for power is that there is no basis because we are all equal. Why, then, do some have the position of ruler while others are ruled? Many factors may dictate this: for instance, birth, wealth or force. Democracy – that is, politics proper – means the rule of the *demos*. A radically democratic government would be one where the governors are chosen by drawing lots.

Hence, political acts display the power of those who are no more qualified to rule than those who are being ruled. 'Democracy' refers to an anarchic structure where the rulers and the ruled are the same and can at any time change places. Politics as dissensus or disruption means that all qualifications are supplemented by the power of the unqualified. The essence of the power of the people, and thus of democracy, is the power of those who have no qualifications. It does not matter what individual features they have, what kind of persons they are, or whether they are skilled, wise, good or bad; the power of the people is impersonal.

Rancière would ask whether Rousseau, after all, breaks down the people into isolated individuals, which become the presupposition for the social contract. The same criticism could be addressed to Sieyès' first phase of individual wills, and more generally to the whole contractual idea. Nancy is helpful here because he reminds us that instead of a contract, we should speak about a difficult contraction in the birth of a political community. The people 'must be produced as a public or communal (communism) thing, even though an untameable anarchy presses from within'.[40]

---

[38] Jacques Rancière, 'Democracies Against Democracy', trans. William McCuaig, in Giorgio Agamben, Alain Badiou, Daniel Bensaïd, Wendy Brown, Jean-Luc Nancy, Jacques Rancière, Kristin Ross, and Slavoj Žižek, *Democracy in What State?* (New York: Columbia University Press, 2011), pp. 76–81, at p. 80.

[39] Jean-Luc Nancy, *The Truth of Democracy*, trans. Pascale-Anne Brault and Michael Naas (New York: Fordham University Press, 2010), pp. 50–53.

[40] Jean-Luc Nancy, 'Populism and Democracy', trans. Sarah Clift, *Los Angeles Review of Books*, 17 February 2019.

It is worth noting that even though Rancière and Nancy have their reservations about social contract theories, for Rancière the staging of equality in the form of becoming a political subject is decisive. For Nancy, what is crucial is not equality but freedom in the form of singular plurality that 'constitutes the essence of Being, a constitution that undoes or dislocates every single, substantial essence of Being itself'. This is not just a way of speaking, Nancy continues, since 'there is no prior substance that would be dissolved'.[41]

Rancière emphasises disagreement and the ways in which equality is opposed to police order. In the end, Rancière comes closer to Rousseau than Nancy because he sees the people as defined by interchangeability. Singularity is not a core issue of Rancière's – and understandably so, as his concept of equality is so strong that it blurs all distinctions between singularities. This does not mean, however, that Rancière considers people only as abstract subjects. For him, 'history is made by people who have only one life'.[42]

According to Nancy, Rousseau assimilates the social contract with humanity, as he gave the initial version of the aporia of common institutions. To have human society, there must be human beings capable of entering into a contract, and to have human beings there must be a contract about human society that inaugurates their humanity. Rousseau took the concept of 'contract' from the tradition of the social contract but recognised its paradox and interrupted this tradition: 'man precedes man, the common precedes the individual, and the individual precedes the common'.[43] Therefore, Rousseau's social contract includes a double anteriority, which, Nancy adds, allows singularity: 'each after the other, one by one, but every one together. Being-in-common without common substance.'[44] Neither 'an individual nor any other alleged entity (race or nation, for instance) would be able to incorporate the people'.[45]

By bringing together the general will and the social contract, we can now present three conclusions. First, political events split the subject into particular and generic subjects without any stable identity. There is a necessary tension of the common in relation to the singular, and the particular in relation to the general. Second, this divides the foundation of the political community. The social contract creates the people but does not annihilate singularities.

[41] Jean-Luc Nancy, *Being Singular Plural*, trans. R.D. Richardson and A.E. O'Byrne (Stanford, CA: Stanford University Press, 2000), pp. 28–29.

[42] Rancière, 'Democracies Against Democracy', p. 80.

[43] Nancy, 'Politics and Beyond', p. 92.

[44] Nancy, 'Politics and Beyond', p. 92.

[45] Jean-Luc Nancy, 'Neofascism', trans. Sarah Clift, *Los Angeles Review of Books*, 17 February 2019.

Third, the social contract is neither a historical event nor an a priori theoretical or speculative precondition of the legitimacy of a state. It is split between these two versions, since the general will always already includes in itself the renewal of the social contract. If this were not so, then the people would be either an abstract legal concept or an ideological nationalist construction. For us, the people comprises a political event where the aforementioned splits and tensions form a constant circulation that produces and legitimises the people. Or, as Nancy says, 'the common thus becomes a singularity that exists in the act or event of its becoming singular' (for example, a people).[46]

People

The general will as the constituent power means the people willing itself 'a sense of existence *here and now and for everyone*'.[47] Due to the revolutionary concepts of the general will, the social contract and the people, a subject does not have to be considered as subjected to a transcendent divine or secular authority; rather, it can be a free and equal political subject – as noted above, a split subject – and simultaneously an autonomous subject of the positive law, split between particular and general interests.[48] Who, then, belongs to the 'everything' of the people?

Rousseau's answer is that only those nations which are mature enough may be subjected to the laws. The nation is here understood in territorial terms. The size of the land and the populace should not be too large or too small. Rousseau stresses the importance of a strong 'social bond of unity'.[49] For him, the people found the state, and its true constitution is engraved in their hearts.

In the collective body of the constitutional state, the general will would be the common will of those who are called citizens. Those who do not have the status of a citizen are excluded from the formation and acts of the general will.[50] They are mere subjects, the objects of the law. This is an exclusive definition of the people, which marginalises migrants and other non-citizens from public and political action.

Nancy considers that Rousseau risks falling into an essentialist presupposition of united consent among individuals. When 'the community gives itself (as) an interiority', and when popular sovereignty no longer resides in the 'autojurisdiction' of the social contract and the general will, the

[46] Nancy, 'Politics and Beyond', p. 94.
[47] Nancy, 'Politics and Beyond', p. 97.
[48] Power, 'Towards an Anthropology of Infinitude', pp. 190–191.
[49] Rousseau, *On the Social Contract*, p. 204.
[50] Birmingham, *Hannah Arendt and Human Rights*, p. 43.

community is seen as expressing itself as an essence.[51] Even if subjects constitute a political community, the contract seems to be made by those who pre-exist as individuals and who are capable of associating and making contracts. In this case, the political community would always already be an essentialist association.

Rousseau says that human beings 'are what makes up the state', and he continues by speaking about 'instituting a people'.[52] The people does not comprise a natural phenomenon based on ethnic or any other kind of identity, but a political one. Politics breaks with nature and the natural law. It is 'based on the concepts of popular sovereignty, association, rigorous equality and collective autonomy understood as the self-determination of a people'.[53] In this sense, the people and the citizen are open concepts. The problem, however, is that after the social contract has been made, the citizen may become an exclusive concept in the constitutional state. The laws establish limits, circumscribe the political community, assert coherence and stabilise actions.

Nevertheless, if we consider the social contract as a pure assembly where the people unites and acts, then there is no obstacle to understanding it as the general will that founds and re-founds simultaneously both the political community and those who are part of the people.[54] Rousseau explicitly declares an inclusive principle: 'this act of association produces a moral and collective body, composed of as many members as there are voices in the assembly, which receives from this same act its unity' and, this is central, 'its common *self*'.[55]

We argue that the self of the body politic, the republic, the state and, on the other hand, the people, being associates as a collective, and the citizens, being associates as individuals, are created by a political event. In such an event, everyone has equal liberty and force, an equal position without any other foundation except the act of placing oneself under the general will. The status of a citizen is not based on any particular identity but only on being an associate in the formation of the social contract and the general will. Therefore, no one would be a priori excluded from the act of the will, since everyone would become an associate in this common and united will.

---

[51] Jean-Luc Nancy, *The Sense of the World*, trans. J.S. Librett. (Minneapolis, MN: University of Minnesota Press, 1997), p. 106.

[52] Rousseau, *On the Social Contract*, pp. 168–169.

[53] Critchley, 'The Catechism of the Citizen', p. 170.

[54] Denis Guénoun, *L'Enlèvement de la politique* (Paris: Circé, 2002), p. 15.

[55] Rousseau, *On the Social Contract*, p. 148, emphasis added.

According to Nancy, we should not be seeking the essence of community. Thinking of community through a unifying feature like nationality, religion or language can lead to closure of the political. This happens when community is assigned a common being. For Nancy, community is something different, namely, having existence in common but without common substance. To have existence in common does not mean that people are fused into one united substance or social body. On the contrary, it means not having such a substantial common identity and sharing this lack of identity.[56]

In Nancy's thinking, the concept of community has a specific meaning. The lack of essence makes the community, and a community cannot have any unified identity. If it becomes a single thing – a body, mind or fatherland – it necessarily ceases to be *in common*.[57] However, the opposite fate is also possible, and this also endangers community. An individualised society, moreover, risks losing community. Thus, the tricky question is how to think of community in-between these two negations.[58] How can the community be without essence, nation or destiny? What kind of politics does not stem from the will to unify? And, on the other hand, what kind of politics allows people to exist singularly together?

For Nancy, Rousseau is 'the thinker par excellence of compearance', the sharing of community 'in every sense'.[59] However, Nancy warns that when the community becomes a single thing, it loses 'the *in* of being-*in*-common' and 'the *with* or the *together* that defines it'.[60] The truth of community resides in the retreat of this kind of common being. If the general will is the truth of the people, it ought to be thought of as residing in what retreats from the single communal body.

Perhaps the general will may be understood as the will of everyone, who together form the people and the citizens in their acts. Then, constituent power does not reduce singularity, even though it denies individual particularism. The people itself is a singularity, which is not a united identity but formed in a singular event of becoming a political subject, the people of constituent power.

Popular sovereignty consists essentially of the general will and the constituent power in – and as a ground for – the political community. No one is outside the law, but simultaneously everyone is part of the popular sovereignty. There are, however, 'foreigners among citizens', says

---

[56] Nancy, *The Inoperative Community*, pp. 29–30.
[57] Interesting contrasts can be drawn to Schmitt here. On political unity and constituent power, see, e.g. Jacques de Ville, *Constitutional Theory: Schmitt after Derrida* (Oxon, NY: Birkbeck Law Press), pp. 74–87.
[58] Nancy, *The Inoperative Community*, p. xxxix.
[59] Nancy, *The Inoperative Community*, p. 30.
[60] Nancy, *The Inoperative Community*, p. xxxix.

Rousseau.[61] They are not pre-determined aliens, migrants or refugees. The distinction is political. For Rousseau, only those who oppose the social contract or resist the general will are foreigners: 'To inhabit the territory is to submit to sovereignty.'[62]

Constituent Power

Constituent power seems to be absolutely immanent without any reference to the transcendental. The law's legitimacy and validity lie in the general will. It is inherently legitimate. The general will declares itself by itself. It is conditioned only by itself.[63]

The concept of the self-constituting general will makes the subject and the sovereign identical correlatives. This dyadic relationship is 'the republican democratization of power'.[64] For Rancière, 'politics is the foundation of the power to govern in the absence of foundation'.[65] A will that wills itself in the act of willing is a political event in which the general will and the people are created or constructed. The general will is the power of the people, which is not, to quote Rancière again, 'the power of the population or of the majority'.[66] For him, *demos* is a dividing and disrupting force in a community of sharing the given sensible. Political subjectification is heterology. It does not only entail the simple assertion of identity. It is always at the same time the denial of an identity given by another, by the prevailing order. Where order is about right names – names that put people in their places and dictate their social roles – politics is about 'wrong' names. These are misnomers that 'articulate a gap and connect with a wrong'. *Demos* refers to being that is non-being. The *demos* consists of people who are not identified with anybody; they are nobody, nothing, the Third Estate. For both Nancy and Rancière, democracy has no *arche*, ground or foundation. It is an-archic. Demo-cracy is the force (*krinein*) of the people (*demos*), that is, the power of the people. Thus, democracy is based on a double absence. There is nothing else to base democracy on but the people, and the people is without any essence, nature and identity. Nancy confirms, 'the word *democracy* seems to contain an internal barrier to the possibility of a foundational principle'.[67]

---

[61] Rousseau, *On the Social Contract*, p. 205.
[62] Rousseau, *On the Social Contract*, p. 205.
[63] Alain Badiou, *Monde contemporain et désir de philosophie* (Reims: Noria, 1992), p. 21.
[64] Power, 'Towards an Anthropology of Infinitude', p. 193.
[65] Rancière, *Hatred of Democracy*, p. 49.
[66] Rancière, *Hatred of Democracy*, p. 49.
[67] Jean-Luc Nancy, 'Finite and Infinite Democracy', trans. William McCuaig, in Giorgio Agamben, Alain Badiou, Daniel Bensaïd, Wendy Brown, Jean-Luc Nancy, Jacques Rancière, Kristin Ross, and Slavoj Žižek, *Democracy in What State?* (New York: Columbia University Press, 2011) pp. 58–75, at p. 65.

As individuals give themselves to others, they enter into a contract with a people yet to come through the contract. By 'giving himself to all', Rousseau says, 'each person gives himself to no one'.[68] That is, in the act of the contract one gives oneself 'to an imagined generality, to a people *which does not in fact exist*'.[69] Then again, Rousseau claims that the 'constant will of all members of the state is the general will'.[70] Here we come back to the question of the exclusive/inclusive concept of the people. 'Constant' seems to exclude those who have not been the associates of the body politic. However, it is the will that is constant. It does not refer to those who give themselves to the generality of the will. Because the constituent power creates the people, whoever is part of the general will is immediately created as a member of the people, the political community. The general will is a will by and through which the social contract is time and again renewed. The covenant is every time a new beginning. In this event of political natality, the 'citizens' – that is, whoever – are born time and again as equal political subjects. We should understand today the sovereign power of the people as the corporate and collective body composed of everyone – citizens and paperless, residents and refugees – since for Rousseau the people included not only the elite or particular individuals but the people.

The constituent power is the necessary empty ground of democracy, an event of the constitution of the political community and the constituent power itself that constitutes the people. The constituent power is not only a beginning as a one-time act but something that should, as Bonnie Honig says, beset 'democracy every day'.[71] Rancière and Nancy would definitely share this. Also for Rousseau, 'The act of legislation is indeed never anything but the Social Contract combined, repeated, and reactivated at each "moment".'[72]

This justifies our dialogue between the revolutionary past and our times. The revolution is not to be reduced to the night of the revolution. The concepts we have discussed – as well as revolution itself – are an immanent power in the foundations of our democratic-constitutional rule of law states. Hence, revolution always already comes from tomorrow.

In the end, the dialogues between Rousseau, Nancy and Rancière do not end in consensus. All three circle around the general will and constituent power as non-foundational foundations of democratic politics. The general will – as a political event, co-appearance or coming together of equal beings – always

---

[68] Rousseau, *On the Social Contract*, p. 148.
[69] Critchley, 'The Catechism of the Citizen', p. 174.
[70] Rousseau, *On the Social Contract*, p. 206.
[71] Bonnie Honig, *Public Things: Democracy in Disrepair* (New York: Fordham University Press, 2017), p. 18.
[72] Althusser, *Montesquieu, Rousseau, Marx*, p. 148.

already includes the tension between unity and differences, genericness and singularity, commonality and immeasurability.

We hope that we have shown that Rousseau, Nancy and Rancière share, in their own way, the definition of the people that is our premise. For us, the constituent power, as we have understood it through their thinking, is a central concept of emancipatory and egalitarian politics without any foundation other than the constituent power that constitutes the people exposed to this very same power. The constituent power of the people, which echoes revolutionary possibilities in times of impossibilities dictated by the liberal democratic executive power, can neither be extradited from parliamentary democracies nor totally subordinated to constitutional forms and legal processes. The constituent power is an inalienable power of the people, which cannot be reduced to nationalist sovereignty and xenophobic authoritarianism. The people is always already something else than nothing, and this something is not an essentialist identity but the power of the people that constitutes simultaneously the people as political subjects and democratic politics.

We have understood the social contract, the general will and the power of the people as constant necessary possibilities of democratic and egalitarian politics – necessary because without these three (more or less) revolutionary concepts, there would not be a political dimension. Concurrently, the people as a political collective is formed in, as and through the political event of the general will. Individual subjects are exposed, on the one hand, to the absence of any pre-given essential identity and, on the other hand, to each other and the general will. The general will is simultaneously the declaration of the people and the political becoming or subjectification of the people.

Conclusion

Liberal democracies have reduced this radical constituent power, first, to constitutional-parliamentary institutions and representative-constituted power and, second, to the necessities of capitalism and security. At the same time that the legal-constitutional discourse formalises popular sovereignty, its neoliberalist fellow turns citizens into right-owners, clients and consumers. Due to this double movement, the people as a collective political subject has lost its relevance. Consequently, 'the very idea of a people, a demos asserting its collective political sovereignty' is abolished.[73] The rule of law and global capitalism have become everything, and due to this, the people is, once again, nothing.

---

[73] Wendy Brown, *Undoing the Demos: Neoliberalism's Stealth Revolution* (New York: Zone Books, 2015), p. 39. See also Honig, *Public Things*, pp. 17–21.

For Nancy, the failure of liberal democracies brings 'discontent, bitterness and revolt to the people who no longer recognise themselves as a people'. Auto- and ontocratic patriotism, nationalism and autonomism attempt to show that democracy is linked with national unity, as they replace the people 'without identity with one falsely identified as the avenger or the savior of its own identity'.[74] The constituent power of the people is lost as it becomes nationalist identity politics.

Based on Sieyès' definition of the people, we have attempted to advance the idea that constituent power is not to be reduced to liberal constitutionalism or nationalism. A third alternative could be an emancipatory identity policy that propagates various social, gender, sexual or ethnic groups based on a shared identity or essence. Even if these kinds of progressive identity policies have their merits, they reduce universal political issues into, Rousseau would say, questions of particular social interest groups. With this kind of identity politics comes the new political correctness discourse, which dissolves solidarity and the egalitarian power of the people.

We have attempted, citing Nancy, 'to remake "people," to repopulate' it by rethinking the revolutionary concepts of general will, social contract, direct democracy and constitutive power.[75] On the one hand, these revolutionary concepts remind us of the possibility of the power of the people. On the other hand, the dialogue between Rousseau, Nancy and Rancière affirms that there is an egalitarian and democratic way to understand the people beyond the triad of abstract liberal democracy and the opposing concrete versions of law and politics, nationalism and progressive identity policy.

'To take back control' means for us that the people, as the constituent power without any pre-given authority or identity, acquires the power to control the global, transnational and local processes. Beyond legal subjects and particular identities, there is the people as the power of political events 'based' on equality and solidarity, a nothing that is always already everything. The power of the people is mobilised 'on a truly revolutionary scale', while 'the formation of a common or a popular will' is up to political subjects.[76] Time and again, the power of the people constitutes the people as the empty ground of the popular sovereignty, and the power of this constituent people, with no Napoleon Bonaparte declaring himself to be the constituent power.[77]

---

[74] Nancy, 'Populism and Democracy'.
[75] Nancy, 'Populism and Democracy'.
[76] Peter Hallward, 'The Will to Leave?', in *The Brexit Crisis: A Verso Report* (London & New York: Verso, 2016), pp. 35–40, at pp. 38–39.
[77] Arendt, *On Revolution*, p. 163.

The power of the people may be naïve utopianism. Yet, when utopias are condemned as impossibilities, we may still have a theoretical and political duty to consider them possible. Nancy concludes that 'Europe today does not have a general will because it is unable to create a political representation of itself'.[78] Then again, the eruption of the constituent power repeatedly creates the people. The surging of the general will as a force of 'disagreement' and 'confrontation' – or *mesente* (Rancière) and *affrontement* (Nancy) – necessary for the constitution of the general will, the social contract and the people includes the democratic and egalitarian power of the people. The power of the people is the constituent power that refers only to itself as people, recognising itself as the political event of this power. As Rousseau says, 'the general will is indestructible'.[79]

---

[78] Nancy, 'Politics and Beyond', p. 94.
[79] Rousseau, *On the Social Contract*, p. 203.

10

Populism: Plebeian Power against Oligarchy

Camila Vergara

Introduction

Since the wave of neoliberal policies implemented in the 1970s and 1980s, liberal democracies have experienced a process of oligarchization in which wealth and income inequalities as well as political corruption have steadily increased. In the United States, for example, while the share of wealth held by the top 0.1 per cent sharply increased from 7 per cent in the late 1970s to 22 per cent in 2016, the bottom 90 per cent of the population saw their wealth shrink during the same period, currently owning only about 22 per cent of US wealth.[1] Growing inequality has increased together with political corruption, a phenomenon that has become 'endemic' in the majority of representative governments and that according to Transparency International 'violates human rights, prevents sustainable development and fuels social exclusion'.[2] This process of oligarchization, in which the rich get richer and increase their undue influence on representative government while ordinary citizens are impoverished and politically disempowered, has increasingly become a dominant trend among liberal democracies.

As a response to the imposition of the Washington Consensus in Latin America and austerity measures in Southern Europe, populist politicians claiming to represent the people and advocating for redistribution quickly gained traction. The so-called Pink Tide of populist leaders and parties embracing non-communist left-leaning projects begun with the election of Hugo Chávez in Venezuela (1998), who campaigned on a platform of social justice and constituent change. While in Latin America the populist

---

[1] Anthony Atkinson, Thomas Piketty, and Emmanuel Saez, 'Top Incomes in the Long Run of History' *Journal of Economic Literature* 49:1 (2011) pp. 3–71; Emmanuel Saez and Gabriel Zucman, 'Wealth Inequality in the United States since 1913: Evidence from Capitalized Income Tax Data', *The Quarterly Journal of Economics* 131:2 (2016), pp. 519–578.

[2] Transparency International, *Corruption Perceptions Index Report 2016*, 25 January 2017. Available at https://www.transparency.org/news/feature/corruption_perceptions_index_2016 (accessed 13 September 2019).

revolution and its '21st century socialism' has been relatively successful, taking power in Bolivia (2006) and Ecuador (2007), resulting in new participatory constitutions and an expansion of social services,[3] in Southern Europe Podemos, even if it managed to become the third-largest party in Spain, has been unable to exert control over the government and implement its populist agenda. The Syriza government in Greece, even if rhetorically populist in its electoral phase, was ultimately unable to reject austerity policies imposed by the EU after taking power in 2015.[4]

The populism of the Pink Tide – which denounced the increasing material deprivation of the masses and the collusion of economic and political elites, and seek to empower the common people against oligarchy – has little substantive resemblance to far right, ethnocentric parties appealing to the people-as-nation, which have recently been on the rise in liberal democracies. After the Sweden Democrats, a party with neo-Nazi roots, entered the Swedish parliament in 2010 with a platform against multiculturalism and immigration,[5] nationalist parties have sprung up in almost every country in the European Union.[6] Even if academia and the media have also labelled this wave of ethnonationalist politics as populist, these right-wing parties have little in common with populist parties in Latin America and Southern Europe, and do not fit into the long history of populism that begun in 1860s Russia. This classificatory confusion is partially rooted in the identification of populism mostly with a style of politics, the repertoires and discourses leaders and parties use to canvas votes and achieve power. Conceiving populism *exclusively* as a form of political discourse,[7]

---

[3] For an overview of the Pink Tide, see Carlos de la Torre, *Latin American Populism in the Twenty-First Century* (Baltimore: Johns Hopkins University Press, 2013). Note that he analyses populism as an embodiment theory of power, which emphasises leadership over movements.

[4] For an analysis of populism in Europe see Giorgios Katsambekis and Alexandros Kioupkiolis (eds.), *The Populist Radical Left in Europe* (London: Routledge, 2019).

[5] For an analysis of how the salience of nationalist ideas brought into the public debate by the Sweden Democrats allowed it to mobilise around anti-immigration policies see Anders Hellström et al., 'Nationalism vs. Nationalism: The Challenge of the Sweden Democrats in the Swedish Public Debate', *Government and Opposition* 47:2 (2012), pp. 186–205. See also Leila Brännström's contribution to this volume.

[6] For an overview of parties and their platforms see Jens Rydgren (ed.), *The Oxford Handbook of the Radical Right* (Oxford: Oxford University Press, 2018).

[7] David Howarth, Aletta Norval, and Yannis Stavrakakis (eds), *Discourse Theory and Political Analysis. Identities, Hegemony and Social Change* (Manchester: Manchester University Press, 2000); Ernesto Laclau, *On Populist Reason* (London: Verso, 2005); Kirk Hawkins and C. Rovira. 'What the (Ideational) Study of Populism Can Teach Us, and What It Can't', *Swiss Political Science Review* 23:4 (2017), pp. 526–542.

performance[8] or strategy[9] neglects the different conceptions of the people, goals and relations to liberal democracy of the political parties and leaders currently being labelled as populists.

Even if the difference between class-based politics – aimed at emancipating and empowering the popular sectors (plebs) – and ethnic-based politics – aimed at re-establishing a lost dominance of the ethnic majority (nation) – are clear, democratic theory has been analysing the *politics of the nation* as if it were part of the *politics of the plebs*: the 'good' or 'less bad' version being ideologically left-wing, advocating for redistribution of property and political power, and the 'bad' or 'worse' version being right-wing, pushing for anti-immigration and anti-pluralist laws. In this chapter, I provide theoretical grounds to move away from this normative ambiguity by situating populism within the republican tradition of thought. Different from democratic theory, which is premised on the idea of the people-as-a-whole, republican theory is premised on the socio-ontological split between the ruling elite[10] and the common people, and the need for establishing a productive conflict between them to achieve liberty as non-domination. Populist leaders and parties – conceived as champions of the plebs, a partiality – are *virtuous* because of the positive role they play within the constitutional structure to empower the people against the overgrowth of oligarchic power. As a form of *plebeian* politics, populism springs from the de-naturalisation and politicisation of inequality and seeks to emancipate and empower the people-as-plebs not only through redistribution of property and political power but also through legal and political reforms aimed at curtailing the entrenched power of oligarchy.[11]

A conception of populism as a plebeian, anti-oligarchic form of politics that pursues the empowerment of the people-as-plebs is not only more in tune with the long history of populism, but also allows us to better understand the *extraordinary* authority that populist representation claims. In what follows I offer a brief analysis of the origin of extraordinary plebeian

---

[8] Benjamin Moffitt, *The Global Rise of Populism: Performance, Political Style, and Representation* (Stanford: Stanford University Press, 2016).

[9] Kurt Weyland, 'Clarifying a Contested Concept: Populism in the Study of Latin American Politics', *Comparative Politics* 34:1 (2001), pp 1–22; Robert Jansen, 'Populist Mobilization: A New Theoretical Approach to Populism', *Sociological Theory* 29:2 (2011), pp. 75–96.

[10] I follow Charles Mills' structural conception of the power elite as the ruling class. See C. Wright Mills, *The Power Elite* (Oxford: Oxford University Press, 1956).

[11] For an extended analysis of plebeian populism see Camila Vergara 'Populism as Plebeian Politics: Inequality, Domination, and Popular Empowerment', *Journal of Political Philosophy*, 28.2 (2020), pp. 224–246.

representation in the late Roman Republic, then a brief historical overview of the use of the term populism, and finally an analysis of populism as a form of plebeian politics.

Plebeian Politics and the *Popularis* Tribune

Recent reinterpretations of Machiavelli coming from radical democratic and republican thought have reintroduced the people-as-plebs as a central category of analysis within liberal democracy, highlighting the productive role of class conflict in preserving and regaining liberty.[12] Against the predominant elitist reading of Machiavelli that equates liberty with the rule of law,[13] John McCormick's 'populist' interpretation[14] shows that for Machiavelli a free republic is based on a conflict in which ordinary people are powerful enough to restrain the ambitions of the ruling elite and keep their independence, which requires low socio-economic inequality.[15] Even though the theory of popular sovereignty that underpins liberal representative government[16] has obscured the fundamental division between the ruling elite and the common people – and the *humours*[17] that according to Machiavelli animate each constitutive part – this split is factual and unavoidable. A republican conception of non-domination requires the recognition of this split and of the people-as-plebs as a political subject whose role is to protect liberty.[18]

[12] See also Gabriele Pedullà, *Machiavelli in Tumult: The* Discourses on Livy *and the Origins of Political Conflictualism* (Cambridge: Cambridge University Press, 2018), published in Italian in 2011.

[13] Quentin Skinner, 'Machiavelli and the Maintenance of Liberty', *Politics* 18:2 (1978), pp. 3–15; Philip Pettit, *Republicanism: A Theory of Freedom and Government* (Oxford: Oxford University Press, 1999). For an early critique of the Cambridge School's interpretation, see John P. McCormick, 'Machiavellian Democracy: Controlling Elites with Ferocious Populism', *American Political Science Review* 95:2 (2001), pp. 297–313; John P. McCormick, 'Machiavelli Against Republicanism: On the Cambridge School's "Guicciardinian Moments"', *Political Theory*, 31:5 (2003), pp. 615–643.

[14] John P. McCormick, *Machiavellian Democracy* (Cambridge: Cambridge University Press, 2011).

[15] Niccolò Machiavelli, 'Discourses on the First Decade of Titus Livius', in *Machiavelli: The Chief Works and Others*, trans. Allan Gilbert (Durham: Duke University Press, 1989), pp. 175–529, at p. 310 (I.55).

[16] Perhaps the most influential is John Locke's theory of the sovereign community composed of individuals with equal natural rights, who create a government for the protection of private property. John Locke, *Two Treatises of Government,* 2nd edn. (Cambridge: Cambridge University Press, 1988).

[17] Following Hippocrates' theory of humours based on the influence of fluids on the body, Machiavelli argues that there are two basic *umori* that comprise the body politic: the great, who want to command and oppress, and the people, who desire to live in freedom and security. Machiavelli, 'Discourses', p. 203 (I.4).

[18] Machiavelli, 'Discourses', p. 204 (I.5).

Throughout history, the plebeian political actor, which according to Martin Breaugh has periodically re-emerged within the 'discontinuous struggle for freedom', should not be conceived as a social category or an identity, but rather as an experience, 'the passage from a subpolitical status to one of a full-fledged political subject'.[19] Moreover, the plebeian actor is determined by the experience of revolt, a refusing of 'the limits of the possible present of the dominant order.'[20]

The emergence of plebeian ideology and its relation to liberty needs to be understood within the institutional structure set up in the constitution of the ancient Roman Republic.[21] A mixed regime combining the three best forms of government (kingship, aristocracy and popular government), the Roman constitution had a tripartite structure in which its main political institutions gave expression to the divide between the few and the many, and the role of kingly leadership (the Consuls, the Senate, and the Plebeian Council and Tribunate). According to Polybius, in the Roman Republic these three forms of authority and institutional power were designed so 'each of them can be effectively counteracted and hampered by the others' to conserve the system so that if one of the part 'thanks to an inflated impression of its own importance,' aims at gaining 'the upper hand' and establishing its dominance, its 'impetus is checked' either by self-restraint or the actions of the other parts.[22] Even if by the late Republic the Plebeian Tribunate appeared as a strong institution able not only to give protection to individuals against the Consuls but also to obstruct the Senate and initiate legislation, it was unable to ultimately thwart the overgrowth of the power of the nobility. The republic kept progressively drifting into oligarchy mainly due to the cooptation of tribunes into patrician ranks and the Senate's disregard of the legislative authority of the Plebeian Council.[23] The emergence of the *popularis* tribune – as a surplus of representation – could be seen as an extraordinary response to the overreaching of oligarchic power, aimed at fulfilling the 'thwarting function'

---

[19] Martin Breaugh, *The Plebeian Experience: A Discontinuous History of Political Freedom* (New York: Columbia University Press, 2013), p. 1.

[20] Breaugh, *The Plebeian Experience*, p. xvi

[21] Livy, *The History of Rome. Vol. 1*, trans. by George Baker (London: Jones, 1834), pp. 47–48 (3§55).

[22] Polybius, *The Histories*, trans. Robin Waterfield (Oxford: Oxford University Press, 2010), p. 385 (6§18).

[23] CH. Wirszubski, *Libertas as a Political Idea at Rome During the Late Republic and Early Principate* (Cambridge: Cambridge University Press, 1968); Andrew Lintott, *The Constitution of the Roman Republic* (Oxford: Oxford University Press, 2009).

that the mixed constitution demanded if liberty as non-domination was to be preserved.[24]

The difference between an ordinary plebeian tribune acting (or ceasing to act) to maintain a deteriorating stability,[25] and a *popularis*, actively empowering the plebs to effectively counteract the power of elites, is made clear in the political struggle to bring about redistribution of land led by the Tribune Tiberius Gracchus (133 BC). Despite commanding a majority in the Plebeian Council – which would have meant a favourable plebiscite and the consequent establishment of the agrarian law – the tribune Marcus Octavius, prompted by 'the prayers and supplications of many influential men', opposed the law, vetoing the motion. Since Tiberius could not pass the law in any other way, he was forced to do something unprecedented: to eject Octavius from his office. Tiberius' speech justifying this illegal motion makes the internal, normative distinction between a *popularis* – the champion of the plebs – and a negligent, ordinary tribune who instead of being a 'guardian and protector' of the people allows for their oppression by siding with the status quo and undermining popular power.[26] According to this distinction, the people's true representative not only resists corrupting tendencies, but also *actively* empowers plebeians against increasing patrician power. *Popularis* activity and ideology stands thus against the mere maintenance of the status quo, as a source of change, actively pursuing the socio-economic and political empowerment of the plebs by going against oligarchic interests and authority.[27] It is this character of the *popularis* leader as guardian of liberty, as directly pursuing the empowerment of the people-as-plebs to protect liberty from the overreaching of oligarchic power, which I argue should define populism as a modern expression of the plebeian struggle for liberty within representative democratic regimes.

[24] Cicero identified the *popularis* as a 'guardian and defender of right and liberty,' concerned with protecting the interests of the plebs for the benefit of the republic. Cicero, *Pro Rabirio Perduellionis Reo Oratio Ad Quirites* (Cambridge: Cambridge University Press, 1882), p. 57 (§12).

[25] Cicero saw the Tribunate as necessary for taming popular power and directing it to the common good. Cicero, *On the Laws,* in Cicero, *On the Commonwealth and On the Laws* (Cambridge: Cambridge University Press, 1999), pp. 105–175, at pp. 166–167 (3§23–26).

[26] Plutarch, 'Life of Tiberius and Caius Gracchi,' in *Plutarch's Lives: A Selection*, trans. Thomas North (Cambridge: Cambridge University Press, 2014), pp. 163–207, at pp. 174–176 (§10).

[27] For an analysis of the origins of *popularis* ideology see Lauren Kaplow, 'Creating "Popularis" History: Sp. Cassius, Sp. Maelius, and M. Manlius in the Political Discourse of the Late Republic', *Bulletin of the Institute of Classical Studies* 55:2 (2012), pp. 101–109.

Populism: History and Interpretations

The most recent precedent of contemporary populism can be traced to the mid-1860s Russian clandestine revolutionary group Zemlya i Volya (Land and Liberty), which sought to pursue the emancipation of the people through redistribution of land and self-government.[28] Informed by the experience of the revolutionary movements of 1848 and the peasant and student revolts of the early 1860s, the ideology of Russian populism (*narodnichestvo*) was centred on the need to 'help the people [*narod*] organize its forces and to throw off the yoke of the government.'[29] The concept begun to be consistently used also in the United States with the establishment in 1891 of the People's Party, which was born out of the electoral coalition between the protest movements of the Southern Farmers' Alliance, the Colored Farmers' National Alliance, and the Knights of Labor.[30] Low agricultural prices and the consequent impoverishment of yeomen and tenants enabled a popular movement organised across racial and gender lines against planter and financial elites.[31] The Populist Party became a considerable electoral force immediately, effectively contesting the Democratic Party's electoral dominance in every Southern state from 1892 to 1896. Populist leaders were egalitarian abolitionists, who opposed a system of power that allowed commercial and financial elites to use the state for their own benefit. Their policy platforms demanded more effective ways to advance the people's interests such as the nationalisation of communication and transportation agencies, progressive taxation, and the opening of state colleges for women and Blacks[32] as well as institutional innovations to better express the popular will and control representatives, such as popular initiatives, referenda and recall elections.[33] This populist experience

[28] Franco Venturi, *Roots of Revolution. A History of the Populist and Socialist Movements in Nineteenth Century Russia* (New York: Knopf, 1960).

[29] Lev Tikhomirov, one of the leaders of *Zemlya i Volya*, in his memoires quoted in Richard Pipes, 'Narodnichestvo: A Semantic Inquiry', *Slavic Review* 23:3 (1964), pp. 441–458, at p. 445.

[30] Jack Abramowitz, 'The Negro in the Populist Movement', *The Journal of Negro History* 38:3 (1953), pp. 257–289.

[31] Even if racial and gender integration was not part of the official populist platform, non-discrimination was 'a point of pride' especially among Knights of Labor members. For an account of the uneasy accommodation of egalitarian ideas and white supremacist ideology coming from the White Farmers Alliance see Laura Grattan, *Populism's Power* (Oxford: Oxford University Press, 2016), chapter 2.

[32] Robert Durden, *The Climax of Populism: The Election of 1896* (Lexington: University Press of Kentucky, 2015).

[33] Frederick Turner, *The Frontier in American History* (New York: Henry Holt and Company, 1921).

was interpreted as a radical, short-lived challenge to capitalism coming from a diverse network of grassroots organisations.[34]

After the populist alliance in the US, the term populist was consistently used during the 1930s–50s in Latin America to describe leaders and governments that enfranchised the popular sectors and developed their national economy to lift the masses out of poverty. Perhaps the most prominent populist was Juan Perón in Argentina (1946–1955), who effectively incorporated the working classes into the political system and increased their socio-economic status through expansive economic policies and a new constitution containing workers' rights.[35]

When neoliberalism began to be forcefully implemented in the 1980s, 'populist politics unexpectedly reappeared' in the region, albeit this time in a new form that departed from the original thrust of populism.[36] This time political outsiders with an anti-elitist rhetoric made vague promises to deal with economic crisis and embraced neoliberal reforms when in government, causing further impoverishment and inequality.[37] This *neo-populism* was analysed during the 1990s mostly in the field of comparative politics, in which there was relative consensus on the labelling of the phenomenon as *neo-* to distinguish it from 'classical' populism, since the later political experiments ended up with further immiseration of the popular sectors and a more robust, discriminatory police state instead of the enfranchisement and increased welfare of the masses. This anomaly in the labelling of populism in Latin America, which combined right-wing economic ideology and a charismatic political outsider, was superseded by another wave of populism possessing the original drive towards empowerment of the popular sectors and control over the market.

---

[34] Norman Pollack, *The Populist Mind* (Indianapolis: Bobbs-Merrill, 1967); Michael Schwartz, *Radical Protest and Social Structure: The Southern Farmers' Alliance and Cotton Tenancy, 1880–1890* (Chicago: University of Chicago Press, 1976); Robert McMath, *Populist Vanguard: A History of the Southern Farmers' Alliance* (New York: Norton, 1977).

[35] Jeremy Adelman, 'Reflections on Argentine Labour and the Rise of Perón', *Bulletin of Latin American Research* 11:3 (1992), pp. 243–259.

[36] Kurt Weyland, 'Clarifying a Contested Concept: Populism in the Study of Latin American Politics', *Comparative Politics* 34:1 (2001), pp. 1–22.

[37] Denise Dresser, *Neopopulist Solutions to Neoliberal Problems* (San Diego: University of California Press 1991); Kenneth Roberts, 'Neoliberalism and the Transformation of Populism in Latin America', *World Politics* 4:8 (1995), pp. 82–116; Kurt Weyland, 'Neopopulism and Neoliberalism in Latin America', *Studies in Comparative International Development* 31:3 (1996), pp 3–31; Alan Knight, 'Populism and Neo-populism in Latin America', *Journal of Latin American Studies* 30:2 (1998), pp. 223–248.

The new populist wave of the Pink Tide, begun as a backlash to austerity measures with the rise in 1998 of Hugo Chávez in Venezuela.[38] After sweeping neoliberal reforms and a sudden hike in gasoline prices and transportation fares were established in 1989, people took to the streets, in a week-long uprising known as *Caracazo*.[39] Chávez is the undisputed, exemplar populist leader in the literature not only because of his expansionist economic policies and the political enfranchisement of the popular sectors, but also because of his flamboyant, antagonistic rhetoric and authoritarian style. He sponsored what he called '21st century socialism' through a new pluralist constitution (1999) containing social rights and equal protection clauses for women and minorities, in addition to a strengthened, but recallable executive. During his fourteen years in office, Chávez achieved a 40 per cent poverty reduction and one of the lowest inequality rates in the region, in addition to free healthcare and other social initiatives.[40]

Following closely the experience of the so-called Bolivarian revolution carried out not only by Chávez in Venezuela but also by Evo Morales in Bolivia and Rafael Correa in Ecuador, the Spanish political party Podemos is perhaps the only ongoing undisputed case of populism outside of Latin America. The party was born out of the 2011 *Indignados* protest movement against the ruling elite and the austerity measures that immiserated the middle and lower sectors of the population.[41] Less than a year after being established, Podemos became the third strongest political force in the Spanish parliament, securing 20 per cent of the national vote. Its egalitarian platform advocated for nationalising hydroelectric power stations, higher

---

[38] For an analysis of this new wave of populism see Carlos de la Torre, *Latin American Populism in the Twenty-First Century* (Baltimore: Johns Hopkins University Press, 2013).

[39] Almost 2/3 of Venezuela's population were living below the poverty line at this point. Edgardo Lander, 'The Impact of Neoliberal Adjustment in Venezuela, 1989-1993', *Latin American Perspectives* 23:3 (1996), pp. 50–73, at p. 65.

[40] See *Economic Survey of Latin America and the Caribbean 2010-2011: International integration and macroeconomic policy challenges amid global economic turmoil.* Report by the Economic Commission for Latin America and the Caribbean (ECLAC) (Santiago, Chile: United Nations, 2011), pp. 61–73. For poverty reduction see Mark Weisbrot, Luis Sandoval, and David Rosnick 'Poverty Rates in Venezuela: Getting the Numbers Right', *International Journal of Health Services* 36:4 (2006), pp. 813–823. Economic and political disarray after Chávez's death should not taint the analysis of his populist achievements. How corruption undermined them, however, should be central to the analysis.

[41] Spain's unemployment rate reached 21.3 per cent with almost five million people out of a job. Youth unemployment rate was 46.23 per cent, the highest in the European Union. See Youth Unemployment Rate, OECD Data. Available at https://data.oecd.org/unemp/youth-unemployment-rate.htm (accessed 10 September 2019).

taxation of the wealthy, increasing the minimum wage, stopping home evictions, and refinancing mortgages.[42]

Theories of Populism: from Discursive to Totalitarian Interpretations

Theorists agree that populism originates in a crisis of representation, a lack of responsiveness of democratically elected leaders to a portion of the population and their inability or unwillingness to satisfy social demands. According to Margaret Canovan populism is born out of crisis as a cure to the failures of traditional forms of representation.[43] Conceiving democracy as the point where redemptive and pragmatic sides of politics intersect, she argues that populist interventions are best understood as invocations of the redemptive face of democracy, as a *corrective* to the excesses of pragmatism. For Canovan, populism is 'an appeal to "the people" against both the established structure of power and the dominant ideas and values of the society', and thus the populist leader is often an outsider who runs against traditional political parties and predominant elite values.[44] According to this view, populism would be a democratising phenomenon aimed at perfecting democratic representativeness, renewing the political system from within. This notion of populism as a 'corrective' was gradually lost within the theoretical discussion, especially after the *discursive turn* in the interpretation of the concept.

Perhaps influenced by the idiosyncratic case of Peronism – which has been able to accommodate different ideological tendencies in its more than seven decades of existence – Ernesto Laclau detached populism from both ideology and material conditions by conceiving it as a discursive process of identity formation open to accommodate different popular identifications. In *On Populist Reason* – the point of departure for most of the theoretical literature on populism coming from the Left – he analyses the process through which the people become a political subject: when unsatisfied demands enter into a 'logic of equivalence' and the populist leader emerges by appealing directly to the people as a collective identity, these demands are retrospectively unified and sublimated under an 'empty signifier'. This 'radical retroactive ontology' is central to Laclau's theory of populism, in which the reconstruction of a collective identity out of the heterogeneity of the social allows for the people to become itself an empty signifier without the need for any previous unity.[45]

---

[42] *Podemos'* policy proposals, even if coherent with the original thrust of populism, are a far cry from the experimental populist experiences in Latin America.

[43] Margaret Canovan, *Populism* (New York: Harcourt, Brace, Jovanovich, 1981); Margaret Canovan, 'Trust the People! Populism and the Two Faces of Democracy', *Political Studies* 47:1 (1999), pp. 2–16.

[44] Canovan, 'Trust the People!', p. 3

[45] Laclau, *On Populist Reason,* p. 69

Despite attempting to depart from democratic theory by engaging with republican thought, arguing the people of populism relates to the Roman plebs, Laclau's theory seems trapped in the logic of the people-as-one, which is rooted not in the Roman Republic, but in the medieval embodiment of power and the myth of popular sovereignty coming out of seventeenth-century social contract theory. The people of populism is for him 'a *plebs* who claims to be the only legitimate *populus* – that is, a partiality which wants to function as the totality of the community'.[46] This *pars pro toto* logic – partiality supplanting the totality – would make populism a politico-theological ideology aimed at the embodiment of power.[47]

Even if Laclau's theory of political identity formation – as a prevalence of equivalence over difference through an empty signifier – is certainly the most sophisticated theoretical description of the constitutive discursive process at work in collective action, the claim that a partial identity would necessarily aim at becoming the only legitimate identity is an unexplained conceptual leap. Why would the plebs aim not only at controlling the state temporarily (the same as any partisan would do) but also at embodying it and supplanting the *populus*? Even if in Rome the plebs certainly desired to set themselves free from patrician domination and punish the nobles for their oppressive rule, there is no evidence of them aiming at taking up 'an incommensurable universal signification' to constitute a 'truly universal *populous*' conceived as an 'ideal totality'.[48]

The 'conceptual stretching'[49] that begun with the severing of populism from ideology and material conditions was paired with a 'minimal' definition of populism coming from empirical political studies, which has produced much research and the further entrenchment of the 'totalitarian' interpretation of populism. The most influential definition of populism in the recent literature is that of Cas Mudde, a scholar of the European far right.[50] Following Michael Freeden's analysis of ideologies,[51] Mudde conceives populism as a

---

[46] Laclau, *On Populist Reason*, p. 81

[47] For a critique of Laclau's theologising of populism see Andrew Arato, 'Political Theology and Populism', *Social Research* 80:1 (2013), pp. 143–172.

[48] Laclau, *On Populist Reason,* pp. 70 and 94

[49] Giovanni Sartori, 'Concept Misformation in Comparative Politics', *American Political Science Review* 64:4 (1970), pp. 1033–1053

[50] Cas Mudde, 'The Populist Zeitgeist', *Government and Opposition* 39:4 (2004), pp. 541–563.

[51] Michael Freeden, *Ideologies and Political Theory* (Oxford: Oxford University Press, 1996), pp. 75–82. Freeden disagrees with Mudde and Rovira's use of his theory to conceptualise populism, arguing that as an ideology 'it is emaciatedly thin rather than thin-centred.' Michael Freeden, 'After the Brexit Referendum: Revisiting Populism as an Ideology', *Journal of Political Ideologies* 22:1 (2017), pp. 1–11, at p. 3.

'thin-centered ideology that considers society to be ultimately separated into two homogeneous and antagonistic camps, "'the pure people" versus "the corrupt elite", and which argues that politics should be an expression of the volonté générale (general will) of the people'.[52] For Mudde the anti-elitism that is at the core of the concept is what makes populism the 'direct opposite' of pluralism. He argues that due to populism's Manichean 'distinction of society' and consequent drive for creating a 'homogenous "good" and a homogenous "evil"' populist actors would go against or weaken the 'broad variety of partly overlapping social groups with different ideas and interests' that characterises pluralism.[53] This false opposition between populism and pluralism stems from Mudde's own definition, which introduces the element of homogeneity as part of the concept's core. Even if an anti-pluralist tendency is evident in cases he labels 'right-wing populism' – his subject of expertise – the claim that it is appropriate to interpret populism as intrinsically opposed to pluralism falls apart when analysing the most paradigmatic cases of populist governments in Latin America, which constitutionally recognised minority rights.[54]

Even if a minimal definition based on populism's undisputed anti-elitism has produced fruitful research due to its easy operationalisation (the people vs the elite), this simplification has also reinforced the false premise that populism is, in essence, a form of anti-pluralism, which in turn increases the conflation of populist and ethnocentric leaders and parties. As an expression of plebeian politics, the formal definition based on the antagonism between 'the people' and 'the elite' refers *only* to the pushback of *plebeians* – the disenfranchised working classes broadly understood – against *oligarchy* – large estate holders, corporations, banks and the political class supporting their interests. I would argue the anti-pluralist premise, based on populism's supposed drive toward homogeneity and the establishment of a totalising hegemonic logic (*pars par toto*), should not be deployed in the study of populism. Never in history have plebeians become hegemonic and established anti-pluralist, totalitarian regimes.

---

[52] Cas Mudde and Cristobal Rovira, *Populism: A Very Short Introduction* (Oxford: Oxford University Press, 2017), p. 6. See previous definitions in Mudde, 'The Populist Zeitgeist', and Cas Mudde, *Populist Radical Right Parties in Europe* (Cambridge: Cambridge University Press, 2007). For a critique of Mudde, see Paris Aslanidis, 'Is Populism an Ideology? A Refutation and a New Perspective', *Political Studies* 64:1 (2015), pp. 88–104.

[53] Mudde and Rovira, *Populism*, p. 7.

[54] See for example the case of Hugo Chávez's policies on race in Barry Cannon, 'Class/Race Polarisation in Venezuela and the Electoral Success of Hugo Chávez: A Break with the Past or the Song Remains the Same?', *Third World Quarterly* 29:4 (2008), pp. 731–748.

Populism as an Electoral Form of Plebeian Politics

Increasing income inequality around the world since the 1980s has enabled growing corruption in politics: the undue influence by powerful citizens on political representatives, who legislate for the interest of the few and not the many. The consequent crisis of representation, in which social demands remain permanently unsatisfied by traditional political parties, further reveals inequality and naked power, making possible the re-emergence of the people-as-plebs under a populist actor who is distinguished by a crusade *against* the domination of the few and *for* the empowerment of the many. Populism as an electoral type of plebeian politics springs from the politicisation of wealth inequality,[55] from the de-naturalisation of the status quo, aimed at rebalancing the scales of social and political power between the elite and the people, by weakening the former and empowering the latter. The same as the *popularis* tribune functioned within the constitutional structure of the Roman Republic as a protector of liberty against oligarchic overreach. The populist representative would come to fulfil a 'thwarting function', empowered to revert the patterns of accumulation and dispossession as a necessary condition for plebeian liberty.

In addition to being a symptom of systemic corruption of the representative system,[56] populism also signals to a subject of representation that has no place in liberal representative governments but nevertheless asserts itself through elections and mobilisations: the people-as-plebs is reconstructed based on the recognition that ordinary citizens are in fact second-class citizens.[57] Different from an ethnic-based identity based on race, religion and language, 'the people' of populism acquires its identity based on a common experience of exclusion and oppression. Even if it is a collective partiality that relates to the Roman plebs, the people-as-plebs are not legally separated from the elites and are not represented in a plebeian institution, and therefore they constitute a *concealed* collective subject. I argue the lack of a plebeian institution serves to explain the emergence and pervasiveness of populism today: as an expression of a *chronic constitutional deficiency,* a lack of institutional power for common people to collectively push back against

---

[55] Kenneth Roberts, 'Social Correlates of Party System Demise and Populist Resurgence in Venezuela', *Latin American Politics and Society* 45:3 (2003), pp. 35–57.

[56] If seen from a structural perspective, political corruption is a long-term, slow-moving process of oligarchization of society's political structure. See my analysis in Camila Vergara, 'Corruption as Systemic Political Decay', *Philosophy and Social Criticism*, Early View (August 2019).

[57] Jeffrey Green, *The Shadow of Unfairness: A Plebeian Theory of Liberal Democracy* (Oxford: Oxford University Press, 2016).

increasing oligarchic domination. Then, it is only under economic crisis and increased oppression, when the veil of legal equality thins out, allowing for the division between the few and the many to become re-politicised and for the people-as-plebs to be reconstituted through extraordinary leadership and mobilisation.

Jacques Rancière's conception of the 'democratic people' also seems helpful to escape the totalising logic wrongly ascribed to populism.[58] By presenting politics as disagreement, as 'forms of expression that confront the logic of equality with the logic of the police order',[59] his democratic people are those who do not have a part in the system of rule, a people subjectified through the performance of an egalitarian logic of disagreement. True political action is always democratic because it attacks inequality and seeks to dismantle patterns of oppression that have been naturalised through the discipline of the police logic. Because politics as disagreement has been completely foreclosed by consensus democracy – a post-democratic regime in which there is an "absolute removal of the sphere of appearance of the people"[60] – plebeian forms of politics – popular performances of the egalitarian logic against the hierarchical logic of police – are sporadic and ephemeral, outbursts of emancipation amid the oligarchic structure of the police order. Moreover, given its egalitarian logic, political action has a specific subject who cannot be constructed along identitarian lines because it 'exists only in the form of disjunction'.[61] The democratic subject is 'not definable in terms of ethnic properties' or identified 'with a sociologically determinable part of a population', but a subject made up of 'those who have no part', who do not 'coincide with the parties of the state or of society, floating subjects that deregulate all representation of places and portions.'[62]

---

[58] Even if for Rancière the label of 'populism' is today just a 'convenient name under which is dissimulated the exacerbated contradiction between popular legitimacy and expert legitimacy', a concept deployed by elites that puts together features that have 'no necessary connection' and that 'amalgamate[s] the very idea of a democratic people with the image of the dangerous crowd.' Jacques Rancière, *Hatred of Democracy*, trans. Steve Corcoran (New York: Verso, 2006), p. 80. See also Jacques Rancière, 'The People Are Not a Brutal and Ignorant Mass', trans. David Fernbach. Verso blog, 30 January 2013. Available at https://www.versobooks.com/blogs/1226-the-people-are-not-a-brutal-and-ignorant-mass-jacques-ranciere-on-populism (accessed 10 September 2019).

[59] Jacques Rancière, *Disagreement: Politics and Philosophy,* trans. Julie Rose (Minneapolis: University of Minnesota Press, 1998), p. 101.

[60] Rancière, *Disagreement*, p. 103.

[61] Jacques Rancière, *Dissensus: On Politics and Aesthetics,* trans. Steven Corcoran (London: Continuum, 2010), p. 53.

[62] Rancière, *Disagreement*, p. 99.

Similarly, the 'people from below' as Juho Turpeinen suggests in his chapter in this volume, could also be conceived as akin to Butler's precariat, constructed based on an egalitarian logic of alterity and disagreement that not only is different from identitarian constructions of the people but also would stand as opposed to them. I would argue that because ethnic constructions of the people are not democratic, but forms of subjectification that reproduce the logic of police and oligarchic domination, they should not be conceived as part of a politics of disagreement, and therefore do not belong in the same conceptual field. Ethnic and plebeian conceptions of the people, and the politics they engender, are not part of a continuum but radically different forms of subjectification; while the ethnic people is constructed within the exclusionary and oligarchic logic of police, the plebeian people disrupts the logic of police by defying the structures of oligarchic rule and appearing as a political actor through a performance that materialises the logic of equality.

Conclusion

Constitutional governments have so far been unable to revert patterns of accumulation and dispossession that are now comparable to those of the *ancien régime*.[63] While deregulation in the financial system ultimately enabled the 2008 financial crisis that produced massive transfer of wealth from the many to the few,[64] there has been an increasing pattern of collusion between economic and political elites[65] that has allowed for a regulatory framework enabling massive amounts of wealth to be accumulated at the top of the income distribution.[66] Populism is a response to the crisis of representation prompted by increasing inequality and corruption and should be conceived as a way of reverting the current patterns of wealth accumulation to regain liberty as non-domination. Therefore, populist leaders may be recognised by the measures they take to increase not only the economic condition of the

---

[63] Thomas Piketty, *Capital in the Twenty-First Century* (Cambridge: Cambridge University Press, 2014).

[64] Between 2009 and 2012 the top 1 per cent of US households captured 95 per cent of total income gains, while bottom 90 per cent saw income fall by 16 per cent. Emmanuel Saez and Thomas Piketty, 'Income Inequality in the United States, 1913–1998', *Quarterly Journal of Economics* 118:1 (2003), pp. 1–39.

[65] Collusion is not a new problem. See John Girling, *Corruption, Capitalism and Democracy* (London: Routledge, 1997), pp. 171–172.

[66] In the U.S. the top 1% per cent holds over 25 trillion dollars compared to the 18 trillion held by the middle class. Isabel Sawhill and Christopher Pulliam, 'Six facts about wealth in the United States', Brookings Institute blog, June 25, 2019. Available at https://www.brookings.edu/blog/up-front/2019/06/25/six-facts-about-wealth-in-the-united-states/ (accessed 10 September 2019).

popular sectors through redistribution via land reform, progressive taxation, subsidies and public goods, but also in terms of their political status, through the establishment of participatory institutions, electoral quotas for oppressed minorities, and new social rights.[67] These actions would necessarily go against some of the rules protecting the status quo, implying the erosion of the elite's ruling power and the established order.

Understanding populist leaders as *popularis,* guided by plebeian ideology based on the logic of equality, seems fruitful because it imposes normativity on a concept so ambiguous that it fails to distinguish between 'good' and 'bad' forms, allowing for genuine champions of the people-as-plebs and tyrants to be categorised under the same banner. The populist as *popularis* needs to be understood as a crusader aimed at *expanding* liberty as non-domination to the people-as-plebs, and thus his authority would *exceed* the power conceded by the institutional structure insofar as in pursuit of that goal. This extra-legal power in favour of liberty, authorised by the many – the part of society that only desires not to be dominated – comes close to the agonistic interpretation of rights in a savage democracy discussed by Panu Minkkinen in his contribution. The same as the *popularis,* the populist should be conceived as the protector of liberty for plebeians – even against the law. However, the crucial difference between plebeian and populist leaders is that while the former were empowered and limited by the Plebeian Council, today the people-as-plebs only exists in the forum,[68] only possible in its relation to a leader or political party, in need of permanent mobilisation. This makes populist elected leaders not only weaker than Roman tribunes in institutional terms, but also less accountable to the unorganised, mobilised masses. The constitutional frameworks of representative democracies are currently unable to adequately deal with the extraordinary authority of the populist leader, allowing for the invocation of sweeping emergency powers with little to no oversight. This is especially troubling given that academia still confuses proto-totalitarian ethnonationalists with populist leaders.

---

[67] Such as indigenous, gay, and third-generation rights. For a radical democratic interpretation of republican liberty and rights see Jean-Fabien Spitz, 'The Reception of Machiavelli in Contemporary Republicanism. Some Ambiguities and Paradoxes', in David Johnston, Nadia Urbinati and Camila Vergara (eds.), *Machiavelli on Liberty and Conflict* (Chicago: University of Chicago Press, 2017), pp. 309–329.

[68] The extra-institutional realm of opinion. Nadia Urbinati, *Democracy Disfigured. Opinion, Truth, and the People* (Cambridge: Harvard University Press, 2014), p. 167.

11

Constituent Power and Constitutive Exceptions: Carl Schmitt, Populism and the Consummation of Secularisation

Jon Wittrock[1]

Constituent Power, Constitutive Boundaries, Constitutive Exceptions

In what can retrospectively be called a great early work of Western philosophy, the fragments of Heraclitus, we find the statement (here, of course, in English translation) that 'the people should fight on behalf of the law as [they would] for [their] city-wall.'[2] We need not regard ourselves presently with the authenticity or exact meaning of this fragment in the context of Heraclitus's philosophy, but simply note that it remains a captivating phrase that points to the ambiguities of what we today may call the normative order of a community, involving a curious entanglement of laws, customs and rituals, raising the question of how these relate to, and should relate to, the boundaries of that community.[3]

Populism may be analysed in terms of its causes and consequences for democratic politics, as a style of politics, or in surveying its recurrent themes.[4] As a number of contributions to this volume make clear, different theorists analyse populism in different ways descriptively, but they also perceive it to a greater

---

[1] I would like to thank the *Japan Society for the Promotion of Science* for their generous support to my research, and Professor Hiroshi Okano of Osaka City University for valuable discussions on the theme of the sacred.
[2] Heraclitus, *Fragments*, trans. T.M. Robinson (Toronto: University of Toronto Press, 1987), p. 33. The brackets indicate words inserted by the translator into the text quoted here.
[3] See also Zakin's contribution in this volume.
[4] See e.g. Ernesto Laclau, *On the Populist Reason* (London: Verso, 2005); Benjamin Arditi, *Politics on the Edges of Liberalism* (Edinburgh: Edinburgh University Press, 2007); Cas Mudde and Cristóbal Rovira Kaltwasser (eds), *Populism in Europe and the Americas: Threat or Corrective for Democracy?* (Cambridge: Cambridge University Press, 2012); and Benjamin Moffit, *The Global Rise of Populism: Performance, Political Style, and Representation* (Stanford: Stanford University Press, 2016).

or lesser extent as either a threat to democracy, or as a possibility for positive renewal of it, or even as an inevitable aspect of it. However, as Vergara puts it, many theorists seem to agree that populism originates in a crisis of representation, a lack of responsiveness of democratically elected leaders to a portion of the population and their inability or unwillingness to satisfy social demands.[5]

Here I believe Carl Schmitt's interpretation of the role of the people in a democratic-constitutional order, although originally presented in the context of debates about the Weimar Constitution, may be helpful to clarify some of the issues involved in contemporary debates. Schmitt argues that the people are anterior to and above the constitution, but also within it. The people is, in other words, on the one hand, the constituent power of the order as a whole, in the sense that it founds it by way of a 'concrete political decision', and on the other hand, it is within the constitution 'exercising constitutionally regulated powers.'[6] The people, however, could also be said to exist *beside* the constitution, in the sense of impacting on the political order by way of public opinion (which is the feature Schmitt highlighted, seeing it as the form that acclamation takes in a modern democracy), civil society organisations, protests and demonstrations, etc.[7] Viewed from this Schmittian angle, the contemporary 'crisis of representation' could be visualised at least partly in terms of the contraction or circumvention of the arteries that bind the people to, and channel their preferences within, the democratic political order.

Fundamentally, however, 'Political democracy', in Schmitt's words, 'cannot rest on the inability to distinguish among persons, but rather only on the quality of belonging to a *particular people*.' This, however, need not rest on an explicitly ethnic conceptualisation of the people; rather, Schmitt observes, 'This quality of belonging to a people can be defined by very different elements (ideas of common race, belief, common destiny, and tradition).'[8] While this is obviously true in the sense that conceptualisations of communal identity vary historically – and Schmitt parades a few examples to illustrate this – the identity of the people may also be constituted symbolically and legally *simultaneously* by elements that do not form a coherent whole, but rather seem to oppose each other.

To reconnect to the quotation from Heraclitus, we may observe that a democratic people is constituted symbolically, both by way of legal regulations

---

[5] See Vergara's contribution in this volume.

[6] Carl Schmitt, *Constitutional Theory*, trans. Jeffrey Seitzer (Durham, N.C.: Duke University Press, 2008), p. 268.

[7] See e.g. Schmitt, *Constitutional Theory*, pp. 131 and 275, and Mikael Spång, *Constituent Power and Constitutional Order: Above, Within and Beside the Constitution* (Basingstoke: Palgrave Macmillan, 2014).

[8] Schmitt, *Constitutional Theory*, p. 258.

and other norms, as well as narratives and ritual practices, that comprise what I propose to call the *constitutive boundaries* of a community. It is clear that when we consider populism as a contemporary political phenomenon within the Western World, we are confronted exactly with core questions concerning boundaries and their legal regulation. 'Build that wall' was indeed one of Donald Trump's most famous slogans, and as a call for action to reduce immigration, as well as pertaining to concerns about cultural and economic globalisation, it is powerfully symbolic, and points to crucial issues connected to the interrelations between norms and constitutive boundaries.

When it comes to modern and contemporary nation states, constitutive boundaries of at least three variants will concern me in the following. Firstly there are, of course, *territorial* boundaries. Secondly, there are what I will call the *tribal* boundaries that determine who does and does not belong to the community, and in the case of modern states, those boundaries are constituted by criteria for nationality and citizenship. Thirdly, there are those *totemic* boundaries that are constituted by the publicly recognised symbols of the identity of a community. All of these types of boundaries may be more or less fuzzy or sharply defined, but in modern nation states, territorial and tribal boundaries tend towards precision, whereas totemic boundaries are constituted by symbolic border stones, as it were – for example, a national flag, anthem, monument, or holiday[9] – which are open to widely different interpretations, and hence totemic boundaries could be compared to a frontier rather than a clearly marked border. These border stones, however, may be abstract as well as concrete: norms, narratives and key concepts – e.g. human dignity – may also function as symbolic border stones, drawing the line between insider and outsider.

These symbolic border stones, in turn, comprise merely one instance of what I propose to call *constitutive exceptions* – exceptions that are constitutive to an order. It is my contention that Schmitt operates, throughout his works, with a fundamental figure of thought exactly concerning constitutive exceptions, that, as becomes clear with his major later work *The Nomos of the Earth*[10], include a range of exceptional domains that either produce new concrete orders, or reproduce existing ones. This dichotomy between production and reproduction should be understood more precisely as an analytical polarity – empirically, interventions in exceptional domains may more or less significantly alter an existing order, depending on where the results are situated along a continuum of continuity or transformation. It is exactly this

---

[9] See e.g. Gabriella Elgenius, *Symbols of Nations and Nationalism: Celebrating Nationhood* (Houndmills, Basingstoke: Palgrave Macmillan, 2011).

[10] Carl Schmitt, *The Nomos of the Earth in the International Law of the Jus Publicum Europaeum*, trans. G. L. Ulmen (New York, NY: Telos Press, 2003).

ambiguous constitutive function of production/reproduction that makes it necessary to bind exceptional domains to established orders, and, Schmitt argues, these bonds should be theorised. It should be noted, however, that my reading of Schmitt does not aim for faithfulness or conceptual-historical accuracy – rather, my reading constitutes a creative-constructive wrestling with Schmitt's major concepts, and the ultimate aim is to use his concepts, as well as my own conceptual developments following from my engagement with them, to cast light on contemporary dilemmas pertaining to populism and the role of the people as constituent power, and how these, in turn, open up for a wider reflection on alternative socio-political constellations.

Indeed, the themes of the protective, concrete and physical borders of communities and their *nomos*, involving the curious entanglement between law, customs and rituals are not simply archaic issues but remain key contemporary topics. Thus, I will present the major dimensions of Schmitt's thinking on the political, which I will relate to Schmitt's concept of sacred orientations. Finally, I will relate these issues to the contemporary constellation of liberal democracy, with its tensions between and within different interpretations of popular sovereignty and human dignity, and pose the question of what a *consummation of secularisation*, or a consistently secular order, could entail.

Populism and the Political: Dichotomies and Polarities

While 'politics' refers to a host of shifting phenomena, *the political*, Schmitt maintains in the various editions of his compact essay on that subject, concerns the distinction between *friend* and *enemy*.[11] This could entail, according to a somewhat simplistic reading, that the political is simply a matter of declaring more or less arbitrary dichotomies and enmities; or it could be read, as Brännström shows in her chapter of this volume, as pointing to specific enemies and enmities.[12] In another important text, however, Schmitt traces movements of *depoliticisation* and, we might add, *politicisation*.[13] These, then, are two core conceptual pairs we may use in interpreting Schmitt's theory of the political as consisting of two major dimensions. Firstly, there are the stabilised, publicly declared, points or dichotomies of enmity, and secondly, there are gliding scales or trajectories of the increasing intensity of contestation or politicisation, peaking in the eruption of deadly violence. Later on, developing his earlier approach from *The Concept of the Political*, Schmitt speaks of *conventional, absolute* and *real* enemies, although it is not exactly

---

[11] Carl Schmitt, *The Concept of the Political*, expanded edn., trans. George Schwab (Chicago and London: The University of Chicago Press, 2007), pp. 25–6.

[12] See Brännström's contribution in this volume.

[13] Schmitt, *The Concept of the Political*, pp. 80–96.

clear how these categories should be interpreted.[14] At any rate, they need not concern us, presently.

If the opposite of the friend is the enemy, however, and if the two can be conceptualised in various pairings according to different criteria and interpretations, what is the polar opposite of politicisation? Supposedly the absence, not only of violence, or of open enmity, but of even the 'real possibility' of collective, violent, conflicts.[15] A plane of absolute depoliticisation, as opposed to peaks of politicisation. The rising intensity of politicisation, when viewing the political as a free-floating potential, something that can erupt anywhere, points towards deadly violence. Any path in this direction is the path towards the intensification of the political, but if we trace these paths backwards, it is far from clear that we will find anything resembling what we would even remotely consider as 'friendship'. The actual opposite pole of the polarity of politicisation, then, is not friendship, but depoliticisation, the absence of conflicts, and ultimately, of even the possibility of conflict.

We could thus visualise Schmitt's theory of the political in an imaginary space as focusing on two dimensions of movement. On the one hand, we may trace the increasing intensity of processes of politicisation, with their opposite counter-movements of depoliticisation – here we may think of a more or less flat or mountainous landscape or, with the entrance of time, of a bubbling surface or stormy sea, or a calm ocean, with dark undercurrents. On the other hand, we may consider declarations of friendship and enmity, and categories of these. Here, we can envisage horizontal dichotomies or delimitations, which can potentially occur anywhere on the scale of politicisation. Logically, there could be a peak of politicisation without any decision on dichotomies of enmity (an absolute zombie apocalypse with cannibalistic zombies comes to mind) but in the real world, and when dealing with human beings, this strikes me as an unlikely scenario.

The art of the political thus consists in channelling processes of depoliticisation and politicisation by gathering and steering their trajectories, in pointing to enemies to be combated, deciding when and how to combat them, deciding the limits for conflict and avoiding trajectories of politicisation that venture into unwanted directions. For example, while painting the image of a conflict or tension between common people and corrupt elites could be a common trait of populist movements, different kinds of populists would point towards different types of elites – e.g. academic, cultural, political, or financial – and articulate different notions of who constitutes the people

---

[14] See Carl Schmitt, *Theory of the Partisan: Intermediate Commentary on the Concept of the Political*, trans. G.L. Ulmen (New York: Telos Press, 2007).

[15] Schmitt, *The Concept of the Political*, p. 33.

(those belonging to certain ethnic groups, or adhere to certain values, or belong to certain socio-economic strata, etc.).

Populism thus actualises questions pertaining to the composition of both the people and the elites. It also, however, raises the question concerning the relation between the two. If, as Schmitt famously maintains in *Political Theology*, 'All significant concepts of the modern theory of the state are secularized theological concepts' both in the sense of being derived from, and analogous to, theological elements, what is the best theological analogy for the role of the people in a democracy?[16] If the democratic machinery could be viewed as a machine running according to the input of the people, but also founded by them in the first place, would that make the people analogous to God in an absolute monarchy? And if so, is there a centre of power in a democracy analogous to a monarch?

Basically, we could raise two counterarguments against that view: the people is not a unified force with one will, analogous to God, and no single centre of power, in a democracy, wields the power of an absolute monarch. Rather, the people is split into a myriad of different groups and individuals with different interests and preferences, and the exercise of power, even in a parliamentary, unitary state, is divided between different institutions.[17] However, if the people were to be conceived of as unitary, and if there were a strong executive power unencumbered by countervailing forces, then a modern democracy would move closer to the theological analogy.[18] This, too, is a key issue involved in contemporary debates, hopes and fears concerning populism. It should be noted that Schmitt mentions 'the authoritative identification of a minority as the people and . . . the decisive transfer of the concept from the quantitative into the qualitative.'[19] Even if this is not exactly what Schmitt had in mind, it is difficult to avoid thinking of the 2016 US presidential election: the peculiar American election system indeed turned a minority of voters into the majority of 'the people', and when the voters are analysed in terms of race, this indeed raises questions about 'the qualitative' composition of 'the people'.

What is involved in debates about populism is thus the movement of key pieces pertaining to the composition of the people and the leaders, as well as the relation between them, and struggles around these issues involve the attempts of antagonistic actors to channel the dangerous forces of the political in their own preferred directions. These conflicts concern the characteristics of

---

[16] Carl Schmitt, *Political Theology: Four Chapters on the Concept of Sovereignty*, trans. George Schwab (Chicago & London: The University of Chicago Press, 2005), p. 36.

[17] See e.g. Spång, *Constituent Power and Constitutional Order*.

[18] See e.g. Carl Schmitt, *The Crisis of Parliamentary Democracy*, trans. Ellen Kennedy (Cambridge, MA: MIT Press, 1998), pp. 31–32.

[19] Schmitt, *The Crisis of Parliamentary Democracy*, p. 31.

constitutive boundaries: indeed, one of the key traits of contemporary populist currents and the conflicts they provoke, and one of the major reasons why they are perceived as both dangerous and potentially beneficial, is the renewed urgency with which they actualise questions concerning constitutive boundaries. In so doing, however, they also point to an even wider dynamic, that of constitutive exceptions and their foundational role for political orders.

Spirit, Enclosure and the Constitution of the People

In *The Nomos of the Earth*, Carl Schmitt used the concept of *nomos* to refer not only to the concrete processes of the appropriation of land and the distribution and production of resources, that constitute fundamental elements of any political order, but also tied this notion to the sacred, to 'something walled or enclosed, or a sacred place, all of which are contained in the word *nomos* . . .'[20] As Wendy Brown remarks, in writing about Schmitt, 'The enclosure brings the sacred into being, marking it off from the common and ordinary.'[21] Questions of something 'enclosed . . . sacred place', however, are not simply a matter of concrete, spatial sites and boundaries, but of lines drawn around norms, concepts, narratives and temporal intervals too. Schmitt thus brings to light the curious entanglement between laws, walls and worship in actual political orders.

In addressing the problem of *nihilism*, Schmitt turns to the concrete order, or *nomos*, which consists, he claims, of 'three processes – appropriation, distribution, and production . . . In every stage of social life, in every economic order, in every period of legal history until now, things have been appropriated, distributed, and produced.'[22] Fundamentally, however, Schmitt writes, order is constituted by an original act of land appropriation, a *Landnahme*, a taking of land.[23] This original act, setting in place concrete processes of appropriation, distribution and production, however, is connected to a sacred *orientation*, and sacred orientations are continuously tied to order; it is when this linkage is severed, when the processes of order are devoid of sacred orientations, that we arrive at the crisis of nihilism.[24]

This critique of nihilism is formulated ever so briefly in *The Nomos of the Earth* and does not, honestly, constitute a major theme of it, at least not explicitly. Nevertheless, Schmitt begins to articulate a thematic that remains of supreme interest to current debates on populism and popular power: he highlights, that is, if somewhat obscurely, the relations between political enmity and the control of sacred enclosures. Schmitt writes about the notion of limited

[20] See Schmitt, *The Nomos of the Earth*, p. 78 and pp. 324–330.
[21] Wendy Brown, *Walled States, Waning Sovereignty* (New York: Zone Books, 2010), p. 46.
[22] Schmitt, *The Nomos of the Earth*, p. 327.
[23] Schmitt, *The Nomos of the Earth*, pp. 78–83.
[24] Schmitt, *The Nomos of the Earth*, p. 66.

war most famously in *The* Nomos *of the Earth* when referring to the development of warfare in Europe whereby, ideally, the armies of sovereign princes would meet much like noble duellists on the battlefield, abiding by shared rules and sparing the civilian population. In portraying this somewhat romanticised image, Schmitt contrast war in Europe to the domains of the open seas and the colonial lands beyond them, lying open to unlimited war and brutal exploitation.[25] Furthermore, however, Schmitt also writes more generally of a closing off, tied to the sacred. Sacred orientations, to Schmitt, are a question of what we could call sacred enclosures, and with this, we actually arrive at a highly relevant discussion, armed with a useful concept.[26]

The notion of enclosures, of protective boundaries, could be handled at a higher level of abstraction than that of simply referring to physical walls or spatial lines of demarcation: enclosures may be spatial as well as temporal, conceptual as well as physical. We could thus extend the concept of enclosure and sacred orientation beyond the domains explicitly mentioned by Schmitt himself: the sacred and corresponding categories entail the withdrawing of domains, spatial, temporal, physical and conceptual, from ordinary usage and circulation – e.g. sacred sites, persons, symbols, narratives, norms and temporal intervals (rituals, festivals, holidays). All of these may uphold or challenge an established order.

There is also, however, the decisive question of the event: the event, that is, to which the sacred orientation of an order is symbolically and ritualistically connected. Thus, a Christian order is tied to enclosures which are in turn symbolically connected to foundational events of Christian faith. We can easily extend this reasoning, however, by way of analogy to other orders: for example, enclosures can be tied to the event of political revolution or a foundational war or appropriation or liberation, and they can also be criticised for failing to take such crucial events into account. We could perceive the clear structural similarity with, say, 'real socialist' as well as liberal constitutionalist regimes: the revolutionary event, the original enthusiasm, such as there was, transmitted by the enclosures of temporal intervals, the iconography of Marxist-Leninism, or the sites, symbols and rituals of the American or French Republics, and the like. Now, we must note that the event is defined retroactively here, as how it is constituted by publicly sanctioned symbols, rituals and narratives. We need not be concerned with a typology of actual events, but rather with those 'events' which are symbolically and ritualistically recalled, and publicly communicated, which communication can become contested and challenged. Enclosures are thus symbolically connected to extraordinary phenomenological as well as political events, but they also legitimise or challenge processes of the appropriation,

---

[25] Schmitt, *The Nomos of the Earth*, pp. 140–8.
[26] See e.g. Schmitt, *The Nomos of the Earth*, pp. 78–79.

production and distribution or exchange of resources. So, while Schmitt explicitly emphasises spatial enclosures, and prefers a Christian orientation, his concepts could be extended beyond both. Here it is a question of collective mobilisation, tied to spatial, temporal and conceptual enclosures symbolically connected to crucial events, but also to questions of appropriation, production, distribution and exchange.

Moving to an even higher level of abstraction, we may invoke Schmitt's contrast between that thought which theorises the relation to the exceptional, and that narrower rationality, which seeks to exclude or repress, and hence fails to adequately theorise, the relation between order and exception.[27] Indeed, Schmitt was consistently preoccupied with what we may call the *topology of the exceptional*, the *topos* of the exception and its relation to the reproduction of the normal and ordinary: the state of exception in relation to the continuation of the legal order, transformative political events in relation to the constitution of political order, the sacred site and sacred time, in relation to territorial space and chronological time, and even phenomenological exceptions in relation to ordinary, consensus reality. This topology of the exceptional is the symbolical and discursive battlefield of trajectories of politicisation and depoliticisation. Controlling it is of the utmost importance to any established order.

In the peculiar Schmittian sense, the legal and political orders and establishments of contemporary Western liberal democracies are not nihilistic. That is, they are by no means bereft of what we could call sacred orientations – national symbols, core concepts such as human dignity and autonomy, holidays and rituals, etc. – but there is a fear of a discrepancy between 'faith and confession': that is, a discrepancy between the outer manifestation of belief and reverence in relation to national narratives as well as liberal democratic creeds, and an actual lack of faith in and genuine commitment to all or some of these.

Following in the path of Schmitt, a basic figure of thought could thus be conceptualised as follows: *constitutive exceptions* are *enclosed*, entailing that they are *bound* to normal order, in an attempt to control their dangerous, potentially disruptive and destabilising potential. But what is it that has to be symbolically bound to order, so that it may be rendered less dangerous? We could perhaps call it *spirit*: that which, to speak with Roberto Unger, transcends any attempt at one final interpretation, that which always reveals further possibilities.[28] An elegant understanding would thus result in a division between *spirit*, as the force, surplus, overflow, transcending any delimitation, and *enclosure*, as the circle – concrete, physical, or normative – enclosing constitutive exceptions. Differently put, 'spirit' is the space of possibilities

---

[27] See Schmitt, *Political Theology*, pp. 5–15, 20–21, and 48–49.
[28] Roberto Mangabeira Unger, *The Religion of the Future* (Cambridge, MA: Harvard University Press, 2014), p. 2. I extend Unger's usage.

surrounding any existing arrangement, the space of its potential variations. In a situation of crisis and transformation, many possibilities are open, whereas a stable order closes down or collapses most of these potential trajectories. Thus, the violence of popular revolutions may overthrow an existing order and found a new one, and the phenomenological overflow of religious revelations may found new religious traditions, or renew existing ones. Analogously, deliberation on alternative political arrangements and communal norms, as well as concrete experimentation with alternative forms of life, also reveal the overflow of spirit, of conceivable options, and such discussions and experimental practices are reined in by norms of the restrictions on free debate, or the enclosure of communal festivals and artistic endeavours.[29]

It should be obvious that the above is acutely relevant to debates on the impact of populist politics: constitutive boundaries are intimately linked to constitutive exceptions. Totemic boundaries are constituted by constitutive exceptions – spatial, temporal, symbolic, conceptual, e.g. flags, anthems, memorial sites, core concepts, rituals, holidays – while territorial and tribal boundaries are legitimised by recourse to them. These mechanisms, however, are neither uncontroversial, nor unchanging: constitutive exceptions are open to contestation and reinterpretation, and territorial and tribal boundaries are not only legitimised but also challenged, by recourse to them. In certain countries, there is an obvious discrepancy between different aspects of the public communication of the national community – for example, a flag adorned with a Christian cross, or laws containing clear traces of a specific ethnoreligious heritage may coexist with an insistence on multiculturalism and secularity – and in many, a fierce struggle has erupted concerning the desirable future of this communication.

A concrete example of a conflict concerning constitutive boundaries and their temporal implications is provided by the by now infamous events in Charlottesville, Virginia, in August 2017. The 'Unite the Right' protestors complained about the removal of a statue of Robert E. Lee, and violence with counter-protesters ensued, leaving one of the latter dead. Above all, however, the event was symbolically significant: to the right-wing protesters, removing the statue was interpreted as an element of a wider movement of displacement and,

[29] See e.g. Scott Atran and Jeremy Ginges, 'Religious and Sacred Imperatives in Human Conflict', *Science* 336:6083 (2012), pp. 855–857; Michel Foucault, 'Of Other Spaces. Heterotopias', in Neil Leach (ed.), *Rethinking Architecture: A Reader in Cultural Theory* (New York: Routledge. 1997), pp. 330–336; Philip. E Tetlock, 'Thinking the Unthinkable: Sacred Values and Taboo Cognitions', *Trends in Cognitive Sciences* 7:7 (2003), pp. 320–324; Luke Yates, 'Rethinking Prefiguration: Alternatives, Micropolitics and Goals in Social Movements,' *Social Movement Studies* 14:1 (2015), pp. 1–21; and Richard Schechner, *The Future of Ritual: Writings on Culture and Performance* (London and New York: Routledge, 1993).

ultimately, genocide of white people, in the US and at a global level. To their opponents, however, it was the radical right that could be perceived as ultimately raising the spectre of genocide.[30] The statue itself thus functioned as a symbolic border stone in the constitution of different articulations of community, ultimately pointing to radically divergent conceptualisations of the people. This issue is, of course, symbolically tied to the question of the relative permeability of the totemic and territorial boundaries of the US and, ultimately, other Western countries as well. Furthermore, this question was perceived by both sides of the conflict as connected to a historical axis, entailing opposing interpretations of the past and the future, and their implications for the constitution of the American people in a larger historical perspective and trajectory.

These questions of constitutive exceptions and constitutive boundaries are thus important since they reveal openly articulated and contested as well as latent possibilities of alternative socio-political configurations.

The Consummation of Secularisation?

Throughout his works, Schmitt repeatedly turns to Thomas Hobbes, with great if qualified admiration. Hobbes was important to Schmitt partly because of his 'philosophical-systematic state theory', which set him apart from other early modern thinkers on sovereignty and state power, but also and specifically because of the relationships between his works and the progression of political secularisation in Europe.[31]

Hobbes, however, was hardly an explicitly secular thinker even in a political sense, but called for 'uniformity of Public Worship'.[32] Nevertheless, while indeed endorsing a shared worship for the commonwealth in its entirety, Hobbes, Schmitt claims, left a gap in his theory, in the form of a distinction between inner faith and outer confession, which left the path open for secularisation.[33] Hobbes attempted to counter the dangers of religious fragmentation and contestation not only by reducing the doctrinaire core of

---

[30] See e.g. George Hawley, *Making Sense of the Alt-Right* (New York: Columbia University Press, 2017); Mike Wendling, *Alt-Right: From 4chan to the White House* (London: Pluto Press, 2018); and Heidi Beirich, 'After Charlottesville: Can We Please Finally Put an End to White Supremacy?', *Intelligence Report*, 2018 Spring Issue. Available at https://www.splcenter.org/fighting-hate/intelligence-report/2018/after-charlottesville-can-we-please-finally-put-end-white-supremacy (accessed 30 April 2019).

[31] Carl Schmitt, *The Leviathan in the State Theory of Thomas Hobbes: Meaning and Failure of a Political Symbol*, trans. George Schwab and Erna Hilfstein (Chicago and London: The University of Chicago Press), p. 43.

[32] Thomas Hobbes, *On the Citizen*, eds Richard Tuck and Michael Silverthorne (Cambridge: Cambridge University Press, 1998 [1642]), p. 181.

[33] Schmitt, *The Leviathan in the State Theory of Thomas Hobbes*, p. 56.

Christianity to a minimum but also by advancing sceptical arguments against claims of divine revelation:

> Seeing . . . miracles now cease, we have no sign left whereby to acknowledge the pretended revelations or inspirations of any private man, nor obligation to give ear to any doctrine farther than that it is conformable to the Holy Scriptures, which since the time of our Saviour supply the place and sufficiently recompense the want of all other prophecy, and from which, by wise and learned interpretation and careful ratiocination, all rules and precepts necessary of our duty both to God and man, without enthusiasm or supernatural inspiration, may easily be deduced.[34]

Similarly, the political establishment of contemporary liberal democracies seek to channel such popular enthusiasm as there is through the legally available forms of political action – voting, restricted deliberation, permitted demonstrations, etc. – in the direction of those parties and politicians which are widely perceived as 'acceptable'. There is to be no new revolution just as, to Hobbes, there should be no new revelation. We have had, many assume, our foundational revolutions and other transformations, and are on the progressive path towards a continuous expansion of equal – and, when necessary, unequal – rights to yet wider groups of individuals.

In the last of his books to be published during his life, Schmitt states that Hobbes consummated the reformation 'by recognising the state as a clear alternative to the Roman Catholic church's monopoly on decision-making.'[35] Leaving aside a broader evaluation of Schmitt's critique of Hobbes, we may observe that political secularisation in the sense of a complete lack of 'public worship' has yet to be consistently realised. Contemporary liberal democracies continue to support narratives, norms, symbols and ritual practices that transcend simplified divisions into religious and secular, and arguably inject sacred elements into the public life of supposedly secular states. Furthermore, critical ideologies and norms of human rights, too, draw upon religious legacies, although the extent to which they do so and what that entails has been and remains a fiercely debated topic.[36]

---

[34] Thomas Hobbes, *Leviathan, with Selected Variants from the Latin Edition of 1668* (Indianapolis and Cambridge: Hackett, 1994 [1651]), p. 249.

[35] Carl Schmitt, *Political Theology II: The Myth of the Closure of Any Political Theology*, trans. Michael Hoelzl and Graham Ward (Cambridge: Polity Press, 2008), pp. 125–126.

[36] See e.g. John Gray, *Black Mass: Apocalyptic Religion and the Death of Utopia* (London: Penguin Books, 2008); Jürgen Habermas, *Religion and Rationality: Essays on Reason, God, and Modernity*, ed. Eduardo Mendieta (Cambridge: Polity Press, 2002); Jürgen Habermas, *The Crisis of the European Union: A Response* (Cambridge: Polity Press, 2012); Hans Joas, *The Sacredness of the Person. A New Genealogy of Human Rights* (Washington DC: Georgetown University Press, 2013); and Slavoj Žižek, *The Fragile Absolute – or, Why is the Christian Legacy Worth Fighting For?* (London and New York: Verso, 2001).

With this in mind, we may ask whether a consummation of secularisation would be desirable. Should we do away with these remnants? In other words, while the concept of *secularisation* is, of course, ambiguous, the question I am raising concerns our relations to the topology of the exceptional comprised of symbols, rituals, norms and narratives that are surrounded by cultural and legal norms demanding reverence and respect. The answer, of course, depends on what we deem to be desirable or problematic. Simply advocating for the rejection of some conceptual or pragmatic element because it is derived from theological and ecclesiastical components, amounts to a poor argument, resting on a genetic fallacy. Likewise, there is no reason to reject an element simply because it is, to some extent, structurally analogous to a theological or ecclesiastical one. Furthermore, we should note that what we are discussing is not simply whether a certain element should be present or allowed to exist, but rather, what kind of relationship should be maintained to it by way of cultural norms or legal regulation. That is, we may consider an entire range of possible relationships, from the prohibition of churches to the maintenance of a 'civil religion' which is explicitly secular.

I will simply treat it as axiomatic in the following that we desire to remain within the confines of a liberal democratic framework. What kind of possibilities does that open up? Are there desirable as well as feasible alternatives to the present range of 'secular' arrangements? The task here is to envisage possible trajectories of secularisation, as I have defined it, and in order to clarify the ensuing analysis, I will distinguish between negative and positive trajectories; that is, between the removal or transfer of religious elements from the public sphere, and their transfer to it, respectively. Drawing upon a Schmittian conceptual apparatus, we may distinguish, then, between negative and positive trajectories of secularisation pertaining to sacred enclosures and processes of politicisation and depoliticisation, agonistically as well as antagonistically.

This thematic area is actualised by contemporary populist politics that raises questions concerning the constitution of the people, the permeability and mutability of constitutive boundaries, and the contested status of constitutive exceptions. As for the last theme, current debates gravitate around the relationships between two crucial normative areas of contemporary liberal democracies, those of popular sovereignty and human rights. The latter infuses an alternative source of justification for political decisions and legal regulation and application, that of *human dignity* – itself arguably an opaque conceptual core that rhetorically legitimises human rights while compressing a host of different normative dimensions into one contested concept. Sadly, however, while, as some theorists argue, it may be a good idea to simply swap *dignity* for *autonomy*, the latter concept is itself ambiguous and contested. Thus, human dignity may be understood as referring to negative or positive liberty to a different extent, as well as questions of the maintenance of any balance between the two over time; and perhaps, such an analysis still leaves an enigmatic remainder of dignity proper, whatever that is.[37] If human rights are to be understood as something beyond mere positive law or international agreement, the way in which we interpret human dignity obviously ought to have some impact on their interpretation and application; and the ambiguities of that core concept leaves room for a great deal of uncertainty about exactly what is to be protected, and why.

As for practices of 'public worship', publicly supported symbols and rituals reproduce symbolic, totemic boundaries of communities: they point to something that binds the community together in a shared identity, albeit by way of elements which are open to widely differing interpretations. Such practices could be perceived as threatening to the autonomy and dignity (in the sense of recognition) of those perceiving themselves as external to the shared identity, or as not being represented and recognised publicly. Furthermore, it may be argued that members of minority cultures are in need of support to ensure that they have meaningful choices, and this may entail supporting their symbols and rituals – the very same argument, however, could support ethnic or racial nationalism, for example.[38] Finally, it may be argued that collective symbols and rituals maintain communal cohesion, and are thus to be maintained, even at the expense of the short-term autonomy of individuals.[39]

In relation to this situation, we find a host of proposals occupying the spectrum from negative to positive political secularisation. At one end, we find anarchist proposals that entail abandoning state coercion, embracing direct consensus democracy, and disconnecting symbols and rituals from state control; such proposals, however, may still defend the relevance of communal, collective festivities, but now entirely disconnected from state coercion.[40] Next in line, logically, we may place libertarian proposals defending a night-watchman state but, again, without any semblances of public worship, state-regulated holidays and publicly communicated narratives, and the like. After that, we may conceive of variants of

---

[37] Many of these issues are succinctly addressed in Michael Rosen, *Dignity: Its History and Meaning* (Cambridge, MA: Harvard University Press, 2012).

[38] See e.g. Charles Taylor, 'The Politics of Recognition', in Amy Gutmann (ed.), *Multiculturalism: Examining the Politics of Recognition* (Princeton: Princeton University Press, 1994); Will Kymlicka, *Multicultural Citizenship: A Liberal Theory of Minority Rights* (Oxford: Oxford University Press, 1995); and Will Kymlicka, *Multicultural Odysseys: Navigating the New International Politics of Diversity* (Oxford: Oxford University Press, 2007).

[39] For example, drawing upon Harvey Whitehouse, 'Ritual, Cognition, and Evolution', in Ron Sun (ed.), *Grounding Social Sciences in Cognitive Sciences* (Cambridge MA: MIT Press, 2012), pp. 265–284.

[40] See e.g. David Graeber, *Fragments of an Anarchist Anthropology* (Chicago: Prickly Paradigm Press, 2004), p. 23.

constitutional patriotism or republicanism devoid of public rituals; combine this with publicly sanctioned symbols, rituals and perhaps narratives, and we arrive at a republican solution, which could be defended by recourse to the need for upholding liberty – negative or positive – over time.[41] Thus, practices of public worship could be considered as instrumental in promoting civic virtue, or even a stronger, Machiavellian understanding of *virtù*. Furthermore, we may think of versions of *civil religion* – publicly communicated narratives, symbols and rituals tied to the political order and its history and formative events, which may be more or less explicitly religious, in the sense of being derivative of specific theological traditions.[42] To such elements, we may add pervasive national norms, narratives, symbols and rituals, thus arriving at the common contemporary model of the liberal-democratic nation state, which has indeed been frequently perceived by scholars as incorporating, by way of nationalism, quasi-religious elements.[43] There are thus temporal as well as spatial issues at stake: we may consider the spatial extension of public worship, as being tied to one state, or there may be several publicly supported, but distinct, 'public worships' within one state (with one or none of them being tied to the national level and the rituals of the political system), or those favouring cosmopolitanism may even advocate some form of cosmopolitan worship transcending national borders – although the example of the EU, the most advanced instance of macro-regional integration to date, may not inspire much confidence in the prospects of such a solution.[44]

[41] See e.g. Jürgen Habermas, 'The European Nation-State – Its Achievements and Its Limits. On the Past and Future of Sovereignty and Citizenship', in Jürgen Habermas, *The Inclusion of the Other. Studies in Political Theory*, ed. Ciaran Cronin and Pablo De Greiff (Cambridge, MA: MIT Press, 1999), pp. 105–127; Maurizio Viroli, *For Love of Country: An Essay on Patriotism and Nationalism* (Oxford: Oxford University Press, 1995); and Quentin Skinner, 'The Republican Ideal of Political Liberty', in Gisela Bock, Quentin Skinner and Maurizio Viroli (eds), *Machiavelli and Republicanism* (Cambridge: Cambridge University Press), pp 293–309.

[42] See e.g. Robert Bellah, 'Civil Religion in America', in Robert Bellah, *Beyond Belief: Essays on Religion in a Post-Traditional World* (New York: Harper & Row, 1970), pp. 168–189.

[43] See e.g. Benedict Anderson, *Imagined Communities: Reflections on the Origin and Spread of Nationalism* (London and New York: Verso, 2002); Carlton Hayes, *Nationalism: A Religion* (New York: Macmillan, 1960); John Smith, *Quasi-Religions: Humanism, Marxism and Nationalism* (Basingstoke: Macmillan, 1994); and Anthony D. Smith, *Nationalism: Theory, Ideology, History* (Cambridge: Polity Press, 2010).

[44] Cf. Immanuel Kant, 'Religion within the Boundaries of Mere Reason' [1793], in Immanuel Kant, *Religion and Rational Theology*, trans. Allen W. Wood and George di Giovanni (Cambridge: Cambridge University Press, 2001), pp 39–216, at pp. 213–214; and Jean-Claude Piris, *The Lisbon Treaty: A Legal and Political Analysis* (Cambridge: Cambridge University Press, 2010), p. 23.

All of the above, however, except a consistently anarchist solution, entail using state coercion in defence of some central principles, which could be considered as elements of a sacred topology of the exceptional. The extent to which such elements themselves are open to public contestation and agonistic challenges, however, may vary: here, we may aim to maximise freedom of speech, to ensure individual liberty, or to restrict it, to protect the dignity of certain groups, or perhaps to safeguard the maintenance of their liberty over time. We may also seek to encourage a culture of respectful and tolerant deliberation, whatever that means. Are we to tolerate that everything can be questioned, or rather tolerate each other's respective sacred elements, and agree to restrict ourselves when dealing with them?

Popular sovereignty is thus tensely related to human dignity, which itself consists of an unclear combination of several normative dimensions, that also clash with each other. Autonomy could be interpreted as entailing different priorities when it comes to freedom from coercion, freedom from structural domination, or the capacity to act or to lead a meaningful existence, and all of these, in turn, are contested when it comes to their extension spatially and temporally, and what that in turn entails. Thus, for example, some may argue that the freedom of movement of migrants has to be restricted spatially to ensure the maintenance of the collective autonomy of a given community over time; others may argue that restrictions on the freedom of speech must be put in place now, to ensure the protection of some group over time, etc. There is nothing about either liberal democracy as a system within states, or hopes for human rights across the planet, that magically dissolves all of these actual and potential conflicts. The political in Schmitt's sense is unlikely to go away.

Ultimately, there will probably be new revelations and new revolutions. We do not live in smoothly running systems which will simply go on forever, undisturbed. Exceptions will intervene, an overflow of possibilities will overwhelm established boundaries, and new orders and new boundaries will emerge. Whether that happens sooner, as a result of populist politics, or later, as the result of some other transformation or crisis (e.g. economic, ecological, technological, or all combined) remains an open question.

Index